The Politics of Culture and Other Essays

The Politics of Culture
and Other Essays

Roger Scruton

St. Augustine's Press
South Bend, Indiana

Manufactured in the United States of America.

1 2 3 4 5 6   25 24 23 22 21 20 19

Library of Congress Cataloging in Publication Data
Names: Scruton, Roger, author.
Title: Politics of culture other essays / Roger Scruton.
Description: South Bend, Indiana: St. Augustine's Press, 2016.
Includes index.
"Originally published by Carcanet Press in 1981."
Identifiers: LCCN 2016034009
ISBN 9781587316647 (paperback)
Subjects: LCSH: Arts and society.
Politics in art.
BISAC: POLITICAL
SCIENCE / Public Policy / Cultural Policy.
Classification: LCC NX180.S6 S4 2016 | DDC 701/.03--dc23 LC record
available at https://lccn.loc.gov/2016034009

∞ The paper used in this publication meets the minimum
requirements of the American National Standard for Information Sciences - Permanence
of Paper for Printed Materials, ANSI Z39.48-1984.

St. Augustine's Press
www.staugustine.net

Contents

Preface

THE essays in this volume, written over a period of ten years, are brought together in the hope that some thought, phrase or argument will alert the reader to the importance of the subject implied in its title. When the publisher first suggested collecting some of the reviews and essays that I had written, it seemed unlikely that unity could be either elicited from or imposed upon the results. As I considered the reasons which motivated this selection, I began to discern an underlying theme and purpose. The political spirit is present in all of the pieces; but it is a spirit that concerns itself with culture, and with the institutions and practices through which culture is upheld. The tone is reactionary, a fact for which it is useless to apologize. It is always to be hoped that the strong expression of a point of view will be of service to someone.

In the writing of these pieces there was the satisfaction of self-discovery, of becoming aware, for a while, of the doctrines that motivated thought and action. Perhaps, in providing instruction for myself, they also provided amusement for the *Davidsbündler* for whom I imagined myself to be writing. But the book is logically no more than a beginning, a first survey from one narrow point of view of some of the cultural landmarks of our time. If it points the way to a more cogent and consecutive formulation of the standpoint that speaks through it, then it will have served a purpose. All of the essays have appeared elsewhere, and I wish to express my obligation to the editors and publishers of the periodicals and collections mentioned in the text. They include no articles that a professional philosopher would regard as written specifically from within the confines of his discipline. On the contrary, they try to steer round the complexities of philosophical argument, in order to make direct assault, perhaps at surprising places, on questions that are of concern to every educated person in our time.

London, 1980

Language and Art

1   The State of the Language

The State of the Language, edited by Leonard Michaels and Christopher Ricks (University of California Press, 1980) from the *Times Literary Supplement*, 22 February 1980.

WE ARE fortunate in possessing no genuine equivalent of the Académie Française. Our language is disciplined not by the majestic fragments of a constitution destined to remain provisional, but by the enterprises of such bootleggers as the Oxford University Press, who give us the whole truth whenever we ask for it, and pretend to no authority that is not derived, at secondhand, from the customer whose demands they satisfy. The market in logophilia is encouraged by large and eager colonies, who absorb the surplus product of rules and principles, providing raw materials in exchange. One by one American English, Black English, Punjabi English and a thousand other varieties find their way home for processing, are included in the Oxford Corpus, and exported again in the form of rules. Of course, the customer is given to understand that his demand is the sole standard of legitimacy, and that the rules which he receives will merely reflect his own eccentricities. Such, however, is the authority of Oxford English that, insensibly, people come to accept it as prescriptive. A monopoly with a free market is the same as a tyranny without one. Besides, it is the tone of voice that turns custom into command, and who would disregard the tone of the *OED*, if it is not someone either ignorant of the *OED* or fired by subversive ambitions?

Over sixty writers have contributed to *The State of the Language*, and they are more or less evenly divided between those prepared to accept that there ought to be authority and obedience in matters of grammar, and those who think that any such conception is arbitrary and tyrannical. The dispute is in no way trivial. It is as deep, and as difficult, as that (of which it is but a special case) between the conservative and the liberal in politics. Only free beings can be governed, but government creates the conditions which make freedom possible. Which, then, comes first: government, or freedom? Even the Tory Party has begun to throw in its lot with freedom, having traditionally considered that, until constrained by this or that allegiance, 'freedom' names no ideal but only a sickness for which government is the remedy.

But many people take the opposite view, and advocate a freedom from which all conditions have been extruded. Some Americans are still surprised to find that this 'freedom', and the abundance which it generates, are actually unwelcome to peoples who for centuries have described their

11

innermost aspirations with the Arabic word for 'submission'. The pathological form of the ideal, which recognizes no authority that is not self-imposed, exists in varying degrees. As one proceeds West across the continent of America its fervour intensifies, until, confronted by the abruptness of the Pacific ocean, the free-born lemmings congregate, looking for the opportunity to throw away freedom and the desire for it together. Some results of this—Californian 'psychobabble', the neologisms of feminists and homosexuals, the blessed rage for disorder and its murderous opposite in Jonestown—are discussed in this book, which is edited, appropriately enough, by a professor from Berkeley, California, and another from Cambridge, England, two places with which the rival conceptions of political life might fairly be associated.

Since the editors have found no issue or concept with which to unite their contributors, I propose to see them united in the strife that divides them, and will consider the battle between linguistic liberalism and linguistic conservatism. But first it must be said that the writers are very diverse, ranging from the pedantic to the witty, from the barbarous to the decadent—with several intervening spells of civilization. A refreshing aspect of the volume is the abundance of serious and intelligent contributors prepared to defend some aspect of common speech which the educated reader might wrongly criticize as a vice of grammar or style. In one of the more daring protests against the *idée reçue*, Christopher Ricks even tries to defend the one thing that we all unthinkingly dismiss as linguistic unthinkingness—cliché. His elegant essay gave me pause, partly because of its characteristic literary criticism, partly because of the arresting nature of its theme. It soon became clear that what Professor Ricks was defending was not cliché, but the exploitation of cliché to say something new. But it is no defence of cliché to say that it is acceptable when used against nature. In its common use, cliché is a way of avoiding the reality of what it describes: hence people become disturbed when they notice its proliferation.

David Reid, reflecting on the Jonestown massacre, laments the 'horrible ease with which we find categories for enormity', wishing on language the function which cliché denies: the function of showing what is there. (It does not occur to Mr Reid that even Aeschylus might have found it difficult to pin tragic sentiments on to this rubbishy affair; but it is the destiny of journalism to miss the insignificance of what it describes.)

A cliché is not just what the dictionary defines it to be: a worn-out expression. (Though full marks to Marshall McLuhan's schoolboy who, asked to use a worn-out expression in a novel way, wrote 'The boy returned home from school with a cliché on his face.') A cliché is a tired and inattentive figure of speech. ('The winter of our discontent' is no cliché in the mouth of Richard III, even now, when it is a cliché in the mouths of politicians.) Cliché, in other words, is a form of falsehood; journalism relies on comparisons which, because they say nothing, can be assimilated at once; you can no more expect it to convey the moral truth about Jonestown than you can expect it to convey the moral truth about anything. When Geoffrey Hill (Ricks's example) uses cliché to convey the truth of things, it is by piercing the hardened shell of an old comparison and exposing its meaning. The wounded cliché makes you feel the truth which injured it. You no more defend cliché by defending such usage (even if your defence is as imaginative as that of Ricks) than you defend barricades by referring to the joy of pulling them down.

Other contributors to the volume make similar efforts—often more brazen, and usually far less sophisticated—to outface the critics of sloppy habits of speech, sometimes by adopting them (as in Geneva Smitherman's affected use of Black English: 'what we bees needing is teachers with the proper attitudinal orientation'), sometimes by turning the kaleidoscope of novelty before our eyes, letting the fragments of untutored usage pattern themselves in academic mirrors (thus Angela Carter: 'Many of my sisters studied the social sciences before they were "freaked out" by the authoritarian patriarchal bias of the methodology of sociology and "got into" personal growth, itself a conceptually vague area that has . . .'). But the balance against the careless neologism is redressed by a tough bunch of linguistic conservatives. Several of these—notably Kingsley Amis and John Simon—point to the frequent illiteracy of modern habits, both popular (the use of 'refute' for 'reject', of 'hopefully' as a modal auxiliary, of 'gamut' for 'gauntlet', 'alternatively' for 'alternately', 'paradigm' for 'paragon', and so on), and also professional (the big business of semiotics, accurately satirized by Mr Simon).

The world used to contain two classes of people, those who could write and those who could not. Now it seems to contain only one class: those who can sort of write if they really try, but don't much relish it or see the point. I suppose that is what an egalitarian would call progress. Illiteracy is clearly of great political interest; it must, therefore, enter our discussion. There is an illiteracy which comes from being unable to spell, and another (more serious) which comes from being unable to use words correctly (or if you prefer, 'correctly'—for we must try to state the question without also begging it). Someone who says 'I refute your allegations totally' unwittingly claims success for an action which he has not even begun. What he says is not merely false, but also ludicrous in its assumption of omniscience. This second kind of illiteracy might, therefore, be expected to have far-reaching implications. It shows itself in two ways; firstly in a lack of awareness of linguistic distinctions, secondly, in the use of jargon whenever it becomes necessary to exercise the mind. Now failure to observe linguistic distinctions may be just one aspect of a general failure to observe. However, there is an intuition, shared by most of the conservatives in this book, that it is really something more than that. What more could it be?

Linguistic distinctions are of two kinds: distinctions of vocabulary, and distinctions of grammar. Suppose someone does not distinguish 'prone' and 'supine', using the two words indifferently whenever referring to the recumbent human form. What does he lack? He can certainly *make* the distinction, using other words—'on his front'/'on his back', for example. Naturally, he will not know what Milton meant by 'a creature who not prone/And Brute as other creatures . . . might erect/His stature . . .'. But he is probably not interested in Milton, nor in the reason why Shelley's 'slave of blind authority' should have been, not prone, but supine. He may even think that a man lying down is described as prone because he is prone to attack, believing (as many people do) that, in this other usage, 'prone' bears a passive meaning. But that too, is only a breach of convention: *he* at least still knows what he means, and could express it in terms intelligible to those prepared to listen to him. So what does he lack, apart from a literature that does not interest him? Most of us, when conversing in a language that is not our own, are used to reconstructing distinctions for which we do not have the exact words. There is a *pleasure* in knowing the right word; but is this linguistic hedonism all that the conservative is recommending?

Consider now distinctions of grammar. In an interesting paper, Julian and Zelda Boyd argue that the complex distinction in the English future tense between 'shall' and 'will' is to be understood as the articulation in grammar of a deep division of attitudes—those summed up in the philosophical distinction between predicting and deciding, the attitudes of observer and of agent. The complex declensions of the two auxiliaries can then be explained in terms of deep differences between states of mind. The suggestion is interesting but, even if it is true, it is not clear that those who confuse 'shall' and 'will' are any worse off than the Italians, who simply lack the distinction. (If it were said that Italians are incapable of renouncing the attitude of agent, it would not be for this reason.) Likewise, those who wrongly think that 'hopefully' is, like 'possibly', a modal auxiliary, obscure a distinction—that between 'I hope she will come', and 'She will come in hope'. But then, I have just *made* the distinction, in other terms, and hopefully the ignoramus can make it, too. (Note that Montaguvian grammar assigns similar deep structure to modal auxiliaries and to adverbs. Does this mean that our ignoramus, like the German user of *hoffentlich*, is right after all, or is it evidence for the falsehood of Montaguvian grammar?).

The examples show how difficult it is for the conservative to advance his case merely by considering individual misuses. There is nothing in the wisdom of Fowler to show that the rules of standard English cannot be broken with impunity, or that something is lost in the degeneration of old distinctions and complexities. It may be that the modern tendency to simplify grammar and vocabulary represents an impoverishment, but of what? If the only impoverishment is of grammar and vocabulary then the complaint is tautological. If, however, there is something else that suffers, we must be told what it is. So let us now turn to the liberal view, and see if it contains any clearer suggestions as to the subject of the quarrel.

In this collection liberalism often advances behind some academic label—'women's studies', 'black studies'—from which it borrows a spurious authority (spurious, since the question whether such subjects are genuine is just the question whether cultural liberalism is coherent). Sometimes they describe an innovation, and argue that innovation has reason in its favour. David Lodge, the imaginative satirist of Californian campus manners, feels called upon to defend the 'poetry' of 'psycho-babble', that grotesque muddle of psychological jargon and machine-made metaphor, named by R. D. Rosen, pertinently ridiculed by Cyra McFadden in her novel *The Serial*, and sounding like this: 'Harvey and I are going through this dynamic right now, and it's kinda where I'm at. I haven't got a lot of psychic energy left over for social interactions. So whatever it is, maybe you should just run it by me right here. Off the wall.' (Example from Miss McFadden.)

Lodge rightly suspects that the outlook expressed by such language is less confused than its grammar. As he puts it:

> Human existence is seen as a process of incessant change, readjust-ment and discovery—no one's condition is static or fixed . . . psycho-babble allays the fear of death by avoiding metaphors drawn from organic life, in which change means eventual decay; its model of experience is drawn from physics, not biology—the individual is pictured in terms of energy and mass, moving about in a curiously timeless psychological space.

Note that Lodge has implied, not only that psychobabble expresses an outlook, but also that it generates and confirms it (it 'allays' the fear of death: it gives a 'model' of human experience, which is 'seen' in a certain way). Through the very accuracy of his observation, Lodge gives fuel to the conservative, who will reply: 'Exactly, that *is* precisely what is wrong with psychobabble. The retreat from death, and the desire to simulate the immortality of machines by sharing in their feelinglessness, make this language a sign, a portent, and a purveyor of social ill.' The battle has shifted ground. It is no longer about language but about the social world as language represents it. We have accomplished this shift, not because we have concentrated on individual misuse, but because we have studied the whole manner in which the act of utterance is performed.

In fact we find that it is the liberals in this volume who make the largest claims on behalf of language, covertly assuming that the relation between speech and outlook is both real and political. In an illiterate piece on the 'political vocabulary of homosexuality' Edmund White wonders whether or not the habit which some men have of referring to one another in the feminine gender is not really 'sexist' (because of the implied sneer). Conscience-struck liberals now avoid calling bitchy men 'she'. Mr White asks himself whether this liberalism has not left something out of consideration. Certainly, it seems to him, the 'rejection of transvestites' (who perpetuate through their antics the invidious distinctions of sexual role) 'has been harsh and perhaps not well thought out'.

Leaving aside the question what a well thought-out rejection of transvestites might be, it is clear that here political and social questions of great profundity are being begged. The choice of innocent-seeming words ('he' and 'she') is seen not merely as a part but almost as the whole of a political struggle, the true nature of which has not been discussed in recent years precisely for fear of offending such as Mr White. The author assumes that homosexuals constitute some coherent but oppressed sub-class of humanity, whose collective assault on the language is simply the legitimate pursuit of heavy breathing space wrongly appropriated by heterosexuals for their self-righteous uses. ('Why not call heterosexuals "sad"?' Vernon Scannell asks, in an amusing poem here reprinted. Why not indeed?)

Reflecting on this matter one is struck by the fact that it is the political liberals—those who found all politics in the doctrine of a right to self-expression which is the natural gift of all, and not merely the privilege of those sad patriarchs whom White calls the 'oppressors'—who are most ready to take offence at the speech of others, to make demands of the language that will change its ideological content and so confirm, even on the lips of the oppressor, the values of the underqueen whose liberty he tramples on. The distinction between 'Mrs' and 'Miss' is pronounced invidious; even the old impersonal 'he' has to be replaced by he stroke she—or rather (to redress the imbalance of sexual roles) she stroke he. For, as we know, the Turks, who lack the grammatical distinction between genders, have always been exemplary in their respect for the rights of women.

Of course, we should always remember the distinction between 'the material transformation of the economic conditions of production' and the 'ideological forms in which men become conscious of this conflict and fight it out'. And language, as the vehicle of consciousness, must be at the centre of the fight. But did Marx (who neglected to write 'men stroke women') imagine that the assault on traditional values would take the form of a tyrannical imposition of 'ideologically purified' rules of speech, and that it would come in the form of a struggle for 'liberation' on the part of a pampered middle class, centred in what Miss McFadden has called 'the consciousness-raising capital of the Western world'? Had he been faced with the sentiments of Mr White, no doubt he would have got on a bummer and freaked out beyond getting behind of anything. But if he retained the power of speech, it would be to utter the words 'bourgeois individualism' with the special sneer that he reserved for everything that had no *obvious* Marxist explanation. The fine frenzy of the self-intoxicated liberal generates dogma after dogma in a system of absolutes from which there is no escape. He will make sure that you feel his freedom where it hurts, and if he gives offence, that only shows how hung-up you are, how unable to swing with the parameters of the gay scene, or flash on human interfaces which are really upfront.

So we have come full circle. It is the liberal who has reminded us of what the conservative does not normally say: that speech is the tyranny of self over other. Take away the order, the manners, and the traditions of hallowed usage, and you reveal the state of nature in its brutishness. What, then, *did* our illiterate specimen lack, besides the language which others, but not he, had chosen? The liberal has forced us to draw inside the veil, and see beneath the 'myth' of freedom and the 'myth' of tradition the common struggle for dominion; but he has given no reason for thinking that *his* form of tyranny is valuable. Nor has he told us *how* values find expression in language, or how any change in the language is able to effect, express or enact (what *is* the right word?) a comparable change in social expectations.

Certain writers from the conservative camp hint at an answer. Margaret Doody, continuing a fashionable discussion, argues that the new Episcopalian prayer book falls short of the 1662 Book of Common Prayer, not because words which we pronounce or hear with special relish are banished from it, but because the style and manner of the new version actually convey new *beliefs*. The inferiority of the new version consists in the paltry, fatuous nature of these beliefs, and not in some independent quality of their expression. There is much to be said about what the word 'belief' might mean, when beliefs are tied so closely to the grammar of their expression. But, whatever it means, there clearly *is* a great difference between the state of mind of those who 'acknowledge and bewail our manifold sins and wickedness, Which we from time to time most grievously have committed, By thought, word, and deed, against thy Divine Majesty, Provoking most justly thy wrath and indignation against us . . .' and the state of mind of those who merely 'confess that we have sinned against you in thought, word and deed'. The first humble themselves; they exalt their Maker through the repentance that possesses them. 'It is quite clear', says Professor Doody, 'that tone is doctrine'. Why? Her answer is that the language of the prayer book is an 'enactment'. This word, borrowed from literary criticism, is not self-explanatory. Professor Doody wishes to say, I think, that in uttering the words of the Prayer Book a man is rehearsing the feelings that are contained in them, and that religious feeling is given both form and substance by this act. The words create the sentiments as much as the sentiments create the words. To remove the words is to remove the sentiments of which they are the indispensable expression.

'Well', the liberal replies, 'that may be true. But all we propose is an *alternative*. In introducing the new ritual, and the new sentiments that are conveyed by it, we do no violence to the old.' That is the more docile form of liberalism, which does not seek to command, but merely to display the infinite variety of disobedience. And now the argument has reached its centre. The conservative has only one reply, which is that the old religious sentiments do not survive the acceptance of 'alternatives'. The old sentiments depended upon an innate sense of their necessity. It is of the nature of religious feeling to regard 'alternatives' as threatening. If expression determines feeling, then alternative expressions are suspect.

It seems to me that the conservative position about language is neither more nor less plausible than such a view about the relation of religious feeling to its ceremonial enactment. The conservative answer to the tyranny of liberalism is that the enforcement of 'alternatives' in the name of 'freedom' is an act of violence against sentiments which require established order for their continuance. And those sentiments have an intrinsic value of their own. The conservative's position is no more (and again no less) difficult than that of the liberal, whose constitutional inability to describe the value of what he recommends is matched only by the conservative's reluctance to make a recommendation.

Returning to the issue of the kidnapping and debauching of the innocent word 'gay', (not so innocent, according to the OED) we begin to see why the conservative, like the liberal, should wish to pretend that the issue is 'merely verbal', and that the connection which they both perceive, between languages and social reality, is too remote to command attention. Conservatives do not find it easy to *say*, but this, I think, is what they believe: the existence of 'alternative' modes of sexual expression, and of the language which 'validates' them, is a threat to nuptial feelings. It is part of those feelings—part of what one could call their 'solemnity'—that they are felt as natural, normal, endowed with an authority that can condone no real alternative. That is why civilization (and its discontents) can be entrusted to them: they contain the seeds of an indispensable continuity. Some such thing *could* be true, even if one is not really allowed to say it. So the issue comes down to this: there are sentiments which depend on traditional modes of expression; and others which depend upon their disruption. Which is to win? In either case the battle becomes conscious in the words that occur to the combatants; but it is *about* words only in the sense that words are the quintessence of style, and style the quintessence of morality. So bitter are the feelings, that neither liberal nor conservative can readily confess to them. However, it takes only a question or two to force them to confess themselves, or, if you prefer, to 'come out'.

There is one author who is shameless in his conservatism—Ian Robinson. Not knowing, or not caring, that there is no greater bigotry than that of liberalism (for after all, is it not fighting for its 'rights'?) he muscles undaunted into the conflict, wearing his opinions on his sleeve. And since, as the conservative insists, form determines content, he loses thereby the first round of a contest which he may well deserve to win. His subject is the language of parliamentary debate (also treated in this volume, in less expletive fashion, by Enoch Powell). This language, as Robinson represents it, is a muddle of mixed metaphors and graceless phraseology. Like Doody, he associates defects of style with deficiencies of content, arguing from the muddle of parliamentary discourse to the paucity and ignorance of the parliamentary mind. But it is worth mentioning a further twist that Robinson adds to the discussion, in his suggestion that the impoverishment of the language of public life consists primarily in a loss of 'ceremoniousness', and that the effects of this are not confined to the public sphere but also invade and disrupt the fulfilments of private life. The thought here is the complex one expressed in the lines from 'A Prayer for my Daughter' (which Robinson quotes): 'How but in custom and in ceremony/Are innocence and beauty born?'

Yeats got away with it, by hiding behind a rhetorical question. Robinson wishes to express the thought as doctrine, and no doubt his expostulating style is the result of the difficulty of such a task. It seems obvious to feeling that the corruption of the public manner erodes the distinction between public and private, and so damages both; but what is obvious to feeling is also recalcitrant to argument. The point which Robinson adumbrates is surely of the greatest interest. The single most obvious recent change in usage has been the loss of formality. English schoolboys may still call each other by their surnames, and occasionally a formal address is heard on the practised lips of underlings: 'sir', 'my lady', 'his lordship', 'your Grace'. But Christian names are now the rule rather than the exception, even between enemies and at a first encounter. Famous people parade themselves on television, making display of their intimacy before those who cannot share it. The last example makes plain how much this seeming informality contains by way of real disdain. But few of the authors in this book choose to mention it, which is odd, for what linguistic innovation could be more political?

There is another change—this time in literary language—which goes unnoticed; strangely, because, in a book containing essays by so many professors of English one would have expected this change to be a main preoccupation. This is the steady erosion, in English, of the subordinate clause, and the consequent loss of grammatical complexity. It is a plausible (if somewhat *a priori*) doctrine, that in a written language the greatest richness of expression will come from complex inflections of grammar and not from fine distinctions of vocabulary. (Compare the syntax of Thucydides with the vocabulary of Homer.) It is one of the effects of an acquaintance with Latin grammar that the logic of the subordinate clause becomes perceivable. The clause is seen to be integral to the thought which constrains and is constrained by it, so that, forcing a qualification into the heart of a sentence, it endows the conclusion with a cadence of mitigated authority.

This returns me again to the subject of homosexuality. At the beginning of *Sodome et Gomorrhe* there occurs a three-page sentence, in which the essence of homosexuality and the pained introversion proper to its social display are not described but—to borrow Doody's word—enacted, in a kind of grammatical ballet, as the prose spasmodically rushes into delights only to hesitate before them, turning backwards on itself with a subjunctive qualification, an imperfect reminiscence, a wavering 'moreover' or a firm, disdainful 'but'. Where in modern English does one find anything like that? You might say that it is purely French (and hence Latin) in its character, but Proust took his immediate inspiration not from Cicero but from Dickens and Ruskin. You find similar effects in Joyce and in Henry James—but not later, or not often. It may be said in reply that meditation is no longer part of the novelist's business: the modern writer seeks to be vivid, and presents his images in staccato form, like this: 'I was left alone in this study, so like the rooms of the monks at Kirkham. The polish. The bare floor. The ugly crucifix on the wall'. (Piers Paul Read). But then, how ineffective that is in comparison with the following sentence, chosen at random from John Evelyn's diary (written long before the supposed eighteenth-century latinization of our literary language):

> Beginning now to descend a little, Captain Wray's horse (that was our sumpter and carried all our baggage) plunging through a bank of loose snow, slid down a frightful precipice, which so incensed that choleric cavalier, his master, that he was sending a brace of bullets into the poor beast, lest our guide should recover him, and run away with his burden; but, just as he was lifting up his carbine, we gave such a shout, and so pelted the horse with snowballs, as with all his might plunging through the snow, he fell from another steep place into another bottom, near a path we were to pass.

You will have been sufficiently engaged by the passage to feel some relief in learning that the horse was unharmed. Just consider the clause 'as with all his might plunging through the snow'; is it not evident that the power of the image is here inseparable from the grammatical tension which controls its expression?

Of course, there is also a modern literary style aimed at complexity, the style of the American 'Creative Writing School'. But complexity is here achieved by accumulation, by the listing and juxtaposing of usually excessive detail, a perpetual stuttering ampersand. The method is often taken to express genuine observation, and moves with a zest for irrelevance which, because it 'contains multitudes', can be mistaken for a zest for life:

> It turns out to be an ancient four-storey hotel with early drunks lying in the hallways, eyelids like tiny loaves brushed with a last glaze of setting sun, and summertime dust in stately evolutions through the taupe light, summertime ease to the streets outside, April summertime as the great vortex of redeployment from Europe to Asia hoots past leaving many souls each night to cling a bit longer to the tranquillities here, this close to the drainhole of Marseilles, this next-to-last stop on the paper cyclone that sweeps them back from Germany, down the river valleys, . . .

You will not be surprised to learn that the sentence (by Thomas Pynchon) does not end but peters out some lines further on in a row of dots. If you read it several times you will see it drooping before your eyes, its vivid images decaying into sparks, its thought becoming darker and odder until nothing remains except a floating subjectivity that has tried, and failed, to take notice of a world.

In general it could be said of this collection that the writers provoke more thought than they express. There are excellent things—such as Michael Tanner's persuasive criticism of the language of modern philosophy, and Frances Ferguson's discussion of the language of letter-writing. But the project is so vast and indeterminate that the reader cannot perceive whether these pieces advance or retard it. And perhaps that is what the editors intended, since they are both too sophisticated to think that anything is advanced or retarded by the exercise of thought alone.

2   Sense and Sincerity

The Living Principle: 'English' as a discipline of thought, F.R. Leavis (Chatto & Windus, 1975), from the *Times Literary Supplement*, 17 October 1975.

IT IS characteristic of Leavis's criticism that every sentence—whether premise, conclusion, or intermediate step—is as much as any other a declaration of outlook. It is foreign to his method and to his style to draw conclusions from otherwise innocent analyses: every phrase and every word is bent to the task of expressing ('intensely', 'irresistibly', 'pre-eminently', etc) the moral and aesthetic vision which he has made his own. This new (or at least partly new) book is no exception to the rule. While ostensibly conceived as some kind of challenge or response to the contemporary philosopher (and in particular, according to a footnote, as an answer to the 'philosophy-addicted Cambridge intellectual' who had asked Leavis what he could have meant in elevating the intelligence of Blake above that of Swift), *The Living Principle* is in fact, like all his recent works, a prolonged, repetitious and yet obscure affirmation of the values which a technological society is now expected to deny.

Despite its putatively authoritative character, the book adds little by way of exposition or development to Leavis's previous publications. None the less, it demands and deserves comment, on two accounts. First because it deliberately addresses itself to the contemporary philosopher, purporting to show that philosophy, at least as it is now conceived in England, cannot have the central place in Leavis's ideal university that he would still wish to accord to the study of English. Secondly, because it contains a criticism of *Four Quartets*, a criticism which attempts to display the weakness and ultimate unacceptability of Eliot's vision in that poem. Sandwiched between these two discussions we find reprinted the fine essays from *Scrutiny*—'Thought and Emotional Quality', 'Imagery and Movement', 'Reality and Sincerity', etc—which would alone justify Leavis's reputation as one of the most important, and also one of the most philosophical, critics of our time.

It is, however, somewhat strange to find these essays reprinted yet again; even stranger is the author's failure anywhere to mention that they were published some thirty years ago. He prefers to treat them as an integral part of the present book, an illustration through detailed analysis of the generalities expounded in the earlier (the 'philosophical') part. There results a blatant discontinuity of style. The first section is written in an abstract, cluttered and private idiom which comes oddly from a self-appointed protector of the English tongue, while the *Scrutiny* essays are both tersely written and entirely persuasive, conveying a far more immediate sense of the author's philosophy than could ever be obtained from the earlier parts.

Leavis spends some time attacking Wittgenstein, and also (less seriously) Russell. Now it is certainly true, as Leavis implies, that contemporary analytical philosophy has had little to contribute to literary criticism, nothing to say about the plight of contemporary man, and only insignificant comments to make on the vulgarization and destruction of our language, that 'shabby equipment always deteriorating/In the general mess of imprecision of feeling.'

. It is perhaps only an analytical philosopher who could now have the effrontery to defend Utilitarianism as a serious account of the moral life, or who could be so illiterate as to think that the problem of self-identity would be solved if we could show that 'person' is a 'family-resemblance' term. And if there is justice in Leavis's passing hostility to Russell it is surely because Russell—like his illustrious godfather, J. S. Mill—presented the code of the philistine in elegant and self-confident accents, sweetening the ugly reductivism of liberal morality with a cultured 'philosophical' outlook.

But Russell was only continuing a more ancient English tradition, the tradition of empiricism, which has never been able to describe what is distinctive in human experience, nor able to leave a place in its fragmented vision of man for history, culture, tradition and the fulfilment characteristic of the moral life. It is the childish common-sense of the free-thinking Anglo-Saxon that disturbs Dr Leavis, but if this spirit survives in English philosophy, it is partly because of Russell and Moore, partly because of Austin and his school, yet emphatically not because of Wittgenstein. For Leavis to direct so many of his remarks against Wittgenstein—seeking to elevate in his stead, as paradigms of the 'relevant', thinkers like Michael Polanyi, Stanislav Andreski and Marjorie Grene—shows a great misunderstanding.

Of course it is true that Wittgenstein's thought finds expression only in 'linguistic analysis', and that he was not given to any but arcane and elusive references to the 'darkness' of our times. But Wittgenstein had a sensibility that was not mere cleverness, which expressed itself in a style that was capable of conveying ideas with life and immediacy, and which united precision of thought with a sensitivity to emotional resonance that is surely unique among all philosophers and not just among those of the linguistic school. It is this which elevates the final refutation of the Cartesian view of mind (a refutation which Leavis applauds but does not, as he should, attribute to Wittgenstein) above the level of a merely formal proof, and gives to it the quality of a vision. That vision is a haunting and eloquent one, and to have seen its force is to have glimpsed, in Wittgenstein's philosophy of mind, a path out of the desert of empiricist and utilitarian thought.

In fact Wittgenstein offers an account of human experience which promises to make sense once again, as the Idealists made sense, of man's being in the world, and of his existence as a cultural, historical and moral figure. But Leavis—whose criticisms seem to rely on an uncomprehending dismissal of the vocabulary of the *Tractatus*—seems not to have appreciated the difference between Wittgenstein and his philosophical contemporaries. And yet if philosophy has not led to the acquisition by its students of genuine standards, why whould we blame Wittgenstein for that? Certainly we do not blame Leavis for the poverty of academic English, or for its failure to provide any bastion against the mediocrity that has swamped the channels of popular communication and now threatens to swamp our universities as well.

We are told that Wittgenstein, in contrast to Marjorie Grene or Polanyi, is not 'useful', which is to say that he does not provide any phrase, word or formula with which neatly to encompass the values that Leavis wishes to urge on the modern man. Polanyi and Grene, however, do provide such phrases, and Leavis quotes them often. But it is almost entirely phrases that he quotes, and all the complexities of argument that would be needed to establish an illuminating position—and that includes the position of Leavis himself—are left out of consideration as 'irrelevant'. What, after all, does philosophical thought amount to for Leavis? 'All three passages', he writes (referring to brief quotations from Collingwood, Polanyi and Marjorie Grene), 'in their different ways register the conviction—the impelling principle, for each of their authors, of his thinking—that "life" is a necessary word.'

The trouble is that what Leavis attempts to sum up in that phrase is a thought far more complex than anything to be found in the passages he quotes, a thought which underlies much of his most penetrating literary criticism, but which he has never succeeded in expressing in wholly adequate words. Perhaps it is impossible now to do so. As he puts it:

> Modern English . . . represents drastic impoverishment; the assumptions implicit in it eliminate from thought, and from the valuations and tested judgments that play so essential a part in thought, very important elements of human experience—elements that linguistic continuity had once made available.

That conception owes much to Eliot, and reflects the tradition of Idealist philosophy from which Eliot himself learned so much. But it is expressed unclearly, and demands a philosophical exegesis.

True, no light will be cast on the problems that interest Leavis by formal semantics, or by the theory of illocutions, or by whatever other fashionable technicalities might happen to have seized the imagination of the philosophical world. And it may be, too, that there is some significance in the fact that, while philosophy contains, in this way, whole branches that are devoid of the human significance that Leavis demands, there could be no such dead branches of English, English being so defined by Leavis that it must necessarily coincide with the realm of serious values. But it does not follow that his own position could not, or should not, be stated in philosophical terms.

On the contrary, a clear statement of Leavis's position would be one that tells us precisely what it means to say, for example, that the assumptions implicit in modern English represent a drastic impoverishment in the experience of English speakers, or that the present corruption of our language is connected essentially with a corruption of consciousness, an inability in the popular mind to embrace the quality of experience that was once made available to it by Shakespeare, or Bunyan, or Dickens or Blake. But to say what such statements mean is to do philosophy—philosophy as Wittgenstein among many others has conceived it. And the position taken up by Leavis—the position, to put it crudely, that our consciousness is created by our language, that our feelings have precision only in so far as our language has precision, and that the precision in question has nothing to do with mathematical or scientific exactitude but rather reflects our whole ability to enter into meaningful commerce with the world—that position belongs to a philosophical standpoint infinitely more subtle than anything Leavis has discovered in Polanyi, Andreski or Marjorie Grene.

It is true that Leavis does not produce any general statement of his views; he has no universal system to which literary criticism could be added as a mere confirmatory appendage. Indeed, in a well-known controversy with Wellek, he expressly denies that such a system (a system of 'value judgments' as modern philosophers might simplifyingly put it) is necessary: a critical judgment can be established, and indeed must be established, through a response to the particular case, and the perception of intrinsic qualities and connections that are made in that response. Leavis's elaboration of that idea must surely be recognized as of fundamental importance in criticism. However, this emphasis on the particular response is by no means alien to philosophical analysis, but leads to the establishing of conceptual connexions of precisely the kind that might feature as the conclusions of a philosophical argument.

Thus Leavis shows, in the discussion of Hardy's 'After a Journey' here reprinted, that sincerity in literature is not simply a matter of the poet telling the truth about himself. Sincerity is a property of the whole manner in which the poet's feeling is expressed, and is inseparable from a detailed attention to the outer world, and a concrete realization of the objects there presented. Sincerity therefore necessitates thought, is incompatible with sentimentality, and reflects a mode of understanding of the world which, while not of a 'scientific' kind, is none the less more important to a man than any understanding that a scientific training might have brought to him.

Now these connections—between sincerity, reality, thought and emotional quality—are not merely connections of fact. It doesn't just so happen that the sincere expression of emotion coincides with an attention to, and realization of, attendant circumstances, or that a sentimental emotion is one that outruns the control of any justifying thought. As John Casey pointed out in *The Language of Criticism*, Leavis's conclusions here are, if true, necessarily true; he is establishing something about the concepts of sincerity and sentimentality, and the connections that he points to must be fundamental to any serious philosophy of mind. It is precisely such connections that form the substance of the later parts of the *Philosophical Investigations*, and it is likely indeed that Wittgenstein would have approved of an analysis of the concept of sincerity that makes so close a connection between genuineness of emotion and the quality of expression.

However, the parallel that most readily suggests itself is with the Idealist philosophy of the nineteenth century, the philosophy that so influenced T. S. Eliot and which finds poetic expression in the *Four Quartets*. In his analysis of sincerity Leavis—as he rightly realizes—is going against the whole Cartesian and empiricist orthodoxy, which assumes sincerity to be merely a matter of correspondence between inner and outer, as though the inner life could be complete in itself and yet all the same not achieve successful expression. On the contrary—and we can see this view again and again in Leavis's early criticism—the inner life is constituted by its outward expression, so that any corruption in the form of expression must bring with it a corresponding corruption of consciousness. There is nothing to the human mind that is not revealed in the elaboration of characteristically human behaviour, and the importance of language, of tradition, of recognized institutions and the rest, is that they determine the quality of our consciousness without being merely ancillary to it. Such a view was, of course, central to the philosophy of Hegel, and it was a view which seemed to provide greatest hope to the thinkers of the nineteenth century, as they sought for a philosophy of human experience with which to resist the crass naiveties of Bentham, Godwin and John Stuart Mill.

In the light of all that, it is of great interest that Leavis should now consider it incumbent on him to show Eliot to be, as he puts it, a major poet but very much a 'case'. A naive reader might have thought that *Four Quartets* contains the most persuasive possible statement of the philosophy upon which Leavis has always surreptitiously relied. Now, in *New Bearings* and *Revaluation* Leavis was for the most part concerned with the *quality of expression*, and hence with the character of the emotion expressed. His concern was to show how faults of form and idiom correspond to shallow and trivial perceptions, and how poetic strength is indicative of deep and serious feeling. On that score, as one cannot fail to recognize, Eliot will always pass muster, and Leavis makes it clear in the third section of this book that if Eliot is a 'case' it is largely *because* he passes muster: he satisfies the standards of sincerity, reality, seriousness and the rest.

But there is a crucial failing. Leavis seems wary of saying what one might have expected him to say, namely that the failing is one of 'intelligence'; however, it is certainly true that the usual contrasts—with Shakespeare, Blake and D. H. Lawrence—are very much in the forefront of his mind. Sometimes, too, one is tempted to think that Leavis will not accept the *Four Quartets* because they seem to him to expound a philosophy which is actually *false*. 'Eliot's affirmation', he says, 'is not coercively entailed in the way he supposes. . . .' But of course it was never suggested that Donne or Herbert or Vaughan had actually to *prove* their metaphysics in their verse: why, then, should one ask the same of Eliot?

What Leavis seems to mean, however, is not so much that the metaphysical assumptions are false, but that an acceptance of them—in contrast, let us suppose, to an acceptance of the philosophy underlying *Pilgrim's Progress*—is at the same time a denial of certain fundamental values, the values of 'life', 'creativity' and so on that we find exemplified in Shakespeare, Lawrence and Blake. It is possible to doubt that Leavis really succeeds in establishing this charge. For one thing he does not discuss Eliot's philosophy in any detail. Consider the lines:

> Words, after speech, reach
> Into the silence. Only by the form, the pattern,
> Can words or music reach
> The stillness, as a Chinese jar still
> Moves perpetually in its stillness.

'It is astonishing', says Leavis, 'that a "practitioner" whose genius manifests itself in its practice as a rare intelligence about the language in which he works should, obviously without self-suspicion, exhibit so grave an unintelligence here. What, when it is said of words ("after speech"), we may ask, does "reach into the silence" mean?' For Leavis the passage has no true coherence and proceeds by a merely associative movement, the implications of which (for example, that words and music are importantly similar) cannot be accepted.

A philosopher might suggest a rather different interpretation. For there is an interesting difficulty that faces the Idealist conception of experience. It is not enough to say that the forms of expression create the possibilities of feeling, and therefore that a disciplined use of words is the manifestation of genuine and controlled emotion. For most emotion is not accompanied by words. Therefore, if the Idealist vision is to be coherent, it must be that a proper understanding of language brings with it, for whatever reason, a corresponding harmony of behaviour.

It might be suggested that Eliot gives poetical expression to such a theory in the passage quoted. For he seems to imply that words, after they have been spoken, none the less 'reach into' (that is, take hold of and modify) those parts of our consciousness that exist in silence; and they impose order in that their 'form' or 'pattern' is conveyed to our unspoken experience. The 'pattern' here might represent the enduring, inherited values through which words master emotions and make them accessible to consciousness. In the acquisition of such a 'pattern' emotion, which in its uncomprehended form can exist only as an anxiety and a burden, becomes instead a living proof of our continuing self-identity. Thus through emotion we reach a stillness which is also a movement, a place where the soul is untroubled without being unmoved: 'as a Chinese jar still/Moves perpetually in its stillness.'

The word 'moves' suggests—to me at least—another meaning, the meaning of 'words move, music moves': namely that *we* are moved by these successful achievements of expression, to share in them, so that our feeling is changed and mastered in the act of understanding expressions made available from another source. It is thus that the activity of the poet—the 'purification of the dialect of the tribe'—is continuous with the search for order that self-consciousness will always demand.

Perhaps, then, the difficulty of creating poetry from the cultural debris of our time is one with the difficulty that ordinary self-consciousness must face, in a world alien to the conceptions which have determined its identity. If that is so, then, as Idealist philosophy has always emphasized, the aesthetic enterprise and the moral task are ultimately one and the same.

The passage suggests another Idealist theme. It is not only words that form, develop, or undo our consciousness. Music may have a similar status, so too may a Chinese jar. Indeed, all the successful distillations of self-consciousness with which history presents us lead to an attempt to understand and sympathize, to seize the Hegelian 'Idea' which gave to such expressions not only an aesthetic but also—and in the same act—a moral significance as well.

Philosophically the idea is a bold one, but it can hardly be dismissed as unserious. In reflecting on it, however, one is reminded of how much Leavisism seems wedded to the criticism of literature, and how much it relies on concepts that have no obvious application to the other forms of art. The Leavisite's 'Great Tradition'—the tradition without which there would be no modern consciousness as we English-speakers know it—is one filled entirely by literary men, and by writers of English at that. In the poetry of Eliot, however, not only Baudelaire and Dante but also Wagner and Beethoven play a part in the formation of perceptions that are, for all their complexity of historical reference, entirely proper to their place and time.

Even when he is not overtly hostile, Leavis seems reluctant to admit that such eclecticism could be poetically valuable. If a passage recommends itself it is most often because of that vigorous use of language which Eliot is supposed to have inherited from the great tradition of English speech and English verse. Thus Leavis says of the lines, 'Out at sea the dawn wind/Wrinkles and slides. . . .' that 'the "wrinkles" and "slides" are Eliot, but we might very well say that they come to him from Shakespeare, and if they come, in a sense, from Shakespeare they came *to* Shakespeare from the multitudes of those who had spoken English before him'. As a matter of fact (and it must surely have been pointed out before now) Eliot's language is reminiscent of the line 'The wrinkled sea beneath him crawls' but clearly Tennyson, not being part of that tradition which gave to English its unique vitality and expressive power (since the uncontrolled feelings in Tennyson's verse *must* be tantamount to a laxity in his use of words) could not, for Leavis, have had any such important influence It is, one might say, a metaphysical impossibility, dictated by the very nature of a living tradition as Leavis conceives it. Here we see another point where Leavis's criticism follows the dictates of a tacit but ambitious philosophical idea.

In general, it seems, Leavis's purpose in this long and interesting essay is to force on the reader the sense of a confrontation of philosophies. Eliot, for Leavis, is against life, while Leavis is concerned to make 'the contrary—the fiercely rebutting—positive affirmation'. But what does that affirmation amount to? The constant insistence that ' "life" is a necessary word', or that Blake had more to say to us when he claimed that 'Jesus was an artist' than Eliot could ever achieve through his examination of spiritual possibilities, is ultimately unsatisfying.

The alternative which Leavis refers to is seriously underdescribed, and acquires what content it has only negatively, through the rejection of Eliot. Having no taste for the Baudelairean sophistication that leads Eliot to give full elaboration to a state of mind even in the act of tacitly withdrawing from it, Leavis seems to take every line of the *Four Quartets* as an utterance of doctrine. For example, the lines: 'Quick now, here, now, always—/Ridiculous the waste sad time/Stretching before and after' must be an expression of Eliot's philosophy, a philosophy which does no more, therefore, than emphasize the epiphanous moment at the expense of an enduring struggle for Life. But is that right? Perhaps we ought not to read *Burnt Norton* as we would read *Little Gidding*. For it is possible to approach the *Four Quartets* in such a way that the first three are only exploratory in tone, the true commitment being postponed until the climax of the last.

After all, it is the hidden laughter of children that rises with that 'quick now, here, now, always', and those hidden children exist only in our 'first world' to which we have returned by following the 'deception of the thrush'. The moment itself will acquire its value (its 'pattern') only later, when it is brought into relation with tradition and history, which is 'now and England'. To insist, in the face of Eliot's mature development of that theme, on the unexplained 'creativity' and 'life' which Eliot's philosophy is held to deny is perhaps also to follow the deception of the thrush, to identify oneself too closely with the hidden children for whom the problem of consciousness has not yet been fully posed. To that solution one might wish to offer, as Leavis would put it, a 'judicious but emphatic no'.

3 The Impossibility of Semiotics

From the *London Review of Books*, 7 February 1980.

SEMIOTICS, semiology, hermeneutics, structuralist criticism—so many labels, but how many things? If there are distinctions here, they seem to be largely hereditary. The term 'semiotic' comes from C. S. Peirce, 'semiology' from Saussure. 'Structuralism' has meant one thing in anthropology, another in linguistics; its application to literary theory comes partly through the work of Propp and the Russian formalists. 'Hermeneutics' once indicated the nice interpretation of Biblical texts; now it denotes the nice interpretation of everything. In all these things, however, the niceties seem to be the same: technicality at the expense of theory, analysis at the expense of content, intensity at the expense of depth—in short, 'vain babblings and oppositions of science, falsely so called' (I Timothy vi, 20). And yet, wherever literature is taught, students have to perceive it through the veil of this new scholasticism, their observations muddled by technicalities borrowed from a thousand premature sciences, distracted by 'methods' which regard Mickey Mouse and the *Mona Lisa*, Superman and *King Lear*, advertising jingles and the works of Schoenberg, as equally legitimate objects of inquiry. Is this movement a reaction against critical moralism, expressed with a hesitancy so great that only massive recourse to technicality can prevent it from knowledge of its impotence? Or is it the first step towards some new critical method, a method sufficiently general as to assign an interpretation to everything that could be regarded as a 'sign'?

Those questions are crucial for the future of literary education in our universities. Any answer to them must begin by recognizing the uncertainty in a movement which now advances behind the banner of scientific inquiry, now slips sideways into the smoke of literary rhetoric. This uncertainty arises from the attempt to combine three independent enterprises, the first modest, the second speculative, the third rooted in fallacy.

The first is the quest for 'levels' of meaning in literary and other works. A poem may allow several readings (literal, allegorical, metaphorical, and so on), which develop with its movement, and take their structure from the narrative which unites them. Dante, in the *Convivio*, describes four such 'levels' of meaning, and the tradition which he exemplifies has continued to the present day. In particular, it can be seen in the French *explication de texte*, whether dressed in its old,

31

cold, surgical garments, or fitted out in the latest jargon of linguistics. The method of much 'structuralist' criticism is that of Dante, the method of stepwise analysis, designed to reveal layers of meaning concealed within the enclosure of a 'text'. The difference lies in a lust on the part of the structuralist for meanings which the author would not have recognized.

Semiotic and structuralist criticism also have their roots in a widespread speculation according to which scientific inquiry does not exhaust the modes of human understanding, being unable to describe the world as we experience it. We stand to this world (the *Lebenswelt*) in a relation not of observation but of 'belonging'. From Kantian metaphysics and 19th-century anthropology arose the idea that a peculiar mode of understanding is reserved for this 'human world', a mode of understanding *(Verstehen)* which would show to be fraught with meaning what science displays as 'neutral' and 'meaning-free'. Meaning belongs to human acts and gestures; it also lies dormant in the world. Perhaps, then, there is a general method that will reveal the meanings of things. Such a method will be unconcerned with explanation and prediction, but it will be of universal significance nevertheless, relating us to artifacts, to art, to things and to one another in a way that restores the centrality of human thought and action. It may even re-create that necessary illusion which scientific explanation took away, the illusion of human freedom.

The third intellectual motive behind this kind of criticism contradicts such speculations. If it is combined with them, it is because the seekers after 'human' understanding have been reluctant to relinquish, in their pursuit of it, the authority and objectivity of science. Hence there has emerged the desire for a 'general science of signs', or semiology. Without the assumption that such a general science is possible, the repeated borrowings from the technicalities of linguistics in order to describe the many things that are fashionably labelled 'signs' is nothing but a kind of alchemy, conjuring the illusion of method in the absence of the fact of it.

The idea of a general science of signs is, I think, rooted in fallacy. What makes a science? There is a science of fish because fish are similarly constituted, obey similar laws, have a discoverable essence, over and above the evident facts which lead us so to label them. (Fish constitute a 'natural kind'.) Buttons, by contrast, have no such essence, and no common identity besides the function which we already know. There can be no general science of the *constitution* of buttons: if there is a science of buttons, it is a science of their function. Now signs are clearly more like buttons than like fish, and a general science of signs will therefore be a science not of constitution but of function. But what is this function? Semiology refers us to language, road signs, facial expressions, food, clothes, photography, architecture, heraldry, basket-weaving, music. Are all these 'signs' in the same sense, or in any sense? The word 'sign' means many things, and points to many functions. Do we suppose that a cloud signifies rain in the way that *Je m'ennuie* signifies that 'I am bored'? Of course not, since no cloud can have the function of a sentence. From a scientific point of view, one suspects that there is not *one* thing here but thousands. What is common is only a small feature of the surface of each, usually as familiar to us as the function of buttons. If there is a common essence of 'signs' it is sure to be very shallow; semiology pretends that it is deep.

But there is more to be said. There are sciences whose subject-matter is contested and speculative, based on analogy and hypothesis, rather than on any intuitive knowledge of the existence of a natural or functional kind. Perhaps linguistics itself is such a science: at least, its subject-matter and its methods are still much in dispute. Semiology leans on linguistics, hoping to base itself on an analogy between language and other sorts of 'sign'. The basis of the analogy is twofold. First, all human behaviour can be seen as expressive. It reveals thoughts, feelings and intentions, not all of which would be spontaneously acknowledged by the agent. Secondly, and more important, the modes of human expression can sometimes be thought to have a certain structure which they share with language. It is this which seems to bring them within the purview of Saussurian linguistics.

According to the Saussurian model, a sentence is a 'system' composed of 'syntagms'. A syntagm can be defined as a set of terms which may replace one another without destroying the system—without rendering the sentence 'unacceptable' to speakers of the language. For example, in the sentence 'John loves Mary,' 'loves' may be replaced by 'hates' or 'eats', but not by 'but', 'thinks that' or 'swims'. Now consider another example, discussed at length by Barthes in his *Eléments de Sémiologie*, the example of the menu. A man might order the following: *oeufs bénédictine*, followed by steak and chips, followed by rum baba. That is an 'acceptable' system: in our society, the same menu in reverse would not be 'acceptable'. Furthermore, each dish belongs to a 'syntagmatic unity': it can be replaced by some dishes and not others. Steak and chips can be replaced by ham salad but not by a glass of Sauternes—for that would be unacceptable. (One can see at a glance that railway trains and classical architecture also exhibit this kind of 'structure'.) What follows?

Consider Barthes's actual interpretation. Steak and chips is supposed to 'mean' (according to an essay in *Mythologies*) 'Frenchness'. Suppose that the 'meaning' of *oeufs bénédictine* is 'Catholicism', and that of rum baba 'sensuality': what now is the meaning of the whole system? Does it mean that French Catholicism is compatible with sensuality? Or that being French is more important than being Catholic? Or being sensual a fundamental part of both? There is no telling, since while the system has structure, it has no grammar. Which is to say that there is no way in which the meanings of the parts determine a meaning for the whole. Hence we should not speak of 'syntax': the idea of syntax is the idea of a potential meaning, so that syntactical rules must depend upon semantic interpretation. (Frege showed this truth to be fundamental to both logic and language.) It follows that the search for 'syntagmatic' and 'paradigmatic' structure plays no part in any science of non-linguistic 'signs'. The two aspects of the analogy with language (expression and structure) cannot be conjoined in the manner that the analogy requires. No amount of technicality can suffice to conjoin them. So it is impossible to assume that the functions of linguistic and non-linguistic 'signs' will be similar, and the grounds for supposing that there might be a general science applicable to both of them collapse.

We must therefore abandon the scientific pretensions of semiology. And in fact we find that semiological criticism has relied on linguistics, not for the latter's scientific claims, but for its technicalities alone. These technicalities nevertheless create an illusion of objectivity. They put the 'semiological critic' in a position of peculiar superiority. They give him a justification for avoiding the question of how meaning is objectively determined in language (since their application makes contact with no semantic inquiry); at the same time, semiology lays claim to a special objectivity of its own. This 'objectivity' consists in the fact that the semiologist will look for those features of a text that 'reveal' things (for example, an attachment to some 'ideology'), while remaining indifferent to the professed intention of the writer. This is what is meant by the claim that semiology explores 'levels' of the text that may not have been apparent to the author. Because Dante was analysing his own poems, he could not raise the question whether the 'levels' that he discerned in them belonged to the writer's intention, the reader's perception, or both. But the problem for the semiologist is no different from the problem for Dante: what makes an interpretation legitimate? No 'method' of 'decoding', as the semiologist would express it, will suffice to answer that question. The semiologist commonly sets about the task of 'demythologizing' the text before him, with the intention of remythologizing it in accordance with his own rival ideology. But that can provide no criterion of legitimate interpretation. This can be seen by reading Barthes's analysis of Balzac's story *Sarrasine*. It is entitled *S/Z* (referring to a problem in phonetics) and consists in a step by step analysis of the story, which is divided into five hundred fragments of text. After a preamble Barthes begins the analysis by turning his attention to the title:

SARRASINE: The title gives rise to the question: Sarrasine, what is that?

It is a promising beginning, and Barthes immediately seizes the opportunity to introduce some technical terms:

Let us use the expression 'hermeneutic code' (which we will write: HER for the sake of simplicity) for the totality of units which have as their function to articulate, in various ways, a question, its answer, and the varied accidents which can prepare a question and delay the answer . . . .

In creating this technical term Barthes considers himself to be analysing something called the writer's 'code'. Soon we have not only HER but also ACT, SEM, REF, and SYM. What function do these terms have? It seems that they are intended to contribute to a 'reading' of Balzac's text, and

to read is not a parasitical gesture . . . . it is an activity (which is why we should rather speak of a lexiological act—or even better, a lexiographic act, since I write down my reading) and the method of this activity is topological. . . .

To put it another way, to read is to understand the 'codes' which are developed in the text. It is to be able (for example) to follow the development of questions raised by the writer (HER), of actions begun but not completed (ACT), and so on. And once again—although this is, of course, entirely trivial—we have syntagmatic structure. At any point in the development of the plot the ways of continuing a question or an action are limited, and until the reader grasps these limitations he does not understand the text.

Now these technical terms belong to no known scientific theory. Nor is the basis of their application clearly described. We may reasonably ask ourselves, therefore, how the analysis would read without them. I venture to suggest that it would read like this: the story consists of actions and characters, and to read the text is to follow the actions and be familiar with the characters. At each point there are associated questions (HER), references to received ideas or commonplaces (REF), the use of rhetorical devices (SEM), and so on. To read the text with understanding is to be aware of these associations and devices, to see how they contribute to the whole. Literary criticism consists in spelling them out for the reader who might otherwise have failed to notice and appreciate them. What, then, does Barthes' procedure amount to? It is no more than a supremely traditional French critical procedure writ large: *explication de texte*. And Barthes' technical coinages add nothing to the theory that lies behind that method, nor do they remove from it that air of pedantry that has so often made it a torture for those who have been exposed to it. Criticism for Barthes is what his compatriots so often take it to be—the analysis of rhetorical figures, together with a culling of associations and symbols, in the framework of a step by step analysis of the literary text. It cannot be denied that Barthes does from time to time notice certain rhetorical figures that had previously escaped academic commentary. For instance he draws the reader's attention to the 'paradoxism' that (we are to suppose) is the ultimate attempt of the writer's code to 'bend the inexpiable':

> Hidden in the embrasure, partitioning the outer and the inner, installed in the interior limit of opposition, straddling the wall of Antithesis, the narrator operates with this figure: he induces or supports a transgression. This transgression has so far nothing disastrous about it; ironised, trivialised, naturalised, it is the object of a likeable idiolect *(parole)* with no relation to the horror of the symbol (to the symbol as horror): and yet its scandal is immediately apparent.

(At this point the reader would do well to remember the active nature of the verb *'délirer'*. *Délirer* is something that the writer—or critic—does: it does not come over him. As an activity it has been made highly respectable by Foucault. Indeed, there are those for whom it is more or less obligatory, and certainly preferable to rational thought, which is tainted with bourgeois categories.)

How does this kind of criticism help the reader to understand Balzac's story? Barthes is unfortunately very unclear about that. There is nothing remarkable in the suggestion that in order to understand Balzac one must be sensitive to the resonances of his style; how could one think otherwise? But it is here that semiology once again raises its head. For having, as he supposes, encapsulated the style in a structural 'code', Barthes thinks that he can force an interpretation on the code in defiance of any 'bourgeois' reading of the story. The writer's codes are demystified, and their true ideology exposed:

> Although their origin derives entirely from books, these codes, by a piece of juggling that is entirely proper to bourgeois ideology, which turns culture upside down so as to make it into nature, seem to be a basis for what is real, for 'Life'. 'Life' becomes, in the classical text, a sickly mixture of commonplace opinions, a suffocating blanket of received ideas . . .

and this is the real reason why it is no longer possible to write like Balzac. For us the ideas of 'life' and 'nature' are discredited, and can find expression in no authentic text. The bourgeois critic, who regards literature as a reflection on life, is disqualified from judging the literature of our time. Similarly literature itself is either 'classical' (and so bound up with a defunct ideology), or else a part of 'our modernity'. Writing becomes modern by abandoning the codes of the *bourgeoisie* and using instead those of the revolutionary consciousness (discernible apparently in the *nouveau*—or rather, *nouveau nouveau*—*roman*).

In short, it is only the bourgeois who seeks for 'life' or 'nature' in a text, only the bourgeois who feels that a story (or a poem or a play) may reflect or illuminate the values and choices of its readers. And Barthes does not like this intrusion of human experience into the critic's sanctum. By demythologizing literature he renders it harmless. No writer can force Barthes to take seriously an ideology that is not his own; no critic of his position can possibly expect to be taken account of. Barthes' claim not to be making value-judgments is no more than a ruse. The mesmerizing pedantry of his criticism is simply a mask for a moralism that brooks no opposition. And yet, such criticism, intent as it is to go *behind* the text, to root out its secret meaning, can give us no proper understanding. It allows nothing to literature except acts of codification which occur equally in fashion, advertising and ordinary speech. Literature, by being demystified, is also denatured. All that is distinctive of it—for example, its ability to imagine and examine human situations, to express and clarify emotions—is left out of consideration as irrelevant. To decipher Balzac's codes 'semiologically' is to ignore the demands of Balzac's representation. And that is precisely why people have disliked the *explication de texte*—it too often dehumanizes literature, degrades it into a vehicle for whimsical pedantry, removes from it every vestige of a moral idea.

The central question raised by such step-by-step analysis is the question of relevance. What *makes* this into a 'reading' of Balzac's story? What is the criterion of legitimate interpretation? If there is none, why all the concealed moral fervour? If the criterion exists, how do we discover it? That these are serious questions is shown by another, much simpler, example, this time from the philosophy of mathematics. Arithmetic can be derived from logic in various ways. Frege, Russell and Zermelo each attempted such a derivation, and their proofs have a common intellectual structure. But where Frege speaks of 'concepts', Russell refers to 'classes' and Zermelo to 'sets'. Applying semiology, we could say that in each case the choice of vocabulary 'reveals' (or better 'codifies') certain 'meanings'. For Frege arithmetic is the objectification of the inner life; for Russell it is the expression of class consciousness; for Zermelo it is the description of a collectivity. The bourgeois individualist, the aristocrat and the egalitarian each reveals himself in the language that he chooses. Such an account could be given all the rhetorical and 'structuralist' support that Barthes gives to his analysis of *Sarrasine*. But we know that it is irrelevant to an understanding of the texts. *How* do we know that?

A question like this bewilders the semiologist, since his technicalities can generate no solution to it. In the last analysis, his answer must be the same as Dante's: an interpretation is a legitimate 'reading' if it develops *through* the text, acquiring its strength and elaboration from the movement of the literary surface. But perhaps there is more to be said. And it is characteristic of 'semiotics'—the new discipline which sometimes forswears, but at other times endorses, the scientific pretensions of semiology—to attempt to say something more than the obvious in answer to our question. Does semiotics, then, represent some new departure, and does it escape the strictures that I have laid upon the general 'science' of signs? The principal exponent of semiotics is Umberto Eco, who holds the only existing chair in this possibly nonexisting subject, and whose writings—which take their initial inspiration from the general classification of signs put forward by C. S. Peirce—have proved influential in Italy, France and America. Eco himself has shown a tireless energy in collecting and applying the results of modern semantics, putting forward (in *La Struttura Assente*) a 'semiotics' of architectural forms which has been studied, if not for its content, at least for the enterprise that it represents. He has looked for his theories of the non-linguistic 'sign', not only in Peirce and his followers, but also in Chomsky's transformational grammar, in the theory of speech acts, and now in the 'possible world' semantics of the modal logician. And while this may seem to be just another case of *Tel Quel* dilettantism, Eco's enterprise is distinguished by spasmodic attempts at clarity, and by a relative freedom from that café-table Marxism which recently transferred its favourite point of observation from Les Deux Magots to La Coupole, acquiring in the process a profound respect for the commodities of the consumer culture, and a keen desire to participate in their fetishization. For such reasons–and because he writes also in English—Eco continues to attract attention, and his awareness that there are important intellectual questions that semiology leaves unanswered has led to a transfer of faith to the newer 'semiotics'. It seems to express a greater plasticity of outlook, and, being able to regard Julia Kristeva and Saul Kripke as equally relevant to its intellectual enterprise, it draws attention from every corner of the academic world.

Let us, however, ignore the higher reaches of semiotic speculation, and attend for a moment to that mundane application through which it first proved influential: the application to architecture. We find the old semiological fallacies enduring uninterrupted. This can be seen at once from reading Donald Preziosi's *The Semiotics of the Built Environment*, which puts forward a theory of the significance of architectural forms. This theory, where intelligible, is palpably erroneous, consisting in a renewed iteration of the fallacy that sequential organization is a kind of 'syntax'. Like most practitioners of semiotics (and in architectural theory they are increasingly many), Preziosi begins by assuming what he ought to be proving: namely, that architecture is sufficiently like language for the methods of analysis appropriate to the one to be usefully transferred to the other. And he masks this assumption by using the word 'code' to refer to both. By what pre-established harmony of folly has this word 'code' come to be brandished in so many places and in the name of so many disciplines, as though it were sufficient to call a thing a 'code' to achieve some special claim to be able to decipher it? 'Like verbal language,' Preziosi writes, 'the *built environment*—what will here be called the *architectonic code*—is a panhuman phenomenon.' The italicized words are held by Preziosi to have a technical meaning; they are assembled, with others, in a glossary, which explains the crucial term 'code' thus: 'the *system* (qv) of ordered relationships among significant formations'. For further elucidation one turns to the entry for *system*, which says '*system:* see *code.*' From which one can deduce what significance these terms have for the author. As one can see already, 'code' is going to be used whenever there is sequential pattern: the idea of semantic interpretation has been brought in by a sleight of hand.

Pressing on, despite this unpromising start, one learns that 'a built environment is an ongoing, dynamically unfolding array of signs, existing' (one is happy to note) 'spatially and temporally.' In other words, the architectonic code consists of signs. What is a sign? The answer is that 'an architectonic sign is a combination of a formation with a *meaning*.' So Preziosi is committed to semantics after all. And perhaps that is no bad thing: for do we not speak of the meaning of architectural forms? Do we not regard buildings as in some sense speaking to us, even, as it were, observing us, with something on the tip of their (our) tongue? Perhaps a 'semiotics of the built environment' will solve the mystery which such speculations generate. But how should it proceed? Preziosi begins by isolating the architectural vocabulary, which he identifies with the 'geometrical properties' of formations. This suggestion is already highly implausible. Imagine two buildings with identical geometrical properties, in an identical arrangement (or 'syntax'), the one built in limestone, the other cast in steel. Is it not absurd to say that they *must* have the same 'meaning' for us?

Let us suppose, however, that we have isolated the architect's 'vocabulary'. No progress can now be made without the assumption that meaning is determined by convention. If it is not, then the reference to vocabulary, and later to syntax, is spurious. Now it is fairly clear to anyone who has thought about these matters that, while what is sometimes called meaning in architecture (but which might equally be called aesthetic character) is influenced by convention, it is not merely the result of convention. An architect cannot guarantee the 'meaning' of his work by obedience to rule. It is hardly surprising, then, if Preziosi's attempts to interpret his architectural 'syntax' are hesitant and vague. After extracting the 'syntactical' rules which generate the forms of ancient Minoan houses, he writes as follows: 'If we take an "architectonic code" as meaning, among other things, sets of elemental units, relationships among those units, and rules governing relationships . . .' What he is saying, clearly, is that architecture 'means' its own 'syntax'. In other words, we have failed to advance from syntax to semantics. We have syntax without semantics, and therefore neither. None of Preziosi's discussion advances beyond this point, which is hardly surprising, since there is no advance to be made, and however much he may seek to draw our attention to the 'ongoing semiotic bricolage of daily life', his observations concerning its principal manifestation remain at a level of vagueness that no linguistic alchemy can conceal.

Umberto Eco's book of essays (*The Role of the Reader*, Indiana, 1979) promises something more substantial. The collection reports and explores specimens of 'unlimited semiosis' (the creeping tendency to accumulate meaning). These specimens are the 'texts' of the semiotician, and the word 'text' applies to everything that might be read as a sign, and so be infected by this disease. Imitating the Barthes of *Mythologies* (but with rather less wit), Eco explores the narrative devices of Ian Fleming and the emotional significance of the *Superman* comics. He also pays attention to modern music, to the once popular melodramas of Eugène Sue, and in the piece which enunciates his latest theoretical advances, to a literary joke by Allais, culled from Breton's *Anthologie de l'Humour Noir*.

Like Preziosi, Eco introduces, and relies upon, the unexplained notion of 'code'; and since he recognizes that a literary work has a writer and a reader, he regards textual codes as the property of both. The title of his collection derives from his supposition that the reader may be in part the creator of what he reads, according to the extent to which the text is, as he puts it, 'open' or 'closed'. It is rather difficult to understand the distinction between the open and the closed text. It is clearly meant to provide some substitute for the (ideologically unacceptable?) distinction between high and popular culture. But Eco's account is odd and sometimes contradictory. The closed text (such as the *Superman* comic-strip) aims at what a more old-fashioned critic might have called 'stock responses'. Paradoxically, this also makes it 'open'—open, that is to any possible 'aberrant de-coding'. Such texts purportedly generate no standard of what is 'right' or 'wrong' in reading them, since they elicit no creative participation from the reader. The truly open text, by contrast, because it makes demands, aims also to discipline its reader into the adoption of those 'codes' (or habits of interpretation) which would be appropriate to it. The open text is addressed to an ideal reader (whether or not suffering from an ideal insomnia), and is therefore 'closed' to aberrant interpretations. Ian Fleming is a writer of closed texts, James Joyce a writer of open texts. We have here an important critical distinction, corresponding to the more familiar distinction between mechanical contrivance and creative art. Unfortunately, semiosis soon sets in, and the distinction rots away. The text becomes 'blown up', and then 'narcotised', a purveyor of 'topics', 'isotopics', 'semantic markers'. Words like 'extensional', 'intensional' and 'macro-proposition' enter without explanation. As well as phonemes and sememes, we eventually acquire the inscrutable 'styleme'. None of these technicalities is either explained or seriously exploited. When it is said, in the conclusion to the introduction, that 'ruled by a constitutive mechanism of unlimited semiosis, the semantic space can be reduced only through the co-operative activity performed by the reader in actualising a given text,' all that is meant is what we already knew: that since a work of art bears many meanings, the reader must choose between them.

But the difficulties for the ideal reader of Eco are compounded by a far from ideal author, who goes on to confuse 'openness' with indeterminacy, as exemplified by improvisatory music, and then with 'suggestiveness', so that the paradigm switches first to the auditory confusion of Stockhausen and then to the fastidious impressionism of Mallarmé and Debussy. What had begun by seeming to be a genuine theory ends as a concatenation of independent distinctions, none of them adequately characterized.

In his final essay, Eco brings forward a truly formidable body of technicalities, in the attempt to arrive at a satisfactory 'reading' of a short story by Allais. This story is a joke, directed against the reader, who is encouraged to fill in its lacunae. In the course of doing so, he involves himself (the implication is, through no fault of the author's) in a startling self-contradiction. A story like this is, of course, a gift to the semiotician. Professor Eco uses it to introduce the latest (and most fashionable) developments in modal logic—in particular, the theory of possible worlds. The result scarcely makes sense, and it appears to me that the author may well be aware of this.

The semantics of modal logic arose in the following way. Certain words, such as 'possibly' and 'necessarily', which seem to be in-dispensable to ordinary as well as to scientific discourse, present problems in the theory of meaning. In particular, they generate 'in-tensional' contexts, contexts like 'It is possible that . . .' which, when completed by some sentence 'p', yield sentences which may be true or false independently of the truth or falsehood of p. Ordinary logic is 'extensional': the truth or falsehood of any complex sentence depends on the truth or falsehood of its parts. And modern logic has developed almost entirely on the assumption of extensionality: without that assumption logic seems hardly to proceed. How then can ordinary logic either represent or elucidate sentences about the necessary and the possible? It is clear that these sentences have a logic. Following a suggestion of Leibniz, the modern logician translates 'It is necessarily p' as 'p is true in all possible worlds.' 'Necessarily' then becomes a 'quantifier', and the logical properties of quantifiers can be described in extensional terms. This theory is capable of systematic development.

It might seem natural to suggest that a work of fiction is nothing but the (partial) description of a possible world. Perhaps, then, the theory of possible worlds can be used to elucidate our understanding of fiction, and thereby show us how jokers like Allais can tie us in impossible knots. This, I suppose, is the intuition that underlies Eco's attempt to introduce the technicalities of this branch of 'model theory' (as it is called) into his discussion of Allais's story. Unfortunately, there are two serious drawbacks. The first is that Eco does not seem to understand the theory from which he persistently borrows. Even his grasp of extensional logic is tenuous, as is shown by the fact that when he chooses to express himself in logical notation rather than in English, the result is usually ill-formed (examples on pages 213 and 236). When he comes to write of model theory itself, the result is strictly unintelligible.

Secondly, it is doubtful whether model theory can do anything to elucidate our understanding of fiction. The difficulty here was pointed out over two millennia ago. In the *Poetics* Aristotle drew attention to the fact that impossibilities are frequent in fiction. But, he argued, there is no reason to complain about a 'probable impossibility', which is always preferable to an 'improbable possibility'. (Consider the many difficulties that surround the idea of incarnation, so brilliantly dramatized by Wagner in the *Ring*. It is impossible that Wotan should be identical with Wälse, but, were he to be so identical, it is probable that he would have fathered Siegmund and Sieglinde.) In other words, a fictional world may not be a possible world. What then happens to the semantics of fiction? A determined model theorist could think of ways around the problem. But neither problem nor solution is hinted at by Eco. Moreover, it is clear that he would not wish to get entangled in such inquiries. All he seeks in the abstruse regions of model theory is the rhetoric of technicality, the means of generating so much smoke for so long that the reader will begin to blame his own lack of perception, rather than the author's lack of illumination, for the fact that he has ceased to see. Therein lies the disease of semiosis. What is true of Eco is, so far as I can see, true of all the practitioners of his art. Perhaps it needs another Ben Jonson to reveal the complex motives behind all this. But we can be sure that, while there was a humane beginning to this madness, its 'method' leaves humanity behind.

4 Deconstruction and Criticism

Deconstruction and Criticism, Geoffrey H. Hartman and others (Routledge): text of a talk broadcast on BBC Radio 3 in 1980.

'SINCE the introduction of printing,' Oscar Wilde observed, 'and the fatal development of the habit of reading amongst the middle and lower classes . . . there has been a tendency in literature to appeal more and more to the eye, and less and less to the ear, which is really the sense . . . which it should seek to please.'

Perhaps Wilde would have taken comfort from the fact that, after some years of research, several well-known professors of literature at Yale have concluded that reading may be impossible. Or at least, to borrow the words of Professor Paul de Man, 'the impossibility of reading should not be taken too lightly.' Professor Jacques Derrida endorses the thought, adding that the critic should aim not to read but to 'deconstruct' the text before him. Others of similar persuasion have joined them in producing a book—called *Deconstruction and Criticism*—in which a new critical stance or theory is presented to those prepared to take the impossibility of reading a little more lightly than the authors.

According to the dust-jacket, the authors are known among their antagonists as the 'hermeneutical Mafia'. They are also known by other names, but it would be wrong to think of them as a school. They consist of critics catalysed into verbal activity by Jacques Derrida, a late product of the linguistic criticism which flourished in Paris during the sixties. But Derrida speaks only in inverted commas, denying in the act of utterance any commitment to the words which stream from him. He mentions schools only to deny his membership of them. Despite that, he has a growing influence, and this book is evidence of the respect in which he is held in America. It will also be read and perhaps made canonical by all those many English critics who still admire the Parisian intellectual movements of the sixties.

The relation between criticism and literature has always been an uncertain one; and it is unlikely that it will be changed by the invention of a critical label. All the same, the rumour that criticism is now deconstructing literature is ominous. Perhaps we should take some heart from Professor Hillis Miller's assertion in this book that 'the word "deconstruction", like other words in "de-", "decrepitude", for example, or "denotation", describes a paradoxical action which is both negative and positive at once.' But that only serves to remind us of those words in 'de-', like 'destruction' and 'depravity', from which all suggestion of positive meaning is absent. I hope I shall be forgiven if I add to this list of destructive words a neologism, the verb 'to derridize', derived from 'to rid' and 'to deride'. I shall be discussing the attempt to rid literature of meaning in order to deride the common reader.

Let me first justify the invention of this new word. The central essay in this book consists of an extended text and an extended footnote, each printed over the same hundred pages. The subject is—well, there is no subject exactly. The pretexts are Shelley's 'The Triumph of Life' (a vainglorious poem which Shelley refuted by drowning before getting to the point of it); and also a story by Maurice Blanchot called 'L'Arrêt de Mort'. The second title is ambiguous. It can mean 'the death sentence', or 'the stopping of death'. Derrida (the author of the article) therefore describes it as unreadable. Shelley's title, by implication, is also unreadable. If you translate it, as by now you will have done, into French, it comes out as 'Le Triomphe de la Vie', which can mean either the triumph of life, or the triumph *over* life. Of course it does not read like that in English. But that makes no odds, since reading is impossible. The point of derridizing a text is to make this impossibility apparent. Here are some of Derrida's own words, which will illustrate my meaning:

> Even before it 'concerns' a text in narrative form, double invagination constitutes the story of stories, the narrative of narrative, *the narrative of deconstruction in deconstruction:* the apparently outer edge of an enclosure, far from being simple, simply external and circular, in accordance with the philosophical representation of philosophy, makes no sign beyond itself, towards what is utterly *other*, without becoming double or dual, without making itself be 'represented', refolded, superposed, *re-marked* within the enclosure, at least in what the structure produces as an effect of interiority.

I think you will agree, when you read this aloud, that while you have made certain sounds, even uttered certain words, it is far from clear that you were reading anything. Reading *can* be impossible.

The sounds that you emitted were a translation from the French. The sentence 'Reading is impossible' comes out in French as 'Lire est impossible'. By a natural transition we could re-write this as 'Délire est possible'. This transition is not logical. However, as I shall show, derridization proceeds by non-logical slides from sense to sense, making no distinction between meaning and association. The word 'délire' is another of those interesting words in 'de-'. As verb it means 'to un-read'; as noun it means 'delirium', from the extraordinary verb *délirer*, which names an activity for which English has no term. The implication is that deconstructive criticism, by adopting the stance of delirium, unreads its text, and therefore . . . Well, and therefore. What is involved in 'unreading', 'deconstructing', a text?

Our distinguished professors from Yale agree on one point, which is
that the language of literature is often, perhaps always, figurative, and
that this presents a difficulty to the reader and an opportunity for the
critic. Professor Harold Bloom, commenting on the nature of figurative
language, writes: 'I do not agree wholly with de Man that reading is
impossible, but I acknowledge how very difficult it is to read a poem
properly . . .'.

Suppose we were to discover that it is *easy* to read a poem. Think of the
consequences for criticism! There is a vested interest in the theory that
figurative language is difficult. Even if figures of speech seem simple to
you and me, we should expect to find theories that make them appear
quite beyond our comprehension. In the ancient science of rhetoric, we
find bewildering classifications of the figures of speech, using technical
terms from the Greek, and accompanying these terms with explanations
as vague as they are pretentious. The Greek terms are still in use, ful-
filling their ancient purpose of inspiring panic in the common reader. The
professors of Yale do not hesitate to use them. They refer to trope,
metonymy, metaphor; synéchdoche, prosopopoeia and catachresis.
Professor Bloom, encouraged by these terms, manages to transfigure the
figurative in a theory which spirals away into abstraction. He writes:
'Metonymy and metaphor alike I would trope as heightened degrees of
dialectical irony, with metaphor the more extended. But synéchdoche is
not a dialectical trope, since as microcosm it represents a macrocosm
without necessarily playing against it.'

If we think of figures of speech in that sort of way, then it is no wonder
if we come to the conclusion that they present an obstacle to reading. We
might even, in our bewilderment, beseech the people who invented these
complexities to remove them. We find that the deconstructive critic is
more than willing to oblige. Paul de Man describes his own attack on 'The
Triumph of Life' as a 'disfiguring' of Shelley. Shelley's poem begins like
this:

>   Swift as a spirit hastening to his task
>   Of glory and of good, the Sun sprang forth
>   Rejoicing in his splendour . . .

Most readers would imagine that if there is a serious critical question
raised by those words, it is on account of their falsehood. The sun never
does 'spring forth', and the movement of Shelley's lines seems entirely in-
appropriate to the rhythm of sunrise. We shall want to know whether
there is anything in the form or content of the poem that overcomes the
seeming ineptness of this description. For de Man, however, the main
interest lies in the fact that the sun is personified. Or, to use a technicality
of rhetoric, the lines exhibit prosopopoeia. How can we read the text,
then, until we have disfigured this figure? De Man has uncovered a diffi-

culty of which the innocent reader had been unaware. No doubt such a reader will not be relieved to learn that disfiguration consists in 'the repetitive erasures by which language performs the erasure of its own positions'. But by the time he gets to that thought, he might be so muddled by rhetoric as to blame himself for failing to understand it.

The fundamental idea behind deconstructive criticism seems to be this: figurative language closes the door between the reader and the meaning. We must open the door, with the Yale key provided. But it seems to me most odd to believe that the door is locked. Figures of speech are open to their meaning. They are vivid, immediate, unambiguous. They are used all the time, and indeed clichés are composed of them. A sly fox, a loving heart, a sullen anger, a serious face—all those are figures of speech. Some seem more figurative than others. But they are all figurative (in the literal sense of the term). They transfer a word from the context which provides its meaning to a context where its meaning is exploited in some novel way. You might think that figures of speech must therefore bear a double meaning. But that is not so. The literal meaning is usually lost in the transfer. When I read 'His heart was in his mouth', the literal sense of the words does not occur to me. If I understand them literally I shall be guilty of a misreading. Sometimes, it is true, a writer can play with figures of speech so as to trap us into a literal reading. And the effect of this might be very powerful. It might seem as though a reality were being displayed behind the commonplace. Consider the effect produced by Geoffrey Hill when, in describing the search for the bodies of drowned men, he suddenly forces us to literalize the metaphor 'scraping home': 'Quietly they wade the disturbed shore;/Gather their dead as the first dead scrape home.' But if a figure of speech can be given this kind of impact this is because it does not normally possess it. The figures I have mentioned are no more inherently ambiguous than literal descriptions.

There is a moral that I wish to draw from those observations. Meaning, it seems to me, is a collusive activity. It requires speakers, hearers, and the social context which permits understanding. The reader brings to literature an experience of language which the writer cannot ignore: the meaning of a text is the meaning which a speaker of the language can find in it, and this is as true of *Finnegan's Wake* as it is of *Gulliver's Travels*. If criticism seeks to elucidate meaning it is elucidating something public and publicly accessible. It must therefore presuppose a reader for the text which it purports to analyse, and it must direct its remarks towards that reader. The critic may guide the reader, but he cannot dictate to him, since the critic's words, like the words he studies, gain their significance from the public practice of speech. This practice defines the reader of literature. The 'common reader' to whom I have referred is the reader who conveys to the text the accumulated meanings of the language. Criticism that is not addressed to the common reader strays from its point, losing sight of language and literature together.

This prompts a second observation. I said earlier that deconstructive criticism ignores the distinction between meaning and association, and it is time I explained what I meant because if language is public, then this distinction must be real, and fundamental to every form of literature. An association is not part of a poem's meaning but a more or less arbitrary contribution by a particular critic. Let us take an example. In John Ashbery's poem 'Sunrise in Suburbia' there occurs a line which marks the change from passionless routine to a glimpse of history and faith. The line reads: 'And then some morning there is a nuance'. The thought is surprising. Why should a mere nuance effect the transition from dearth to fulness, from death to life? It is the purpose of the poem to display the answer to that question in cogent imagery. Bearing the answer in mind, we might reflect on the line which introduced the transition and try to understand its power. We find a concealed double meaning in 'nuance'. Taken as a participle this may be understood as the 'making new'. That leads us to subtract the syllable 'new' from 'nuance', so hearing the echo of the word 'once' in what remains. The 'newing' happens once, at once. Ashbery has avoided an obvious banality, writing 'some morning' where he might have said 'one morning'. This now seems newly significant. By avoiding the word 'one' he has covertly introduced it. The 'once' that is heard at the line's conclusion affirms the 'once' that is rumoured in its beginning. The line reverberates with the expectation which it does not quite describe. 'And then some morning there is a nuance'. I don't know whether what I have just said is true or useful. But I do know that it is not for me to determine the matter. I am appealing to an independent idea of relevance. I was trying to describe the meaning of Ashbery's line, not a private association. The difference is between that which endorses, and that which distracts from, the meaning that is there. The meaning is there because the language embodies it. This language, which is the property of the common reader, is inherently resistant to critical whimsy, and if it resists my interpretation, then the fault is mine.

Deconstructive criticism does not admit the collusive standpoint of the common reader. It prefers to deny his existence. That is what it means to say that reading is impossible. Such criticism therefore makes no distinction between meaning and association, between the arbitrary and the relevant. It is an exercise in critical narcissism. Consider the derridized version of Blanchot's 'L'Arrêt de Mort'. As I said, this title has two clear meanings, which endorse each other and reflect the character of the narrative. (The story, I should say, concerns the courage of a young woman in the face of certain death.) These two meanings are genuine meanings; they are not private associations. Derrida associates the title with a third idea that is, I think, absolutely foreign to it, the idea of a ridge or backbone—*arête,* in French. He then looks for this ridge in the story. It is not described there: it would add nothing to the meaning if it were. (The word *arête* is normally used in common speech when cooking or eating fish.) So Derrida concludes that the ridge must be concealed in the structure of the story. It is this structural ridge which is of supreme importance, and which provides the point of departure for the impossible task of reading. There is no admissible distinction between meaning and association, and so nothing that we could say to suggest that he is straying from the point.

Such sideways slithering through associated ideas is in fact wholly characteristic of deconstructive criticism, which treats the text as a pre-text, and speaks a private 'metalanguage' of its own. The term 'metalanguage', now extremely fashionable among critics, is an interesting one. It belongs to the philosophy of logic, and means a language which talks about another language. The implications of the term are, in the present context, fairly clear. The critic is refusing to speak the language of the reader, or of the writer, of poetry. He uses only a metalanguage of his own—a firm stance from which the frailty of readers and writers can be more accurately observed.

But there is a penalty to pay for that. The language of the critic has become private, since anything is permitted by its rules. Any association, any technicality, can be presented as though it were a contribution to the meaning of the whole. You, the common reader, do not share this language. Therefore you are in no position to know whether what is said is meaningful or true. But that only means that the private language of the deconstructive critic creates the distance that it pretends to discover, the distance between text and meaning. Why, then, should it have been invented, and why have so many critics been persuaded to adopt it?

I can think of an answer, but it is not a pleasant one. A language which rids literature of meaning alienates the reader from literature. He is therefore free to bestow his attention upon the critic. But the critic is glamourized by his 'metalanguage', since it seems to be a repository of knowledge that the reader is despised for lacking and unable to acquire. In denying literature, criticism thereby affirms itself. It begins to seem indispensable.

The critical metalanguage is, then, an expression of the will to power. To understand meaning requires patience and humility, while to revel in association is to release the inner man. It is to accept no authority that is not self-imposed; it is to grow in stature and immunity. As private association takes precedence over public meaning, so does the art of reading shrink into nothingness. And as the reader feels smaller, so does the critic loom large.

Deconstructive criticism does indeed have a negative and a positive side. Perhaps we can best describe them by borrowing again from the words of Professor Hillis Miller: 'There is no deconstruction which is not at the same time constructive, affirmative. The word says this, in juxtaposing "de" and "con".'

5   The English Connection:
Williams, Hoggart and Eagleton

Keywords: a vocabulary of culture and society, Raymond Williams (Fontana/Croom Helm, 1976); *Only Connect,* Richard Hoggart (Chatto & Windus, 1971); and *Exiles and Emigrés: studies in modern English literature,* Terry Eagleton (Chatto & Windus, 1970), from the *Times Literary Supplement,* 26 March 1976; *Spectator,* 1 July 1972; *Spectator,* 24 October 1970.

I

KEYWORDS, the author tells us, is neither a dictionary nor a glossary of any particular academic subject. Nor is it a series of footnotes to dictionary histories, nor even a sequence of definitions. It is 'the record of an inquiry into a *vocabulary:* a shared body of words and meanings in our most general discussions in English, of the practices and institutions which we group as *culture* and *society*'. The book is written with one eye on the methods and conclusions of *Culture and Society,* but words are here considered not in their literary but in their everyday senses, and one purpose seems to be to expose the confusions of thought and laxities of argument that lie hidden behind the ambiguities of current intellectual jargon. The book is about words which the author finds 'difficult' or 'complex', and the words owe these qualities to their occupation of key positions in fashionable controversies, being compelled to bear the burden of conflicting currents of thought. There are over a hundred entries, and each one is as compact as it could be without being obscure.

There is no doubt that *Keywords* represents a great amount of patient industry, considerable breadth of reading, and a gift for clear and concise presentation. The author has a serious and characteristic point of view which retains some of the original freshness even here, in its fifth or sixth reincarnation. The book will prove popular not only among students of English, but also (no doubt to Raymond Williams's dismay) among those anxious to equip themselves with the language of contemporary debate without troubling to understand its origins. And it will prove the more popular on account of its ideology, an ideology which Professor Williams feels himself under no obligation to hide or moderate, thinking indeed that the attempt to hide one's ideology is itself only the expression of a particular set of defunct values—the values of bourgeois humanism, manifest apparently in the 'neutrality' of the *Oxford English Dictionary.*

In contrast to the *OED* Professor Williams is unashamedly radical. Moreover his radicalism has taken a distinctly fashionable turn since *Culture and Society*. Professor Williams is now able to describe our society without a hint of self-doubt as an example of 'late bourgeois' civilization; and able too to regard the sense of the word 'media' in which newspapers are regarded as media for other things (for advertising, for example, or—presumably—for propaganda) as a specifically 'capitalist' sense of the term. And indeed one detects the belief that if the words of which Williams writes were used less confusedly the result would be not only clarity but socialism.

Such dogmatism is in itself no defect. On the contrary, it lends interest to what might otherwise appear a dry and laborious inquiry. However, Professor Williams's ideological assertiveness leads to weaknesses in his discussion of individual terms, and also gives rise to a general sense of intellectual fatigue. Despite the immense labour that must have gone into the compilation of this book, one wonders how much Professor Williams has really thought about the presuppositions on which it rests. Take, for example, the entry on 'family'. It is interesting and useful to know that this word derives from the Latin *famulus* (a servant), and that it used to have a much wider meaning (both of kinship and of household) than it now has. None of that is of any great relevance to contemporary discussions of the nature and value of primary social relations, as Professor Williams realizes. Consequently, in his discussion of the modern usages of the term he contrives to introduce something called the *bourgeois family*, such use of the term 'family' bringing with it, apparently, a sense of 'household and property'. The simplification involved in that— implying as it does the existence of a non-bourgeois family, which presumably does not have associations of household and property, of a kind of family which is not, as Professor Williams puts it, an 'economic unit'—goes quite unnoticed. But consider some typical 'non-bourgeois' families. The Homeric *oikos* (from which word our own 'economy' is derived) had associations of household and property; the modern proletarian family has such associations; so too did the extended aristocratic family of the Renaissance. And all these represent 'economic units'. The implication which Professor Williams attempts to put across—that the particular family structure which exists at present is integral to the institution of private property and that both are somehow dispensable—that implication depends upon the shallowest of observations, none the less shallow for being commonplace.

From the same corpus of received ideas comes Professor Williams's description of literary criticism as 'ideological'.

> Not only in the sense that it assumes the position of the *consumer*, but also in the sense that it masks this position by a succession of abstrac-

tions of its real terms of response (as *judgment, taste, cultivation, discrimination, sensibility, disinterested, qualified, rigorous,* and so on). This then actively prevents that understanding of response which does not assume the habit (or right or duty) of judgment.

The implication is that Dr Johnson, F. R. Leavis, and the other great 'consumers' of literature rely for their authority on the questionable assumption that literary response and literary judgment are one and the same. Having rejected that assumption we recognize the possibility of a response to literature which is spontaneous, remaining on the level of 'specificity' characteristic of 'practice'.

Professor Williams—invoking in that word 'practice' the praise-worthy associations of a Marxist view of art—seeks in a few lines to dispose not only of the entire tradition of English literary criticism, but also of the aesthetic philosophy which has its roots in Kant, and which holds that aesthetic experience and aesthetic judgment are inseparable. Professor Williams conveys no sense that anybody might actually have *argued* for the view which he rejects. On the contrary, he presents it as though it were an unconscious assumption of the language of criticism, an assumption from which we can free ourselves simply by changing our words.

It is disconcerting to find how often in this work Professor Williams is prepared to abuse the privileges of the etymologist, to profit from the necessary brevity of a dictionary entry in order to put forward as authoritative opinions which are at best contentious and often (as in this case) indefensible. Consider the parallel case of moral experience. Could there be such a thing as a response to someone's cruelty or cowardice which involved no judgment? And if there could be such a thing, would it have any value? Clearly, judgment is here *part* of the response, and the man who always observed the wickedness of others without the faintest stirring of contempt or indignation could only be described as insensible. It is some such model of insensibility that Williams must be recommending as the ideal stance towards works of art, for here too we are compelled to recognize (once we begin to think about it) that response and judgment go together, and that an attitude towards art that left no place for taste or discrimination would be an attitude which showed no understanding of its object.

But perhaps the most serious shortcoming of this book—and of the enterprise which it represents— lies in the author's failure to consider the relation between the history of words and the history of concepts. The fault is not peculiar to Professor Williams; he shares it, for example, with Michel Foucault, whose 'archaeological' approach to intellectual history has manufactured some startling conclusions from a deft confusion of concept and word. Clearly, the history of the word 'family' is not the history of the concept, for the concept has had a history in China, where the word has not. We have the same concept whenever we have the same classification, coexisting with a sufficient body of common knowledge; the words used to effect a classification may change, but that is irrelevant to the history of the concept. It would seem to follow that conclusions about the nature and history of ideas—even of commonplace ideas—cannot be derived in any simple way from the study of etymology.

Moreover, while some concepts (such as the concept of man) must be common to all who speak and reason, other concepts derive their character not from common knowledge but from theories, and must share the history of the theories to which they belong. Now Professor Williams does not distinguish between the two kinds of concept. He discusses not only words in common speech—such as 'city' and 'educated'—but also words which have only a technical significance, such as 'alienation', 'formalist' and 'dialectic'. Superficially Professor Williams gives the same kind of treatment to both classes. In either case he first traces the history of the word (which in one case is long and interesting, in the other short and dull), and then attempts to create some order among its contemporary senses. But it is not clear why one should treat the two kinds of word together. To understand the meaning of 'alienation' is to understand a political theory. To understand the meaning of 'city' is to have a competent grasp of contemporary English. The true history of the word 'alienation' is the history of a theory of human nature. It is not clear that an extended dictionary article can accommodate such a history, any more than it can indicate the history of 'force' from Newton to Einstein.

This perhaps provides some explanation of the dullness and aridity of Professor Williams's articles on theoretical terms. It might also explain why he is prepared to ignore altogether some of the important theoretical meanings that hide behind common words. Thus he ignores, for example, in his entry on 'tradition', the entire Idealist philosophy concerning that term and confines himself to a few dismissive journalistic remarks about one coffee-table meaning. But it is possible that here there is another explanation of Professor Williams's crudeness. For the concept of tradition is a key concept in the view of society which rivals Professor Williams's own, and it suits his dogmatism to pass over its intellectual content in silence.

II

In *The Uses of Literacy* Richard Hoggart tried to describe the collapse of working-class culture under the impact of the mass media. He argued that the genuine culture of the working class was being replaced by 'the mass opinion, the mass recreational product and the generalized emotional response'—what he called 'a poorer kind of classless culture.' In this valuable book Hoggart showed himself more capable of describing the concrete phenomena of decay than of investigating its causes. He did not, surely, intend to denounce the 'classless culture' merely as the instrument of 'mass opinion' or of 'generalized response.' In one sense these phrases apply equally to the old-fashioned class culture that Hoggart defends. *The Uses of Literacy* in fact gives support to a far less contentious theory—the theory that a culture is *necessarily* inward-looking, closed to direct influence from outside, founded on a sense of reality that is achieved through traditional expressions and traditional forms of behaviour, and not through the appeal of fantasies manufactured by people from another sphere, with an alien set of values. To defend the working class culture against the assaults of the media was, for Hoggart, simply to defend reality against fantasy, the meaningful against the meaningless.

In view of all this, it is rather surprising to find Hoggart in his Reith Lectures mounting an extraordinarily devious defence of 'the mass recreational product.' Of course broadcasting no longer comes under quite that description. For there are, it seems, standards in broadcasting which will, if adhered to, make it a force for good in society. Broadcasters have it in their power to 'widen our options,' by virtue of which they may become 'critically involved, a sort of yeast in society. They will be active agents of change.' This power goes with an exciting access to 'new forms, and new audiences, a new kind of audience'—to an unspoiled public that has 'no set expectations,' no 'habitual responses.' It is not the banality of these pronouncements that is stunning so much as the extraordinary solemnity with which Hoggart professes his faith in them. Gone is the sense that the 'widening' of options might not be in itself the best of social endeavours; gone too is the scepticism with which Hoggart once viewed the enterprise of mass communication. As long as our broadcasters are open-minded, he now tells us, as long as they tell the truth at all costs, then we have nothing to fear from them. The suggestion that a medium might propagate fantasy in virtue of its form and irrespective of its content—whether or not it is open-minded, impartial, well-informed and true—seems to have been finally buried.

It would not be fair to suggest that Hoggart has changed his mind about all this. His mind has not so much changed as sunk to its lowest resources. He is not an optimist, but he has had from the beginning a touching faith in the need to be well-informed, and in the possibilities that are open to us once we condescend to know. His defence of broadcasting rests upon this premise alone. He has nothing further to say. His desire to 'connect' seems to have replaced the need to think. He tries to disarm his readers by citing the experiences that have moulded his ideas, chief among them being a recent move to France. But things were already at work within him long before this cataclysmic episode. 'I have been making notes for years,' he writes, 'about things which have struck me—incidents, remarks, gestures.'

For example, he has noticed that certain phrases in common use, such as 'You should have seen the look he gave me' or 'Who do you think you're talking to?' do not only express thoughts but also describe and establish relationships. He has noticed that silence can be a form of communication between people, that tones of voice carry implications, that people from one class may not understand the code of 'signals' proper to another. He has discovered that 'the individual matters; and he matters more than society,' that 'we all have a great deal to learn about other styles of life,' and that one cannot expect 'gentle public relationships in Paris.' ('I suppose,' he writes, 'this may be related somewhere to the acceptance of violence as a part of the process of political life; though I'm not sure of that yet.' One is left wondering what decisive experience might clinch the matter for him.)

The book contains a certain amount of information. We learn for example that many of the *chambres de bonne* in Paris are still occupied by servants; that a lot of experiences are to be had through working in UNESCO, that George Orwell was able to say, à propos a collection of dirty postcards, 'When it comes to the pinch, human beings are heroic'—a remark that Hoggart greets with enormous admiration. As Reith Lecturer Hoggart feels able to speak of 'the idea of fellow-feeling' as though it were new and important, or to refer to the fact that men can communicate with each other (or, in his cant phrase 'reach each other') as a 'very large, and so far as I know, unproven assertion.' Whatever the effect of such thoughts spoken on the wireless, coldly recorded in a book they are simply risible. They awaken no more interest than the fact that Hoggart finds such phrases as 'now and forever we are alone' moving, or the fact that he feels sad at the extent to which intellectuals and artists can conform to particular national ideologies, or the fact that he feels specially at ease in the company of elderly ladies.

One leaves the book with a sense of disappointment that the author of *The Uses of Literacy* should feel constrained to talk in this way. He enters with ease into the task of explaining 'culture'; but he expresses himself in a language that makes culture meaningless. He has opened the floodgates of his mind, but what has issued forth is a very shallow trickle indeed.

III

Except for Conrad, Eliot, and D. H. Lawrence, the 'exiles and émigrés' studied by Terry Eagleton get only passing mention. What Mr Eagleton is trying to show is not very clear; he seems to think that, because recent English literature has been dominated by 'foreigners', there must be something about contemporary English culture which renders it comprehensible only from outside. This is a promising idea, one might think, until one remembers that Yeats and Joyce were no more foreigners than Swift, Scott or Goldsmith, that Pound seldom wrote about English society, Joyce never, and James and Conrad only half the time (at most). Perhaps there is some significance in the fact that Conrad *chose* to write in English, rather than, say, French or Polish. But is this more significant than Kafka's choice of German, or Rilke's choice (in his middle years) of French? I suspect that Eagleton would not consider this sort of evidence relevant to his theme; his approach to literature is far more metaphysical. The true writer, for him, is the one who 'totalizes' the experience of his culture, and so 'transcends' it. A culture is only 'totalized' in a work of art which can present all the elements of the culture in their 'living relation'; through 'totalization' an artist can 'transcend' the pressures of his immediate situation and present impartially a complete vision of the 'culture' in which he writes. And English culture in its decline can best be 'totalized' from an alien vantage point.

This suggests that Eagleton is reproaching (and he is always reproaching) Waugh, Greene, Orwell and Conrad for some fault or unfairness in their presentation of English life. They do not totalize their culture (what it would be to do this Eagleton does not say). But when it comes to the point, the real crime is that of the writer who does not 'belong to his own experience'. There seems to be no limit to the number of ways in which this sin can be committed. A piece of clumsy melodrama (the street scene in *Antic Hay*), the portrayal of a hero who cannot value himself as highly as his self-knowledge requires (Scobie, Querry and the other 'reluctant heroes' of Graham Greene), an irony which is too persistent and which offers no alternative to what is criticized (Waugh): these are only some of the ways in which a writer and his experience may fail to belong together.

Above all, Eagleton is hunting for ideologies. This task is rather difficult for the critic of the modern novel. James, Conrad, Joyce, and their followers have cultivated, in general, a Flaubertian *impassibilité:* they try to express not their own beliefs and feelings, but those of their characters. This makes matters difficult for the ideology hunter: like Eagleton, he will tend to direct his attention to those works in which the 'sacred office' of the dramatist is from time to time betrayed—the works of minor novelists such as Aldous Huxley, George Orwell, and Graham Greene. Thus we often find in Eagleton's book a lengthy diagnosis of the faults of some novelist whose work, set beside his own solemn didacticism, can only look forlornly out of place, like a child suffering from measles who has strayed by accident into the cancer ward.

When he turns his attention to a great novel—*Under Western Eyes*—his method leads at once to a false interpretation. He cannot see Conrad's technique of oblique narration as a formal device; instead he thinks of the narrator as included in the subject of the novel. Conrad wished to awaken a response to the distinctive features of Razumov's character and experience, while preserving for the reader some of the mystery of their cause. In order to do this it was necessary to employ a narrator whose understanding of the politics of autocracy is limited. It is Razumov who is the whole subject-matter of the book. For Eagleton, however, the book is really about the conflict between the narrator's English conservatism and the revolutionary anarchism of the Russian exiles in Geneva, into whose society Razumov comes as a police spy. He accuses Conrad of 'endorsing' the narrator's attitudes, and dismissing those of the anarchists, without any true examination. This is characteristic. Eagleton often talks of novels as 'posing problems' for which they 'find solutions'; the solution is the 'thesis' which the novel upholds. If that is the case, why has literature not been replaced by sociology?

The real failure in this interpretation is its indifference to Razumov's internal struggle, and to the effect in him of a terror which, under Western eyes, seems so strange and so strangely founded. The novel is not an account of Razumov's 'destruction at the hands of the radicals'; their punishment of Razumov affects us as a purging of his own self-destructive terror.

There are better moments: the essay on 'T. S. Eliot and the Uses of Myth' is intelligent and interesting, and many of the criticisms of Greene hit the mark. But the whole is spoiled by a nagging and insistent bigotry. One suspects that it is not *literature* which has any importance in the author's eyes. Eagleton is interested only in ideologies, and these he hunts out everywhere, fumbling for them even in the early comedies of Evelyn Waugh, with the effect, here, of some humourless policeman rummaging for hand-grenades in the garments of a clown.

6   Art, Language, and Nelson Goodman

The Arts and Cognition, edited by David Perkins and Barbara Leondar (Johns Hopkins University Press, 1977), from the *Times Literary Supplement*, 12 August 1977.

EVER SINCE Hegel wrote of art as the 'sensuous embodiment' of the idea, the theory that art is a symbolic activity has provided the most popular conception of its nature. But nobody has been able to give a convincing account of this 'symbolism'. Is it one thing or many? Is it a matter of evocation or convention, of personal response or linguistic rule? And what does art symbolize? Ideas, feelings, objects, states of affairs? From all the confused speculations of the later idealists one firm distinction has emerged—the distinction between representation and expression, between the description of the world outside us and the expression of the mind within. The latter, according to the Expressionists, is the true aim of art, and representation is at best no more than a means to it.

More recent philosophers, wishing to preserve the distinction, but lacking the confidence to dismiss either part of it, have admitted both representation and expression, as the separate but complementary processes through which art presents its intimations of the world. Perhaps the most distinguished of these philosophers has been the American, Nelson Goodman, inventor of a profound paradox in the philosophy of science, whose *Languages of Art* was the first work of analytical philosophy to make any sustained contribution to aesthetics. While writing that work Goodman founded an association, called Harvard Project Zero, the purpose of which was to carry out research into all aspects of artistic appreciation and performance. The work of the Project, here brought together, consists of both philosophical and psychological studies, many of which assume, reiterate, vary, modify or purport to apply the general theory of artistic symbolism put forward in *Languages of Art*.

Goodman's project is a familiar one. It seeks for the nature of art in symbolism, and for the nature of symbolism in some general theory of signs. The project has been pursued, in a manner that is as spectacular rhetorically as it is intellectually vacuous, in the French and Italian coffee-houses, where it goes by the name of 'semiology', but in Anglo-Saxon philosophy, because of the prevailing respect for elementary logic, 'semiology' has little place.

Goodman's 'semantic' theory of art is derived from the uncompromising nominalism expounded in his earlier work, a nominalism which represents the relation between language and the world as largely inscrutable. This fact is not always appreciated by Goodman's critics. Nor, as the present volume shows, is it very clearly appreciated by his followers. According to Goodman the relation between words and the world can be described, like any relation, in terms of its formal structure—in terms of the logical categories of symmetry, reflexivity and transitivity—and in terms of the objects related (in this case words and things). But apart from that formal analysis there is nothing to be said. Words are labels which attach to things, but the attempt to describe the process of 'attachment' must, in using words, presuppose what it seeks to explain.

Goodman uses the word 'reference' to express the relation between word and thing, and on his view both names and predicates refer. The difference is that, while a name refers to one thing, a predicate refers to many. It is a further aspect of his nominalism that reference to 'properties' is dispensable; it suffices to speak of predicates, since to be red and to be referred to by the predicate 'red' are one and the same thing.

Sometimes the process of 'labelling' goes both ways. A colour sample is a sign for the colour which it possesses—the colour red, say. It therefore refers to the label 'red'. So that in this case, the predicate 'red' both refers to and is referred to by the sample. Goodman analyses expression as a special case of this mutual labelling, representation as a special case of non-mutual labelling. What makes it possible to speak of a 'special case' is not some fact about the internal structure of the labelling relation—for, being inscrutable, it has no internal structure—but certain formal properties of the 'symbol system' to which the label belongs.

It is the sparseness of Goodman's theory which allows it to apply so directly to art. For it can easily be shown that the formal properties of the relation between a painting and its subject—the relation of pictorial 'representation'—are identical with the formal properties of reference, QED. We should not worry if that leads us to no new understanding of the relation: for what we are being told is that there is nothing to be understood. That is what nominalism says.

As a matter of fact, if we think of reference as the relation between name and object, it is wrong to regard it as wholly inscrutable. For it can be shown that certain properties of the 'symbol system' destroy the appearance of inscrutability, and make it possible to say something further about the relation between words and the world. Frege showed how the *syntactic* properties of language display and illuminate its semantic relations. He showed that the reference of a word (the object referred to) must make a systematic contribution to the conditions for the truth of sentences in which it occurs.

Tarski developed the theory formally, showing how to derive the conditions for the truth of any sentence from the reference of its parts: he thereby demonstrated the existence of a 'generative' connection between reference and truth. Recent philosophers and linguists have taken advantage of these insights. For they show how, by understanding the primitive parts of a language, a man can understand the whole. They therefore begin to show *how* words relate to the world in the minds of those who use and understand them.

Now the distinguishing feature of representational systems, such as painting, is that they are, as Goodman puts it, 'syntactically dense'. Between any two painted representations there will be a third, differing, however minimally, from each. Hence there is an infinite syntactic continuum. It follows that Frege's theory of reference—which requires syntactic disjointedness—cannot be applied.

But if that is so, then the principal advantage of a semantic theory of art is lost. For the semantic theory seemed to suggest how we *understand* works of art: we understand them as we understand language, and the classical theory of reference can be invoked to explain what 'understanding' means. But Goodman's 'reference' is generalized beyond the point at which the classical theory expires, so that we cannot apply our knowledge of language to the field of painting, and cannot assume that there is some common process of understanding exemplified in each. The inscrutability of the relation between painting and subject remains, and the assimilation of representation to reference seems little more than a sleight of hand.

The objection is an important one; for it is only if the analogy with language is sufficiently strong that the semantic theory will provide any account of artistic understanding. Even if we admit the objection, however, there remains an important difference between Goodman's theory and other accepted philosophies of art. For the theory suggests that art, like language, is a matter of skill, a matter of being able to formulate in symbols a reference to the world.

The way seems open to a proper psychology of artistic creation and response, a psychology of the skills and abilities involved in the manipulation of artistic signs. It is this aspect of Goodman's theory which seems to have aroused the greatest interest among the writers in *The Arts and Cognition,* most of whom have devoted their research to problems in the psychology of artistic creation and performance, and to the nature of skills. A certain measure of coherence is imposed on the book by a continuous and clever commentary, written by the editors in a Goodmanian style, with the dry facetiousness and slick figures of speech for which he is admired. But the contents of the book, for all that, are highly varied, and touch on many themes besides the central one, of the nature and psychology of aesthetic choice.

A characteristic piece by Goodman himself is followed by a long philosophical discussion of the 'codes' of the cinema. This article, written with admirable clarity by Soren Kjørup, reiterates the theory of *Languages of Art*, and attempts to apply it to the cinema. The writer refers to the 'codes' used in the cinema as though there were no significant difference between a dramatic portrayal and a traffic sign; indeed, on the level of Goodmanian semantics, there is little distinction to be made between the two. As a result, the aesthetic significance of the cinematic 'codes' seems impossible to grasp. Of course, it does not matter which term is used to denote the relation between a film and its subject, but the use of the term 'code' suggests a specific theory of that relation, a theory which Kjørup's analysis belies. All that we understand from the analysis is that, looking at a film, we learn about its subject; which is simply to repeat our most basic intuition about representation. The intuition is taken up by T. G. Roupas, in an article which attempts to analyse the concept of representation in terms of the transfer of information.

The article is remarkable in that it contains some pertinent criticism of Goodman's views. (Whether or not the editors noticed the fact is unclear from their mellifluous commentary.) But it is possible to doubt that Roupas's thought requires for its expression the ungainly theoretical apparatus which he provides for it.

The remaining articles, whether philosophical or psychological, pay much attention to the understanding of artistic skills. Now it is a striking feature of Goodman's theory that it seems partly to destroy the Idealist distinctions between art and science and art and craft. It has been a commonplace since Kant that the aesthetic understanding is neither theoretical nor practical, but in some way *sui generis*. As the title of the present collection suggests, the authors do not accept that view. It would have been valuable, therefore, if they had clearly stated their disagreement with it, instead of plunging into the half-light of psychological aesthetics with little more than a dogma to guide them.

Consider Goodman's theory of expression. Most students of aesthetics feel a certain amazement at the ease with which Goodman reduces this to a semantic property, to a mode of symbolization. For 'expression' has traditionally been used to denote a peculiar aesthetic achievement, and it is a long-standing Idealist thesis (expressed in their various ways by Hegel, Croce and Collingwood) that there can be no rule or formula for expression, no procedure for the manufacture of expressive objects. Collingwood put the point in the following way: expression is not so much a matter of finding the symbol for a human feeling as coming to know, through the act of expression, just what the feeling is. Expression is part of the realization of the inner life, the making intelligible what is otherwise ineffable and confused. An artist who could already identify the feeling which he sought to express might indeed make use of a rule: a rule of the form 'To express x use y'. But then he would not need the rule, for if he can identify the feeling it is because he has already expressed it. Expression is not, therefore, an activity whose goal can be identified prior to its achievement: it is not an activity that can be described in terms of end and means. And that is one basis for the fundamental distinction between art and craft.

Collingwood's thought is complex and partly confused. But it suggests an approach to art that is both more subtle and more plausible than the semantic theory, and it is strange that the adherents of that theory never bother even to consider it. The entire tradition of European aesthetics stands against the view that the relation of expression can be described in terms of some semantic convention or rule, and against the view, assumed by the authors of this book, that artistic creation is a kind of skill, and that the distinction between art and craft is therefore illegitimate. One wonders whether it is arrogance or ignorance that leads to the authors' total indifference to that tradition, and to all the arguments and concepts to which it has given rise. It is indeed surprising to find in one paper the blank assertion that criticism is a form of 'propositional knowledge' as opposed to practical knowledge (or 'procedural know-how', as the author, V. A. Howard, expresses it). For surely, whatever might be wrong with the Kantian tradition in aesthetics, the tradition which began with the spectacular assertion that criticism is 'free from concepts', it ought to be recognized by now that criticism simply cannot be reduced to a form of 'propositional knowledge', that its end-point is not the acquisition of theoretical knowledge but the transformation of experience.

This indifference to traditional theory would matter less were the enterprise of investigating artistic skills to be more clearly presented. But the concepts provided by the editors—the concepts of a symbol system, of representation, expression and notation—are quickly left behind in the course of the psychological experiments and no others seem to come in place of them: and experiments without concepts are blind. Nor is this surprising. For consider the art of musical composition (investigated by Jeanne Bamberger in a paper entitled 'In Search of a Tune'). It does not need much observation to realize that the first thing in this art is the discovery of the right note, an ability that has little relation to the application of semantic rules. Despite all the *theories* which assimilate music to language, and musical understanding to semantic understanding, sensitive observation will always point the other way.

It may at first seem surprising, but the same is true of poetry. For here too we are concerned with the search for what is right, for the right word, phrase or imagery. And the ability to discriminate the right word is not reducible to a semantic skill. It is the ability to choose between words *despite* their identical semantic properties, to choose, for example, the word *sans* instead of the word *without,* as in a famous Shakespearean example. It is the ability to choose between words with, as Frege would put it, the same sense but different tone. And observation again serves only to disconfirm the assimilation of 'tone' to semantic categories. A word acquires its tone as a consequence of its use and of the rules which govern it. Tone cannot therefore be the *subject* of a rule.

Indeed, it is not at all clear what a 'psychology of artistic creation' might be. If we were to regard the Goodmanian theory as proven, and each form of art as a 'system' of 'symbols', then certainly we could begin to think of artistic creation as a skill. But it does not seem to be anything like a skill, even if it involves skill as a necessary component. And that ought to provide an argument against Goodman's theory. No doubt the composition of a piece of sub-Telemannian *Tafelmusik* could be considered a matter of skill: but that is precisely because it is musically meaningless. The elements are given, it remains only to combine them according to rule. The 'meaningful' quality of a piece of Bach or Mozart stems precisely from its ability to transcend mere versatility. To compose a piece of music is to exploit rules only to transcend them, and if the creative act is defined precisely by the meaningfulness of its results, then it cannot be considered as an exercise of skill.

It is not surprising, therefore, to find that the psychological investigations here recorded have a distinctly sterile air. They record bizarre experiments in which subjects are asked to find substitutes for words in a poem, or piece together a 'reasonable' melody by typing on a computer. In the absence of any concepts with which to describe the results—a failing not peculiar to the psychologists at Project Zero but, as contemporary philosophers have repeatedly and fruitlessly pointed out, common to psychologists everywhere—these experiments strike the reader, in all their confusion of detail, as an amazing waste of time. Despite the confidence of its members, and (in the words of one contributor) their 'elaborate and thought-laden dealings with ongoing works', one is forced to be sceptical about the achievements of Project Zero.

The Project remains an interesting one, and it would be well if minds of the right quality were attracted to it. But if they are attracted it will not be on account of the Project's publications, but on account of the brilliance of its founder.

7 Imagination

Imagination, Mary Warnock (Faber & Faber, 1976), from the *Times Literary Supplement*, 15 October 1976.

IN THE eighteenth century the concept of Imagination rose to usurp the place previously accorded to the notion of Taste, and became the ruling concept in aesthetic theory. Criticism, in consequence, became entangled with the philosophy of mind. From Kant to Collingwood we find the same attempt to unite the aesthetic and the moral under a single mental capacity: and usually the word 'imagination' has been chosen to denote it. This is not surprising. From the beginning of the Enlightenment imagination was studied not only in aesthetics but also in metaphysics and the theory of knowledge. Neither Hume nor Kant thought that there was anything special about it, nor did they regard it as unequally distributed among men. For both of them it was the imagination that knits together the scattered data of the senses into a patterned image of the world. It provides us with our beliefs about the past and future, and with that awareness of what is possible without which there can be no knowledge of what is. While given to occasional flights, the imagination is more usually to be found perched in the cage of the common understanding, peaceably parroting its banal observations of the world.

It was Kant who gave the most powerful impetus to this 'general' theory of imagination. He saw it as a capacity exercised in every act of perception, as a force active in the formation of every image and every cognitive state. There is also a 'special' theory, associated with Sartre and Wittgenstein, according to whom the imagination is manifest only sometimes and only in certain special forms of perception, imagery and thought. On their view memory, for example, although it involves images, is not an exercise of the imagination.

The dispute between the two theories may appear to be a verbal one; in fact it is more serious. If we adopt the general theory then, like Coleridge, we find that the experience of art is no longer puzzling. Precisely the same capacities are exercised in imaginative experience as are revealed in ordinary perception. There is no problem, therefore, in showing how the first can illuminate the second, and the second give content to the first. If we adopt the special theory, however, aesthetics becomes more difficult.

Mary Warnock espouses the general theory, and sees the whole history of the subject as exemplifying it. From Hume to Merleau-Ponty we are encouraged to find the same emphasis on the omnipresence of imagination, and when Coleridge presented the imagination as the highest form of knowledge he was (apparently) only repeating one of the established truths of philosophy. In his theories (or rather, in what would have been his theories had he been possessed of a systematic mind) we find, according to Mrs Warnock, a profound exegesis of Kantian epistemology. It is one of the many valuable qualities of Mrs Warnock's book that she clarifies this chain of influence, and sets the philosophy of *Lyrical Ballads* and *The Prelude* in its true historical context.

Why should we adopt the general theory? Why should we think that there is a single faculty that is exercised in seeing, remembering and imagining, and why should we think that 'imagination' is an appropriate name for it? I am not sure. Hume said that we attribute an identity and continuity to objects despite the momentary and fragmented character of our perceptions. Our beliefs about the world are therefore founded on imagination, which fills in the ragged gaps between experiences. Nobody really believes that. Knowledge of experience is possible only through the prior identification of enduring objects, and the idea that we use imagination to *construct* the world is palpably absurd.

Kant was more subtle. He argued that there can be no perception that does not already postulate its object as continuous and identical. It is not, as Hume thought, that we first have perceptions and then imaginatively unite them; it is rather that perceptions are already organized into the unity required. Our experience comes to us as the result of a 'transcendental synthesis' which accommodates it to the concepts of the understanding. One instrument in that 'synthesis' is the imagination. But the imagination moves in a mysterious way. We can see only the products of its operation; the process, being 'transcendental', remains forever hidden.

Kant's theory is interesting, but scarcely intelligible as it stands. There cannot be such a thing as a 'transcendental' process, nor can we understand what is meant by a 'faculty' the operation of which can never be examined. In fact the concept of a 'faculty' is incoherent. It was a philosophical ruse, an attempt to see the entire structure of philosophy in metaphysical terms and to recast as ontological problems what are really puzzles in the philosophy of mind.

Mrs Warnock seems prepared to admit as much. The language of 'faculties' she says, is at best a metaphor. But what remains to the general theory of imagination when that language is discarded? Despite Mrs Warnock's admirable lucidity it is difficult to derive a coherent answer from her book. Her discussion is primarily historical, rather than critical. And the criticisms, when they are offered, are not always persuasive.

Sartre is attacked for rejecting the general theory of imagination. He describes the imagination thus: it is the positing of an object as not being (as 'a nothingness' to use his portentous phrase). In memory and perception, however, the object is posited as real. Surely that is a sensible distinction? Moreover, does it not capture precisely what is puzzling in those cases which are normally described as cases of 'imagining'? Mrs Warnock objects that the memory image and the imaginative image have more similarities than differences; therefore Sartre's theory is an exaggeration. But surely, it is very misleading to speak of the 'similarities' between images. The principal feature of an image, the feature which determines its nature as a mental act, is its relation to its object. An image is not an object of attention but rather a mode of attention to other things. It is not so much a thing with properties as a way of envisaging the properties of its object.

The important question about an image concerns its object: does it posit the object as real or imaginary? And what is it to posit an object as imaginary? This last question is the central question in the philosophy of imagination. It is the question which must be answered if any of the activities normally described as 'imagining' are to be correctly understood. And it could never be answered simply by attending to those features which all images share. Why then should we try to assimilate perception and imagination when to do so is to leave the most important question in the theory of imagination without an answer? Once we have abandoned the jargon of 'faculties' I cannot see that there remains any attraction in the 'general' theory of imagination.

Mrs Warnock expounds many philosophies, and devotes a considerable portion of her book—indeed the portion with which she seems most strongly to identify—to the so-called 'method' of phenomenology. Nobody knows (or at least, nobody has managed to communicate) what this method involves. It is supposed to be distinct from introspection, but Mrs Warnock is not certain about that. Is she being a phenomenologist when she says that Hume's theory does not fit our experience of imagining? Or is that merely an 'empirical' observation? How would she reply to someone who said that *his* images *were* as Hume described? What is the criterion of correctness here? Is Sartre being a phenomenologist when he says that the imaginative image posits its object as not being? If so, why? Is this something one learns by studying the image, or the language in which the image is described, or the behaviour which expresses it? There is nothing in the jargon of phenomenology to enable us to answer such questions. But, until we answer them, how can we know what an image is?

If I employ the 'method' of phenomenology it is in some way 'up to me' to determine, by some mysterious process of abstraction, the distinguishing features of my mental states. A typical result is this: when I see I am presented with an appearance to which is added, in the 'intentional act' of perception, the unseen depth, the substance, the solidity and the hidden underside of things.

This way of putting the matter points back to the Enlightenment theory of imagination, as a force that is somehow 'active' in perception, drawing together the observable fragments of an object and somehow uniting them with their unseen and unseeable parts. So Mrs Warnock understands it, and she provides many entertaining examples of phenomenological analysis with which to compare the more unworldly speculations of Kant. The fact that Kant's theory is made neither more nor less plausible by these examples leads one to doubt that phenomenology can make any serious contribution to the subject.

Moreover, Mrs Warnock systematically overlooks the fact that phenomenology, whatever it is, cannot present us with the essence of perception, but only with the peculiarities of self-conscious perception. In phenomenological analysis the 'I' is already posited. It is by virtue of this sleight-of-hand that the phenomenological metaphors begin to persuade us. We can now force an artificial separation between act and object, and invent a spurious process through which they are united. Phenomenology does not describe the contents of consciousness; it merely meddles with them.

Now there is perception which is not self-conscious. My dog, not being a *zoon politikon* lacks the knowledge and the concept of self. Yet he sees me in the garden, hears me calling to him, and smells me as he approaches. Is he synthesizing in imagination the fragmentary deliverances of experience? Say that if you will, but do not think that what you have there called 'imagination' is identical with that ability to 'posit the imaginary' without which there is little moral experience and no understanding of art. Once we have rejected the myth of faculties, and the beguiling self-absorption of the phenomenologists, the important fact is no longer the resemblance between imagination and perception, but the insurmountable difference. Only some animals imagine, but all animals perceive. As Sartre and Wittgenstein repeatedly emphasize, the thought process in imagination is active; it is possessed of a freedom which springs from the known unreality of its object. Therefore the imagination lies within our control. I can command you to imagine that there is life on Mars, but not to believe it, perceive it or remember it.

The fact is of paramount importance. For it shows that imagination is peculiar to rational beings, peculiar to beings whose intellectual capacities transcend the fixation with the immediate which is characteristic of merely animal existence. If one continues to insist that there is a process of 'synthesis' involved in all perception (whether 'transcendental' or 'intentional' or what), then one must go on to say, either that such a process is not after all identical with imagination, or that it is, and that my dog, who lacks imagination, cannot see.

8   Through Fiction to Reality

The Fire and the Sun: why Plato banished the artists, based on the Romanes Lecture 1976, Iris Murdoch (Clarendon Press, 1977), from the *Times Literary Supplement*, 25 November 1977.

IRIS MURDOCH'S Romanes Lectures afford a lively introduction to Plato's thought, an introduction which, while ostensibly confining itself to the notorious edict against poetry, adumbrates most of the Platonic system. Miss Murdoch does not argue, she reflects; and her reflections combine robust common sense with quick imagination, in the manner of her novels. As a thinker she is woolly, but serious, and clearly untainted by any fear of the unknown. Miss Murdoch is fascinated by the quality of Plato's mind, and by the unsurpassable genius with which he extracted from every simple puzzle a bold metaphysical answer. Since she communicates her enthusiasm honestly, and supports it with a comprehensive knowledge of the texts, her little book will be as academically useful as it is sure to be popularly admired. It goes without saying that neither the content nor the presentation are strictly orthodox. But a philosopher of Plato's stature cannot suffer from this unorthodoxy, and even the narrowest of academics must be impressed by the confidence with which Miss Murdoch is able to see the entire philosophy of Forms laid bare in Plato's passing animadversions against art.

It is indeed useful to see this issue in its wider aspect. For at first sight Plato's grounds for dismissing poets and painters from the Republic are not only surprising (coming from the greatest poet among philosophers), but also naive. It is not true that poets are liars: there is a distinction, recognized by all reasonable men, between deceit and fiction. Nor is it true that poetry delights in the ludicrous, that theatrical displays are naturally unseemly, or that a painting offers us a mere copy or semblance, as distant from the reality of its subject as the subject is distant from its Form.

In considering this last point it is interesting to contrast painting and photography. A photograph of Monsieur Choquet might certainly be a mere semblance—for it would contain nothing of the man but a fleeting appearance, and would address itself, as photographs address themselves, primarily to sentimental and impertinent emotions. The photograph conveys much, but what it conveys is fortuitous and ephemeral. Cézanne's portrait of Monsieur Choquet is not like that. It attempts to represent the whole man, his character, and his significance. It attempts to speak to those who might never have known Monsieur Choquet, who have no personal interest in him nor any reason to inform themselves of his existence. No fleeting appearance of Monsieur Choquet could convey to us what Cézanne's portrait conveys. The portrait addresses itself to no profane lust for ephemera, no anecdotal musing, no nostalgic revery. It is an attempt to give knowledge and understanding, not of this particular man or this particular moment, but of a human character conceived entire. Such art emancipates itself from any preoccupation with ephemera; in doing so it approaches Plato's ideal of the mind.

It is true that most of what passes for art is nothing but a play of shadows. But it is also true that art has had, and has still, the aim of transcending the ephemeral. Therefore Aristotle, the first to admonish Plato for his puritanism, described poetry as more general than history, and nearer to that emancipation from the immediate, the contingent and the particular which Plato demanded. It is true that a poem or a play represents a particular. But it also expresses a universal. Moreover it has this relation to the universal precisely because what it represents is a fiction: that is to say, a particular detached from the fortuitous workings of reality and understood not as a threat or promise but as an objective and impersonal idea. Far from being deception, fiction—true fiction—is an instrument of understanding. Fiction becomes a lie only in becoming mechanical. For then it responds not to intellect but to impulse. Then it is no more than fantasy, and fantasy, unlike fiction, competes with what is real. (Which is why Coleridge found it necessary to distinguish fancy and imagination.)

Those reflections are not Miss Murdoch's. Nevertheless they suggest a connection which she makes, between the Platonic discussion of art and Freud's scattered remarks on the same subject. But while it is true that Freud considered art under the aspect of 'pleasure seeking', it is surely not true—as Miss Murdoch seems to imply—that he also regarded it as 'self-satisfied pseudo-analysis and pseudo-enlightenment'. In a famous phrase Freud spoke of the artist as creating a path from fantasy back to reality. And that is surely what Aristotle had in mind in his reply to Plato (the reply which included his theory of catharsis).

Fantasy is both easy and (when pursued with no other aim) destructive: for it involves the creation of unreal objects for passions which are real, whereas in true art both passion and object are imagined. There is an outward-looking force in men, which Freud called 'libido' and Plato 'eros', and which is channelled away from real fulfilment by the pursuit of fantasy. When that happens the ego is deprived of its source of integrity and strength. The artist, who awakens fantasy, therefore has the moral task of destroying its superficial charm, of using it in defiance of its own nature, in order to pursue, capture and understand what is real: *hoc opus, hic labor est.*

Miss Murdoch is aware of all that. But she does not put the point with quite the clarity and rigour which it demands. It is not clear whether she is really willing to put forward and defend a forthright view of her own. Startling remarks—such as that it is the attraction of beauty which leads us to study the synthetic *a priori*, or that Western art has 'surreptitiously lent its power to an ossifying of the religion it purports to serve'—stand out suddenly and unsupported in the text: while old platitudes which no philosopher should accept with readiness (art is 'at home with evil and quick to beautify it' or 'a free art is an essential aspect of a free society') emerge from the flow of reflection with an unearned and spurious authority. Perhaps this is inevitable in a book which aims to be (and succeeds in being) succinct and comprehensive. But once in a while the reader might wish for a little more argument and a little less assertion, especially in those passages (and they are many) where it is not clear that the assertions belong to Miss Murdoch rather than to Plato.

Her own contributions—when they are identifiable—are subtle and suggestive; but they cannot stand alone. The thesis just mentioned, that Western art has tended to ossify the religion it purports to serve, is an arresting one. But is it really true? Certainly Dante, Michelangelo, Milton and Bach purported to serve in their works the Christian religion. But have those works lent their power to the ossification of Christianity? It is hard to know what Miss Murdoch means by that. There is no doubt that the Church is ill, and dangerously ill. But those responsible for its sickness have little understanding of the traditions of Western art (as the new liturgies amply illustrate), and no capacity to learn from *The Divine Comedy* or the St Matthew Passion—works which have provided generations of men and women, and not only educated men and women, with the concrete expression of religious feeling. No doubt those thoughts do not refute Miss Murdoch's view, which is more subtle, and more concerned with the historical tendency of Western art, than they suggest. But that only shows how interesting a clearer statement would have been, and how recent an invention is the concept of art employed in it. In one sense, indeed, Miss Murdoch's subtitle is highly misleading. Plato sought to banish poets and painters; not musicians or architects. In making such a sharp distinction he showed that his conception of art was very different from ours. Nor is that surprising, since Plato, unlike Miss Murdoch, had not read Hegel.

9   Pseudo-painting

Concerning Contemporary Art: the Power Lectures 1968-1973, edited by Bernard Smith (Clarendon Press, 1975), from the *Times Literary Supplement,* 25 July 1975.

THE POWER LECTURE in Contemporary Art is delivered annually throughout Australia in honour of John Power, the Cubist artist whose bequest made possible the establishment of the Power Institute of Fine Arts in the University of Sydney. The first six lectures, published together, and written by a variety of distinguished men directly and indirectly concerned with contemporary art, will be of interest to anyone who seeks for an intelligible account of the painting and sculpture of our time. No art-lover can be wholly unaware of the unsatisfactory state of contemporary painting, and occasionally too the writers of these lectures acknowledge that the art-lover's case should be stated, even if it does not deserve an answer. As Clement Greenberg puts it, in the energetic lecture that opens the book:

> It has become apparent that art can have a startling impact without really being or saying anything startling—or new. The character itself of being startling, spectacular or upsetting has become conventionalized, part of safe good taste.

Alas, his criticism goes no farther and when we come to the important question of how a ready-made, an excreting machine, or a plain unornamented box can have value as a work of art, his answer is the tritest imaginable: the box is good art when it is felt, inspired; bad art when it is unfelt, uninspired. But the problem is: how, and when, can a plain box be felt or unfelt, inspired or uninspired?

The truth is that after the experience of the Impressionist, Fauve, Cubist, and more recent revolutions, few critics will dare to say of any contemporary 'school' or 'movement' that it is not what it claims to be, or that painting might have been better without it. Every casual product of fashion must now be taken seriously, and while particular skills of self-advertisement are required if an artist is to enter into the consumer-orientated world of museum and gallery, it is not always clear that any aesthetic standards are, or could be, applied to distinguish the successful from the unsuccessful. Such standards are certainly not always in evidence in this book. Sometimes, as in Patrick Hutchings's interesting essay on contemporary realism, we do find ourselves being led to an understanding of the works of art under discussion. But even there, lively

71

though the presentation is, the approach to intellectual problems is little more than a *jeu d'idées reçues*. The question of the relation between painting and photography is deep and difficult; Mr Hutchings's failure to be aware of the difficulties detracts seriously from his discussion of the work of Chambers, Danby and Colville. The cold, crisp eye and inhuman sensibility of those painters is not happily characterized as realism, for the very reason that their photographic technique removes from the canvas the realist's consciousness of time.

Perhaps the most interesting essay in the book is that by Richard Wollheim, who attempts to describe in philosophical terms one of the crucial difficulties that face contemporary painting, the difficulty of forming a style. Professor Wollheim's thesis is that a modern artist is compelled to pursue recognizability in a manner that is inimical to the formation of style. The compelling force here, he says, is an economic one, and the result of that force is to impoverish the content of contemporary painting and to limit its expressive power. The thesis, which is put forward tentatively, has an important philosophical basis, and is developed with characteristic ingenuity. Were the author more robust in his scepticism his argument would perhaps be a little clearer; but already it must constitute a serious objection to the sillier styles of contemporary art-criticism, exemplified here by Charles Mitchell and Donald Brook.

Mr Mitchell's essay, with its phoney academicism, and its uncritical admiration for artists like Oldenburg, Warhol, and the idiotic Marcel Duchamp, is the most irritating in the book. And the spirit that is most alive in both these essays, and in the art which they purport to criticize, is that of Duchamp, who was more determined than other modern artists to subordinate visual experience to literary ideas, and to replace genuine imagination with sterile fantasy. For, while there is both good modern art and bad modern art, there is most of all time-serving modish modern art, which relegates standards to the dust-heap of history and claims for itself the absolute autonomy of a merely personal experience. Such art was made respectable by Duchamp, or rather by André Breton on Duchamp's behalf. It is art to be accepted rather than judged, and lest one should be unaware *how* to accept it, such art comes already complete with instructions, programme notes, and fanfares of synthetic applause. Indeed, a special language has been developed in order to defeat all criticism before it can be uttered. The combined resources of pseuds and charlatans in every area of intellectual endeavour—from phenomenology to cybernetics—have been tapped to provide the necessary jargon, and a unique style has evolved with which to create an irrebuttable sense of absolute authority:

It is now possible to separate . . . decisions, which are relevant to the object as thing in itself, from those decisions external to its physical presence . . . placement becomes critical as it never was before in establishing the particular quality of the work. A beam on its end is not the same as the same beam on its side.

It is not surprising that some of the new sculpture which avoids varying parts, polychrome, etc, has been called negative, boring, nihilistic. These judgments arise from confronting the work with expectations structured by a Cubist aesthetic in which what is to be had from the work is located strictly within the specific object. The situation is now more complex and expanded.

Those are the words (quoted by Mr Brook) of Robert Morris, whose own work is indeed negative, boring and nihilistic. But the fact is that artists like Morris do not very much object to the use of such labels in describing their works: their art is a 'literary' art, designed to be a subject of controversy, entangled from its inception in a web of half-comprehended ideas. It is an art divorced from the true history of visual perception, and its newness, gaining no value from any previous tradition, remains visually insignificant. It is the excess of foolish verbiage, and the self-conscious concern with uncomprehended 'aesthetic' notions that have destroyed the visual integrity of so much contemporary art, leaving in the place of genuine evolution a mindless flirtation with empty novelties. Nowhere is this more apparent than in the desperate academicism of the art schools, where silly jokes done to death by dadaism are solemnly resurrected in the form of a humourless posturing, sometimes even presented as a 'challenge' to the 'structures' and 'categories' of our 'bourgeois' world.

The final essay is more traditional, reminding one somewhat of Haydon's memoirs. It is written by Patrick Heron, who takes the opportunity to explain his greatness to the Australian public. His arguments are supported by much independent opinion, and contain no fewer than eight long quotations from critical articles (all, as it happens, written by himself). The style is amiable and straightforward, one word in every twenty-five being the first person singular pronoun. And the essay provides some startling insights into the creative process. For example, Mr Heron describes a momentous transition in his own style as follows:

My exhibition of 1956 was categorized *tachist*. But in my case the strokes, or *taches*, increasingly assumed a vertical direction so that each canvas, in the end, consisted solely of large isolated vertical brushstrokes. In early 1957, feeling, I think, that the allover emphasis and the uniform looseness and the too-mechanical scribble of what the French called tachism and the Americans action-painting needed to be harnessed slightly more rigidly to the edges of the canvas, I allowed my arm to extend a number of these vertical brush strokes until they made contact with the top and the bottom edges of the canvas. . . .

While the world of art was still reeling from the effect of this discovery, Mr Heron had taken an even more daring initiative; he had progressed to canvases

> whose total image consisted solely of these long vertical strokes, in differing colours, all reaching more or less from top to bottom of the picture format. It was during this same month, March 1957, that I therefore arrived at the first of a series of paintings which were later to be known as colour stripe paintings.

Surprisingly, although these were of course the first stripe paintings to be painted anywhere, Heron was initially unaware of having changed the whole course of modern painting. 'Something called "colour stripe painting" did not exist at the time, even as a concept.'

This revelation of the creative process, combined with the insight into aesthetic ideas provided by Mr Brook and Mr Mitchell, will make the book a welcome addition to any art school library. Moreover, it is printed in very small type, set in fashionable asymmetry on the page, and has a migraine-inducing quality that ranks it with the best of Bridget Riley.

10 The Semiology of Music

Fondements d'une Sémiologie de la Musique, J. J. Nattiez (Paris, 1978), from *Cambridge Review*, 2 June 1978.

FASHION demands that there should be a book on the semiology of music, and that it should be long, dense, introverted and, if possible, French. M. Nattiez has written the book, spreading his subject over four hundred and forty eight pages of dither and doubt. It is true that the quotations from his fellow *sémiologues* are so many and so lengthy that one can with safety attribute only some two hundred of those pages to M. Nattiez; but to have been responsible even for one of them would have already constituted an offence against his reader's intelligence. For, as Nattiez confesses in the first sentence of Chapter One, '*La Sémiologie n'existe pas*', a fact which in no way deters him from describing its musical foundations. But let us reflect for a moment on the title of the book. We are offered foundations not of *the* semiology of music, but of *a* semiology of music. Does this mean that there could be more than one semiology? Two, perhaps? Or three? A hundred? Infinitely many? Now there is only *one* physics; does that make physics more, or less, scientific than semiology, less, or more, impoverished? The answers are obvious, and would that M. Nattiez and his colleagues had paused to consider them. If there seems to be more than one semiology it is because in reality there is less than one. As M. Nattiez says, this science, so impetuously conjured from the dead remnants of Saussurian linguistics, does not exist.

But whoever said that semiology is a science? Its founder, for one. In his *Cours de Linguistique Générale,* Saussure defined semiology as the 'general science of signs', and affirmed that it had a 'right' to exist. In the sixties it became fashionable to invent it. Roland Barthes presented his *Eléments de Sémiologie* in 1964, borrowing from Saussure, Jakobson and Hjelmslev all the premature technicalities of the unformed science of linguistics, and displaying them with a beguiling irreverence that at times seemed like insight. Less nimble charlatans danced attendance on him, and beheld with bitterness the later antics of their master. Like a true modiste, Barthes sensed the dangers of discipleship. He quickly dropped his 'scientific' pretensions, spun a web of pedantry (on the shocking subject of pleasure), and vanished, leaving only his clothes. But the wardrobe is an enticing one; its colourful disguises have been rifled in the cause of ignorance.

The word 'sign' means many things. Do we suppose that a cloud signifies rain in the way that '*Je m'ennuie*' signifies that I am bored? Of course not. From a scientific point of view there is not *one* thing here, but thousands. What is common is only that small feature of the surface of each, which is as familiar to us as the function of buttons. The common essence of signs is shallow; semiology pretends that it is deep. Thus Nattiez, having suggested that music is a 'sign' can go on to say that '*nous ne savons pas grand'chose sur la musique*' (p. 45). The cure of M. Nattiez's ignorance does not lie where he is seeking it; he has only to close his books, and open his ears.

It is wrong to suppose that we can transfer the few respectable concepts generated by the young science of linguistics to the study of music; much more wrong to transfer, as Nattiez does, that science's infant babble. Of course, the thesis that music is, or might be, a language, has been taken seriously since the time of Rousseau. The late Deryck Cooke expressed it with a plain English innocence that had the singular merit of showing his theory to be wrong. Cooke treated music as a code, correlated step by step with a dictionary meaning. He ignored an essential feature of language, which gives to language its universality, learnability, and descriptive power—the feature of grammar. The meanings of musical fragments, as Cooke interpreted them, led towards no meaning for the whole. Hence his 'decipherings' have never been persuasive. Cooke was describing not meaning but expression, and expression, which obeys no rule, cannot be subject to the rule of a dictionary (otherwise we should all be Mozarts).

What is it, then, that the semiologist hopes to add to this dismal enterprise? Precisely the feature of grammar, referred to either as 'structure' (with a tendentious allusion to the anthropology of Lévi-Strauss), or as syntax. Nicholas Ruwet, for example, treats music as a 'semiotic system' because it 'shares a certain number of common features—such as the existence of syntax—with language and other systems of signs' (*Langage, Musique, Poésie*, Paris, 1972). Nattiez seems bitter towards Ruwet (who was, I suppose, the true founder of musical 'semiotics'), and therefore makes unintelligible murmurs of dissent. Nevertheless, he accepts the idea of a musical 'syntax', and takes this as sufficient confirmation of the semiologist's premise—the premise that music is a 'sign'. And once accepted, the idea of syntax is embellished with every available technical term. The syntax of music becomes a 'system', with 'paradigmatic' and 'syntagmatic' structure. (Barthes did the same for menus, Eco has done it for architecture; I myself have prepared an analysis of the syntactical structure of railway trains. All this means is that, in music, as in railway trains, every item limits what may precede or follow it). Allusions are made to the 'generative' grammar of Chomsky (rejected by Nattiez (p. 53) on the spurious ground that it does not distinguish the theory of utterance from the theory of understanding). Nattiez refers to everything that might add complexity to the description of 'syntax', to every 'model', as he puts it, or 'criterion', for arriving at a description of that 'neutral level' where the music exists in all its grammatical purity, purged of human causes and human effects. Nattiez's gross misuse of logical terms—'variable', 'criterion', 'model', 'metalanguage', 'set'—is in fact a device for mesmerizing his reader into the hallucination of a deep and difficult enquiry, a slow analysis *'remontant de niveau en niveau'*. But since the purpose of this analysis is never revealed, one can only suppose that the difficulties are of Nattiez's invention. Even at the end of the book he is asking simple questions which should have been settled at the outset, questions of method, aim and subject-matter. The description of semiology as an *'exercise aride'* (p. 417) is well confirmed by the statement of what has actually been achieved in four hundred pages: 'the exercise of comparing different analyses of a single work', from which 'there cannot but arise questions concerning the criteria employed by the various musicologists or by their schools' (p. 410). All we have, then, are more 'questions', about 'criteria'; what 'criteria' are, what they are 'of', or 'for', is never clarified. (Nattiez does, however, attempt (p. 264) to define the musical 'paradigm' as an *'ensemble de critères'*, as one might define an elephant as a heap of corners, or a lake as a series of swims).

Nor should we be surprised by this confusion. For what Ruwet and Nattiez call the 'syntax' of music is no such thing. By 'syntax' we mean the system of rules for generating acceptable sentences. The idea of a syntactic structure is the idea of a potential *meaning*. There can be no system of syntax which does not, in its turn, rest on a system of semantics, a system for deriving the meaning of a sentence from the meaning of its parts. In the absence of a semantic interpretation, to speak of syntax is to use a metaphor and a misleading metaphor. It is to suggest the presence of an organization that is not there. The jargon of 'syntagm' and 'paradigm' adds nothing that will remove this difficulty. All that is meant in referring to the existence of musical syntax is that music exhibits linear progression (and also style). But the importance of syntax lies elsewhere, in the semantic implications which it displays. The point was given theoretical foundation by Tarski (who invented the term 'metalanguage', so ignorantly abused by the *Sémiologues*). Naturally, Tarski's work, like that of Frege, and all the powerful studies in the grammar of natural language which have stemmed from it, is ignored by Nattiez. And rightly so, for, since music is not a language, the theories of formal semantics do not apply. Nor, however, do the theories borrowed by Nattiez.

It is surely evident that music, while it is in some respects *like* language, is unlike language in the crucial respect of meaning. (One does not respond to a phrase in music with remarks like 'True', 'False', or 'You're lying'). There is nothing (besides itself) which music means. Nattiez briefly mentions expression (which, in music, has nothing to do with linguistic meaning), but wisely puts it aside. He also toys with the idea that music is a pictorial art (p. 148). This too seems wrong. Or at least, it requires argument to establish it, and argument is no part of Nattiez's style. Music, like clothes and architecture, may *imitate* features of the world. But it is necessary to distinguish imitation from representation, copying from description. In any case, apart from these brief and un-argued allusions, Nattiez makes no attempt to assign a semantic dimension to musical form. His analysis remains schematic, and its purpose, since it defies its author's explanatory powers, must also defy mine.

But should we simply reject the analogy between music and language? At one point (p. 399) Nattiez asserts that the transference of linguistic 'models' to music is not metaphorical. On the next page he describes the linguistic theory of music as an *'immense métaphore scientifique'*. Clearly, then, Nattiez has little to tell us on the subject (or much, if you accept the view that, from a contradiction, everything follows). Nevertheless, he mentions the fact which draws most people to the linguistic analogy, the fact that music may be *misunderstood*. What is it, then, that we understand in music? To put it another way: Is there something *else*, in addition to the music, that we understand? (In language there is the meaning, in addition to the sentence). Nattiez (following Leibowitz in *Schönberg and his School*), notices the concept of musical understanding. But he envisages it as a kind of problem-solving. He goes on to speak of an activity of breaking-down *(discrétisation)*, requiring an 'analysis' of a 'structure', and involving 'models', 'criteria', 'codes'. But that is obviously wrong. Consider the opening bars of the prelude to *Pelléas:*

Nattiez puzzles over the tonality of this passage and over the correct description of the chords which occur in bars 5 and 6. Indeed, in a previously published paper Nattiez had compared no fewer than ten analyses of this passage, representing each one as an approach to its musical syntax, and hence, one supposes, as a step towards decoding it. The problem, for Nattiez, is that the tonality of D minor (or the D minor mode) survives throughout the first four bars. What then of the first chord of bar five? Most people would say—describe it as you like, so long as you hear it correctly. (Janáček, asked by a pupil to describe a chord, wrung his hands, and answered, 'A chord like *that*'). Leibowitz, however, (*Les Temps Modernes*, 1971), is convinced that this is the dominant seventh chord of G with a flattened fifth; while a certain Mr van Appledorn regards it as a second inversion of a French sixth. M. Nattiez has no settled view of the matter, except that it is all very difficult, and that we see how many different '*critères*' are employed in the description of even the simplest musical work. It seems, then, that '*nous ne savons pas grand'chose sur la musique*'.

Fortunately, however, you do not have to engage in these weird enquiries in order to understand the prelude to *Pelléas*. It does not matter how you describe that questionable chord—except that certain descriptions suggest wrong ways of hearing it. (Leibowitz, for example, suggests a chord out of Fats Waller. Debussy never *flattened* a fifth, as a Jazz musician might; he simply used the interval of a tritone). What is obvious to the ear is the contrast in mood and atmosphere between the 'modal' passage and the bars which follow it. The harmony of those bars is in fact derived directly from the whole-tone scale (and the rocking tritone in the bass is used, as in the prelude to *Siegfried*, Act II, to deny the sense of key). The whole-tone harmony supports the whole-tone melody (perhaps the greatest melody ever to be composed out of two notes); it gives to the melody that wandering, poignant air which Debussy exploits throughout the opera. All this can be heard without describing it: anyone who misunderstands can be brought to hear the passage correctly by an acquaintance with the whole-tone scale (for example by listening to *Voiles*). What, then, is the point of establishing a 'criterion' for describing the passage? What is learned from that exercise, and how is our understanding of the music changed by it? According to Nattiez (p. 104), his style of analysis is designed not to 'deepen the manner in which the music is experienced (*vécue*) by its "*utilisateurs*" (does he mean audience?), but to establish *rules* . . . which describe how it functions'. But the function of music *is* our experience: that is where understanding lies. Why then assume that there are *rules* of this game, and why assume, what surely stands to be proved, that the rules are those of a 'syntax'? The fact is that we have nothing here but an immense unscientific metaphor, which bears neither on the hearing, nor the understanding, nor the intelligent criticism, of music.

11   Philosophy and Literature

Originally published as 'Filosofie, literatuur en waarheid' in *Wijsgerig Perspectief op Maatshappij en Wetenschap*, 1978.

'PHILOSOPHY' and 'literature' are words which are now narrowly defined. The first denotes the abstract pursuit of truth (whether, in the Anglo-Saxon style, through the analysis of concepts, or in the continental style, through the speculative perusal of subjective consciousness). The second denotes all those uses of words whose principal aim is art. We include under 'literature' not only poetry and drama, but also novels, stories, prose poems, all those writings where *what* is said, and *how* it is said, matter equally. What do these forms that we call 'literature' have in common? The word 'art' now carries little meaning. Let us substitute another: 'imagination', or, if you prefer, 'creative imagination'. So, what is the relation, and what the difference, between imaginative literature, and philosophy?

Philosophy is the pursuit of truth. Not truth about the here and now, about what is contingent, passing, subject to change; but essential, changeless truth. Philosophy explores the nature of things; not how they are but how they must be. Whether by conceptual analysis, by phenomenological examination, by dialectical speculation, or whatever, philosophy always aims at essence. Its means is argument, and its end is truth.

What, then, distinguishes poetry from philosophy? Does not poetry, indeed does not all imaginative writing, aim to describe the essence of things? Perhaps not always, but always when it is serious. We must make some distinctions. The method of philosophy is argument: a philosopher presents reasons for something which he holds to be true. In argument, the aim of validity takes precedence over every demand of elegance, clarity or style. Great philosophy may be very bad prose. Equally, a great philosopher might be a great stylist, and produce works which are sublime and beautiful, in addition to whatever they contain by way of philosophical argument. Consider the works of Plato, or the remote, magisterial *Ethics* of Spinoza.

Imaginative literature does not proceed by argument, and it has 'conclusions' only in an obscure and attenuated sense. It is significant that a philosopher tries to *state* his conclusions, whereas the 'conclusions' of a novel or poem must be 'drawn'. What are the 'conclusions' of the *Agamemnon*? A critic might tell us; but Aeschylus is silent. Here, perhaps, is one source of our distinction. In philosophy truth is *argued for*; in literature it is only implied. So perhaps truth is a secondary aim in literature. If there is a primary aim (and that too may be doubted), it seems to lie in the creation of an imaginative experience, rather than the generation of speculative thought. The content of a novel, play or poem is not thought, but lived. And it is lived, not as real, but as imaginary. (So let us not agree with Plato; poetry is *not* a kind of elaborate lie).

This suggests a further distinction. Philosophy is abstract, concerned with truth in its most general form. Imaginative literature is concrete, for it is through the concrete image that imagination represents the world. It is indeed a great fault in imaginative literature when some dominant abstraction begins to control the writer's pen, when the desire to prove a point or express an idea outruns the ability to provide the image that would embody it. (Consider the works of Hermann Hesse: here we see the imagination overrun by thought. The art has become didactic, vague, unreal; it has lost all concrete connection with life. Contrast, say, *The Divine Comedy*, where the most baffling of abstractions are translated into images of overwhelming immediacy and power).

What exactly do we mean when we say that the imagination (unlike the intellect) is concrete? Part of the matter lies here: in imagination, what is represented is also realized. Which is to say, imaginative literature does not merely communicate a thought ('Once upon a time . . .'). The thought is conveyed through an experience—as are the thoughts in a painting. As Hegel put it: in art we have the sensuous *embodiment* of an idea. And this means that, in literature, (or at least in successful literature), thought and experience are inextricably combined. It follows, for example, that science fiction, if it is to be imaginative literature, must succeed in transforming science *into* fiction: it is uninteresting as a genre if it amounts only to fiction sprinkled with scientific novelties. It also follows that literature may describe impossibilities, and still be successful, so long as it provides some vivid image that corresponds to them. In this sense a deep philosophical untruth may find its successful expression in poetry—the transformation of Athena into Mentes at the beginning of the *Odyssey,* of Fafner into a dragon in the *Ring*. Thus Aristotle remarked in the *Poetics,* that in dramatic representation improbable possibilities are a fault, whereas 'probable impossibilities' are not. (This remark may raise the eyebrows of the modal logician, but, properly interpreted, must appear to the critical reader as plain common sense.)

But now we come across a difficulty. There is poetry that deals almost entirely in abstractions, such as the metaphysical poetry of George Herbert and John Donne, or the philosophical ruminations of Goethe and Hölderlin. Nevertheless, there is an argument for saying that, even here, it is the imagination, and not reasoned argument that is the principal guiding force, and that the sign of this lies again in the partial inseparability of content from form, and of thought from experience. Thus the thought of a poem can move through deliberate ambiguities; and no such movement can constitute an *argument*. Consider the highly abstract first lines of T. S. Eliot's *Four Quartets:*

> Time present and time past
> Are both perhaps present in time future
> And time future contained in time past.

This has the semblance of philosophical statement; but it is not philosophy. It is poetry clothed in the language of abstract statement. Consider how we might translate the full content of these lines into other words. We find that we cannot do so. It is essential, for example, to note and to feel the ambiguity contained in the word 'present' in the second line. Time past is present in the future, and therefore both remains and also becomes part of what is (now) present; moreover it is a present, a gift, which only the future offers, and the 'presence' of time past (of time *as* past) comes only with our own presence in time future. The future however is not present in the past, but only contained in it: it is embryonic, incomplete, and yet also complete enough to be 'contained'. Here is a further ambiguity: time future can be contained in time past only if it is circumscribed by time past: in which case it can itself contain nothing that time past forbids it to contain. There is, then, hidden in these lines, not merely an abstract metaphysic of time, but an experience of continuity, an experience that can be translated only approximately into abstract terms. The experience is a 'reverberation' of the choice of words, and of their placing in the text, and this reverberation has to be caught and lived in the act of reading. ('My words echo/Thus in your mind'). Consider now what would happen if one were to change the order of the words, and substitute a new word (say 'possibly', for 'perhaps'), while preserving the literal meaning. Consider, for example, the statement 'Past time and present time are both possibly present in future time.' Here we find that, while the *philosophical* thought remains the same, the *sense* of time's continuity, of the subtle identity of time (present, past and future) has been lost, so too has the sense of the peculiarity of time's movement (captured in 'perhaps', with its allusion to what 'happens', lost in the word 'possibly' which merely throws the experience into doubt).

In this example then, is poetry which, while being as near as possible to abstract thought, is nevertheless intelligible only as a concrete experience 'condensed' into the sound, sense and order of the given words. The understanding of the nature of time which Eliot presents, while *based* in a certain philosophy, is *revealed* only in an imaginative experience. The verse invites us to share in an experience of time, and can be understood only by the reader who 'lives' that experience. Eliot himself spoke of metaphysical poetry as providing not thought, but the emotional equivalent of thought. By that he meant simply thought as it is *lived* and enacted by the thinker.

But all that is still unsatisfactory. For we know that philosophy may *express* itself through poetry, and then, do not philosophy and poetry become one and the same? Perhaps the most popular work of philosophy ever written—the *Consolation* of Boethius—consists partly of argument, and partly of verse. And it is the verse above all which, in beautifying the thought, renders it persuasive. From the Dialogues of Plato, through the *De Rerum Natura* of Lucretius, right up to the 'philosophical' novels of Sartre and Hermann Hesse, there is a continuous tradition of illustrating and supplementing abstract argument through imaginative literary forms. That there is this *continuum* between philosophy and literature, and an area of complexity where they meet, should not remove the force of the claim that there is also a polar distinction which defines this ambiguous, equatorial middle. But it imposes on us the arduous task of exploring this equatorial region. What we find is a 'forêt de symboles', with poetry and philosophy working together to make a path for self-conscious reflection.

Now, as we have seen, there is a sense in which philosophy is abstract and argued, while poetry is concrete and narrated, and this difference stems from the overriding aim of philosophy to say what is true. At the same time there is an equally important sense in which poetry aims at truth and is admired for its truth, as it is condemned for its falsehood. (Consider again Eliot's three lines.) Must we then distinguish between kinds of truth, the truth of philosophy and the truth of poetry? Few readers of Eliot, Sartre, or Boethius feel disposed to set aside the 'message' which their works contain, and judge the remainder as though it were only an imaginative exercise, with no thesis to be assessed or rejected. Something is being put across by these writers, and however difficult it may be to express that something in other words, it is something that matters, that demands belief, or something very like belief. Naturally, we are not expected to believe in the *reality* of a novelist's characters: but even in the case of fiction, we can distinguish the true from the false. What, then, *is* this truth in literature? Why should we value it? And why should the imagination have any part to play in conveying it?

Various attempts have been made to distinguish between philosophical and literary truth. Some (for example, Croce), rely on the distinction between statement and expression, arguing that the truth of a work of literature is not the truth of a statement of fact, but rather that of a truthful expression of the writer's state of mind: 'truth' means truthfulness—truth to the experience expressed. So truth has become a kind of sincerity, in a very special sense which connects sincerity with what Croce called 'fullness of expression'. If the imagination is a necessary vehicle for the communication of this literary 'truth' it is because what has to be conveyed is not fact but experience (or, as Croce put it, 'intuition'). In its turn that requires a complex attention to the resonances of individual words and phrases, since it is through words that the writer's mental state is expressed or 'realized'; indeed, until the words are available, neither the writer nor anyone else has full access to the experience contained in them.

Such a view proposes lyrical expression as the essence of literature: under the influence of expressionism even novels and plays have come to be seen as explorations of a single 'experience' or emotion that compelled them. Since truth in every literary sphere has become a matter of sincerity, a complex analysis of 'sincerity' has to be offered to cover these cases, and also to preserve an essential aspect of the concept of truth— that truth is public, openly accessible, and never the possession of one man alone. So we must show how the reader can be the best judge of a writer's sincerity. (How else is criticism possible?). There is nothing absurd in the suggestion. The concept of sincerity is complex, and all the attendant phenomena of insincerity—exaggeration, afflatus, sentimentality—point to a connection between sincerity and style which perhaps makes it true to say that a man is not always the best judge of his own sincerity of feeling. (Wilde wrote that in questions of the greatest importance it is style and not sincerity that matters: here is a distinction without a difference). Indeed, the entire criticism of such writers as Richards and Leavis is based on this expressionist assumption, that truthfulness is, in the end, a matter of style. In their analysis of sincerity such critics are going against the Cartesian and empiricist orthodoxy, which assumes sincerity to be merely a matter of correspondence between inner and outer, as though the inner life could be complete in itself and yet all the same not achieve successful expression. On the contrary—and we can see this view again and again in contemporary criticism—the inner life is constituted by its outward expression, so that any corruption in the form of expression must bring with it a corresponding corruption of consciousness. There is nothing to the human mind that is not revealed in the elaboration of characteristically human behaviour, and the importance of language, literature, tradition, recognized institutions and the rest, is that they determine the quality of our consciousness without being merely ancillary to it.

Nevertheless, the reduction of truth to truthfulness must surely give us an impoverished conception of truth in literature. We value Shakespeare, not because he voiced his own sentiments sincerely, but because he represented the reality of human nature. That is like being true to the facts. One could, if one wished, speak of James Joyce's *Ulysses* as containing a refutation of the Marxist psychology of bourgeois man. For the exploration of Bloom's consciousness, in its very concreteness, defies the description which the Marxist would wish to impose on it. That is literature doing the work of political science, and doing it better than any political scientist.

Because of this kind of example, critics (for example, Wayne C. Booth in *The Rhetoric of Fiction*) make another distinction, that between telling and showing. This is a way of expanding the expressionist's dichotomy between statement and expression. To say that something happened is one thing; to show it happening is another. In the latter case, understanding comes through experience: when things are shown it is the experience that guides us to their reality. We can now take this distinction into the literary realm, and say that there is a similar difference between inventing a fiction and imaginatively displaying it. In the second case the reader can re-live in imagination the experience described; moreover, *how* he re-lives it lies entirely within the control of the writer.

This distinction has much to do with the role of imagination in creative understanding. What light does it shed on our problem? It might seem that what matters in an image—what *moves* us—is not its veracity but its vivacity. So long as the image 'comes home to us', it has succeeded. To refer to its truth seems to be either to confuse imagination with delusion, or else to speak again in the expressionist's way, of the truthfulness of the image to the feeling that conceived it.

It is important to notice that an image may be both peculiarly vivid and yet wholly 'untranslatable', so that it seems difficult to see how the question of its truth could arise. Take Breton's image of the seasons as 'une pomme dont on a détaché un quartier'. Are the seasons like that? Less like than unlike; not really either. There is a core of nonsense at the heart of this image which forbids one to judge. Nevertheless it is both vivid and appropriate. And if we can speak of appropriateness then it seems that we *are* measuring, guessing, or sensing, some relation between the image and reality. And is that not a judgement of the image's truth? Here is a paradox: for there was no way of comparing this image with reality, and yet we sense that a relation is there. The relation is there not in thought but in experience, and it disappears as the experience fades. The correspondence between image and reality cannot be spelled out in the manner of an argument, and its content remains bound to its sensory form.

Let us return again to the vital distinction between philosophical and literary truth. It is now additionally clear that, in grasping the latter, one is *living* something. Philosophy can be understood and then laid to one side; it can be translated, stored, placed in the heap of intellectual debris which we day by day acquire. But our acquaintance with a literary truth, being inseparable from a particular imaginative experience, may have to be constantly renewed. We may wish to be *shown* it, again and again, either by reading, watching, or rehearsing the words in our imagination. It is this dependence on experience that explains the 'inexhaustible' nature of the literary truth.

This is a point at which we can usefully introduce some more distinctions. We can, first, distinguish the intensity of an experience from its depth. There are images which intensely disturb us—images, for example, of violence, death, sexual encounter. There are other images which please us, and seem to speak to us in words that are not our own, yet of things that belong to us and that we once thought lost; images which sink to the depth of the soul and remain there, undisturbed and undisturbing. The first kind of image can be freely traded in. Yet such images do not increase our unstanding; they merely impress upon us their peculiar sensory power. Their very intensity seems to imply their superficiality. Yet the 'shocking' images of the cinema, which in this sense are intense and shallow, are in a literal sense more truthful than the deepest and most valued products of the literary imagination. And indeed it is only because of their absolute *lifelikeness*—their absolute truth to the way things appear—that these images exert their fascination. It follows that truth in imaginative literature is not the same as lifelikeness—just as the waxworks is no paradigm of realistic sculpture. Before the imagination can arrive at its truth, it must pass through the world of fiction. The creation of copies, or semblances, satisfies a different appetite, an appetite for make-believe, and in the cinema this has led to the mass marketing of sentimentality under the guise of imaginative drama. It is odd, but true, that in the work of the imagination, the failure to say anything comes about precisely when the image is too literally and too shockingly (or too absorbingly) true. How is this so?

To conclude, let us make two final distinctions: between imagination and fantasy, and between consumption and understanding. Freud hinted at a profound truth when he wrote that the work of the artist is to create a path from fantasy back to reality. The world of imagination is not a world of make-believe, or a substitute for the lusts of day-to-day. Its greatest effects depend upon the simultaneous consciousness that we are not part of what we read or see. Art leads us on a journey, but it is not the journey of fantasy—which repeats in sterile re-enactment the fascinating scenes of life as we would have it be—but rather the journey of imagination, in which experience is guided by thought yet always transcends it, and departs from reality only to reveal it again in a sudden glimpse. The imagination surprises us. But the surprise is one of new understanding, and to provide this understanding the imagination must always struggle to free itself from the facile tricks of fantasy.

The second distinction will perhaps make this clearer. Among the many artifacts which compete for the now worthless label 'art', there are some designed for consumption—to be sucked and thrown away. (Most films are like this, and can therefore be seen only once. How many film lovers indeed could even imagine seeing their favourite masterpiece as many times as the ordinary music lover has heard the Choral Symphony?). There are other works of art which cannot be consumed, because they have no consumable content: the only consumable content is fantasy, which is gratified when enacted, and must await the resurgence of appetite for its renewal. The content of the imaginative work is only available in contemplation, and contemplation, unlike sensuous delight, does not consume its object. Its aim lies in the reflection on experience freed from that 'fetishism of commodities' which bedevils the world of consumer art. It is in contemplation that the truth of art is shown.

We have seen how difficult it is to define the 'truth' of literature; how near and how far is that truth from the truth aimed at in philosophical reflection. Yet one can and must believe, both in its reality, and in its distinctiveness: for without the latter there is no art, and without the former, no value, in any of the works of the literary imagination.

Writers in Context

12 Graham Greene

The Confidential Agent, The Power and the Glory and *The Heart of the Matter*, reissued in the Collected Works of Graham Greene (Heinemann and Bodley Head, 1971), from the *Spectator,* 15 May 1971.

THE THREE NOVELS which Heinemann and the Bodley Head are currently publishing as part of their collected edition of Graham Greene are not of equal merit. *The Heart of the Matter*, which is the most ambitious, strikes one on re-reading as the least successful. One wonders how much this impression is due to the attempt to portray a relatively complex pattern of human relationships. For it is a strange fact about Greene that he is never very interested in relations between people. His heroes seem immersed in a heartless egotism, in which they can soliloquise but never communicate. If they seem vulnerable it is not because they are really touched by the world around them. They are touched by nothing so much as their own vulnerability. Like Major Scobie in *The Heart of the Matter* they become trapped by this feeling, and the attempt at human relations only serves to strengthen its grip. Ostensibly it is a religious attitude, involving a Christ-like responsibility towards all human misery. But in the absence of any embodiment in personal contact it strikes one as merely morbid. It is because Scobie is not plausible as a human being that his religious experience is unconvincing. We are told at the end that Scobie loved no one but God, but we can attach no more precise value to this love than we can attach to his feeling for his wife. It is characteristically bold of Greene to make so much hang on Scobie's going to communion in a state of mortal sin, though, in the context, this particular dilemma can only strike us as absurd.

Greene is undoubtedly at his best in portraying the solitude of a hunted man. The anxiety-ridden introversion of his characters is made plausible by loneliness. It is for this reason that *The Power and the Glory* is superior to *The Heart of the Matter*. The best parts of the novel depict a kind of self-conscious and unassuageable solitude that has few parallels in modern English fiction. When the priest, in his flight across the hills, encounters an Indian woman and her murdered child, the poignancy of the scene gains from the hero's incapacity for human contact. The result is strangely evocative and moving. The more common experiences in the book, however, are far less credible. Captain and Mrs Fellowes are depicted, like Mrs Scobie, with a facile savagery, and the portrait of the married priest, Padre José, is about as subtle as a moral tale for convent girls. The most convincing relationship in the book—that between the priest and the Judas-mestizo—is no relationship at all, but a mere allegiance based on mutual distrust.

In all his novels Greene has shown a gift for construction. It is often said of him, as it is of Conrad, that he is a brilliant *story-teller*. Like Conrad, too, he has a taste for exotic surroundings, in which to set the thoroughly European self-consciousness of his heroes. Unlike Conrad, however, Greene is unable to bring the exotic surroundings into any true relation with his theme: the effect is of an elaborate, and partly super-fluous, stage scenery. In *The Power and the Glory* the background of Latin America and religious persecution is used simply to create the breathless urgency of a thriller. Latin America is for Greene what Jamaica was for Ian Fleming, although Greene's novel contains an implicit valuing of experience which is quite absent from the ordinary thriller. The passive silence of the Indians, the Spanish fainéantism, and the nihilism of revolution receive only desultory treatment. Their relation to character and feeling is shallow and their poetic value nil. No true picture of the setting emerges and the much-praised 'vividness' remains a kind of cheat, a simple by-product of the remorseless violence of style.

This is, of course, quite unlike Conrad, whose ability to tell an exciting story is an integral part of his understanding of character and feeling. Ir *Nostromo*, for example, the actions and attitudes of Gould would be quite unintelligible without the detailed knowledge of his surroundings which the book provides. We might compare Greene not only with Conrad, but with other English novelists who have written seriously about Latin America: Malcolm Lowry in *Under the Volcano*, and even D. H. Lawrence in *The Plumed Serpent*, both of whom convey a sense of having observed and recorded a unique and communicable experience arising from the sense of place. One may criticize their work (few, I imagine, would find Lawrence's successful), but it must be said that they tried to *observe* the Mexican setting, and create drama out of observation alone. Like Conrad they chose characters in a fertile and meaningful relation to their surroundings.

Greene tends to choose his characters from a limited and predeter-mined range of human attitudes. Either they fear life and know that they do (in which case they tend to take a central role), or else they fear life unwittingly (in which case they serve to illustrate the emptiness of human satisfactions). Sometimes they possess a trusting and childlike innocence, which is the most noxious gift of all: only in the books which Greene used to call 'entertainments' can the innocent escape a horrible destruction (and not always there—witness Else in *The Confidential Agent*). Examples of the first kind of character are usually men, such as Scobie, the Whisky Priest, Querry, and D in *The Confidential Agent*. Examples of the second type tend to be women—Mrs Fellowes, Mrs Scobie, and Ida in *Brighton Rock*. Greene is perhaps least successful in his attempts to portray women. His women tend to be either vague, touching and diaphanous (like Phuong in *The Quiet American*): or else, like Mrs Scobie, helpless, empty, middle-class people, crudely and ruthlessly depicted.

Many critics have been interested by the place of Catholicism in Greene's early novels. In the absence of any strictly personal conflicts to motivate his characters, it is not surprising that Greene should rely on spiritual conflicts to give them life. It is perhaps this constant preoccupation with religious doubts and certainties that has aroused the most serious interest in his work. In a sense Greene's heroes are saved by their Catholicism, for it is used as a surrogate for moral and personal existence. On the other hand, the Catholic faith in no way individuates Greene's characters. They all share similar notions and similar doubts. While this is perhaps inevitable, it is surely a failing in a novel where there is no point except religion in which the characters have individual life. Scobie's religion is almost academic: one can indeed think of it in terms of serious and respectable ideas of God and morality, but the ideas as they occur in the novel are entirely disembodied. Religion is something like a talking-point, recurring from time to time in order to produce an emotional intensity beyond what is yielded by the common thriller. Ultimately Greene's characters do little more than luxuriate in the stark contrasts between their shabby experience and the absolutes of Roman Catholic thought.

In Greene's 'serious' novels one finds very little vivid detail. What detail there is, is chosen at random from a corpus of stereotyped effects—vultures, snakes, heat, sweat, malaria, excrement, etc. Only at a few points in *The Power and the Glory* does an image present itself with true vivacity, as when the priest, returning to the body of the Indian child, takes the piece of sugar which the mother has left at its side. The descriptions are mostly dull and matter-of-fact, for Greene's interest in language often seems slight, and although he attempts to spice his style with similes, these are usually as banal and grey as the phrases they replace: 'Heat stood in the room like an enemy'; 'loneliness seated itself like a companion that does not need to speak'; 'He swivelled round and switched on a smile as he would a cigarette lighter'; 'the rain came perpendicularly down with a sort of measured intensity as if it were driving nails into a coffin lid'; 'faces sprouted like vegetables'; and so on.

On comparing these early novels with more recent work one is struck by how much Greene's writing has changed. The witty and delicate *Travels with my Aunt* seems to bear little relation to *The Power and the Glroy* and *The Heart of the Matter*, which can only be described, for all their brilliance of construction, as ill-written. If one were to look for a connecting link between the two styles it could be found perhaps in some of the books which used to be called 'entertainments', such as *The Confidential Agent*. Here one finds some of the felicitous triviality of

Travels with my Aunt, phrased rather incongruously in the pugnacious language of the more 'serious' works. If one were to read any of these novels again it is certainly *The Confidential Agent* one would choose.

The books are attractively printed on expensive paper, and well bound in cloth, a privilege which the Bodley Head has not thought fit to extend to Ford Madox Ford, Jack London or Henry James. This lavish treatment indicates a widespread interest in Greene. Much of this interest seems to have been directed towards the eccentric moral views and the heresy implicit in his works, although in fact these are no more than offshoots of the literary method. The so-called Manicheanism is merely a projection of a melodramatic view of human character. When this melodramatic quality is subdued the early novels have moments of real power, and there is no doubt about the seriousness of Greene's intention. But as a master of language, rather than of mere construction, we cannot escape the fact that Greene is inferior to that other minor novelist with whom he is often bracketed—Evelyn Waugh.

13 James Joyce

James Joyce, John Gross (Fontana Modern Masters, 1971) from the *Spectator*, 6 March 1971

IT IS easier for the ordinary English reader to come to terms with Joyce than it is for many English critics. Joyce's writings are everywhere ironical, but nowhere satirical; they contain characters but no drama; pathos, but no true suffering. They are executed in a bewildering variety of styles, richly studded with symbols, images and arcane devices; but at the same time it does not seem possible to extract from them any definite moral purpose. In short, they are a delight to the scholar but an anomaly to the critic. We should not be surprised, therefore, to be told that, in frustrating the expectations of criticism, Joyce damaged the artistic quality of his novels and that his work is so heavily riddled with ambiguity that there is no way of knowing how to read it. Mr Gross—in an admirably written and intelligent study—shows a great deal of sympathy with this view, while continuing to believe that Joyce's stylistic and technical eccentricities are compatible with an orthodox reading of the novels in terms of character and plot.

Gross tackles his subject bravely, confronting many of the fundamental questions which Joycean scholars avoid. But in his lucid discussion of these questions, he misconstrues a great deal of Joyce's meaning. Readers of *Ulysses*, for example, face the following dilemma: either Bloom is an adequate hero, and the sole task of the book is to display his day's adventure; in which case what is the point of the structural symbolism? Or else the structure itself is the point of interest, in which case the book must lack a centre. Gross takes a beneficent view of Bloom—he is the 'good man' Joyce intended him to be, passive but well-intentioned, not a modern Everyman, but a fair representant, nonetheless, of 'ordinary, inartistic humanity'. (According to Gross this makes *Ulysses* one of the most democratic of modern novels—an unusually eccentric *non sequitur*.) As a result, Gross is impatient with the Homeric aspect of *Ulysses*, and with the elaborate pattern of symbolism (revealed by Joyce himself to Stuart Gilbert, one of his earliest interpreters) which remains so conspicuously absent from an ordinary reading of the book. Gross argues that the book's success is to be judged on the level of the Bloomsday story, and fails to carry over into the realm of myth; that Joyce's allegory is too cerebral and contrived; and that it is impossible to use mere technical devices to impose on the quotidian adventures of a modern secular man the heroic structure which his experience denies.

The trouble lies more with the incidental symbolism than with the Homeric parallel. Mrs Bloom is not only Penelope but also, according to Gilbert, the Flesh, the Earth, and even Gaea-Tellus, the Ancestral Mother of All Things. Gross retorts that she is simply an unamiable and slatternly adulteress.

This is an extreme view, although in face of the excesses of Joycean scholarship one feels a certain sympathy with it. Yet we must remind ourselves how much the Homeric parallel contributes to the impact of *Ulysses*. It would be wrong to think of the parallel as a clumsy attempt to vindicate Bloom's experience through its relation to some more heroic universal. For in fact a contrast is being pointed, and irony is being used to point it. If critics fail to see this it is because for Joyce irony involves the acceptance, not the rejection, of its object. As for the incidental symbolism, this is unobtrusive, and is justifiable merely as an artist's *aide-mémoire*. The sequence of bodily organs, of arts, techniques and colours, the strange attempts at literary mimesis (as in the *Fuga per Canonem* of the Sirens episode), are all simply parts of the linear variation essential to an episodic structure. If they present a difficulty it is that of attempting to construe a psychological novel in other than dramatic terms. Yet when a single day's experience is recounted as a 'comic epic in prose', all real dramatic conflict is curtailed. In *Ulysses* nothing can be put to the test: there are no moral choices to be made and no great adversity to face up to. When Bloom and Stephen meet at last, the imaginary narrator of 'Ithaca' contrives, in a series of devastating questions and answers, to destroy the sense that anything has passed between them. Dramatic possibilities are deliberately neutralized (no relationship could be formed in this meeting that is not sentimental or banal) and it would be a monstrous disproportion if Bloom's experience should suddenly break through the boundary of day-to-day occurrences. Yet, with a characteristic inattention to Joyce's irony, Gross considers that something might have happened between Bloom and Stephen, and that indeed, in a mysterious way, something did happen.

It is true, of course, that Stephen's presence elicits from Bloom an important feeling. In Stephen's company Bloom senses an ache of paternal responsibility. He sees himself as an individual standing against the current of mere animal life, inheriting consciousness and passing it on. But Stephen is not the object of this feeling, which preceded their meeting and which is wholly characteristic of Bloom. It is in the light of this experience, indeed, that Molly Bloom's soliloquy is to be understood. Molly exists outside the realm of moral knowledge, immersed in sensuality, indifferently reflecting the unconscious currents of organic life. She resents Bloom, who moves in the sphere of personal choice and social struggle. But she complements him too. Her thoughts drift at last towards a vagrant acceptance of her husband as she falls asleep beside him.

Perhaps it was excessive of Joyce to refer to so many female archetypes. But Molly's feelings are as typical of her sex as Bloom's are of his.
She is the perfect counterpart to Bloom, experiencing the feminine
microcosm, just as he experiences in a complete but diminutive way the
fact of being male. There is a natural place for Joyce's symbolism which
does not require us to give way to 'Molliolatry', as Gross derisively calls
it. The book itself explains the symbols; it is not explained by them.

This is something which commentators on *Finnegan's Wake* too
readily forget. Gross thinks that Joyce is to blame if his most difficult
work lies buried beneath a heap of scholarship and if in *Finnegan's Wake*
the symbolism is no longer self-explanatory. The references to books,
political events and mythologies which are central to an understanding of
the work, are, he claims, too private for the effort of understanding to be
justified. Many will find Gross's arguments convincing—they are put
forward with characteristic vigour and intelligence. But they are one-
sided and provide no alternative approach to *Finnegan's Wake*.

Gross contends that 'however great its curiosity-value, as a work of art
on the scale which Joyce intended the *Wake* stands or falls by its central
myth . . .' But what is this central myth? So many myths are woven into
the fabric of the work that it is very hard to think of any one as central.
Gross joins with most commentators in assuming that the content of the
book is to be explained in terms of the cyclical view of history and the cab-
balistic mumbo-jumbo which evidently dictated to Joyce the particular
sequence in which episodes occur. It would seem to follow that the book
cannot be built on one particular myth—that its content is only the *form*
of a myth, into which myths and characters can disappear at will. In a
sense, of course, there *are* characters and episodes, (thanks to Campbell
and Robinson's brilliant *Skeleton Key* we can be reasonably sure of many
of these). But each character obscures another, and behind each episode
lies another, less concrete; nothing occurs in the book which does not
disintegrate on closer scrutiny into endless strata of fact and fable. Every
certainty the reader is offered stands proxy for a greater doubt.

Such an extraordinary way of presenting a novel cannot depend on the
myth which it is supposed to enact. For nothing is enacted. Myth has
entered Joyce's thinking in an unfamiliar and essentially anti-dramatic
way. In *Finnegan's Wake* myth is not embodied in character. On the
contrary, human character is absorbed into fable, fable into myth, myth
into symbol, and symbol itself gives way at last to a bare struggle between
consciousness and sleep. As a result there can be no dramatic conflict. If
'opposites are reconciled' in *Finnegan's Wake* it is for this reason only and
not on account of any doctrine written into the imagery of the work. The
idea of such a doctrine as a structural principle (dictating the activities of a
thousand Shems and Shauns) is really very misleading, for it does not tell
us how to read the book. Is it true? Is it false? Is it being enacted here? Or
here? Those most responsible for Gross's reservations are the scholars

(such as James Atherton and Clive Hart) who insist that we should approach *Finnegan's Wake* in the light of certain structural axioms and motifs—the polarity of opposites, the cycle of history, the necessary dependence of part on whole (all the banalities of occultism are there).

It is impossible to read *Finnegan's Wake* as a dramatization of these doctrines, in the way that the *Ring* is in part a dramatization of Schopenhauer's philosophy of will. No interpretation in epic or dramatic terms seems to produce anything but useless pedantry. Much of the book reads, in fact, like a parody of the modern Joycean scholar relentlessly hunting in the fragments of a scribbled manuscript for the secret of Earwicker's crime. Like the hen which pecked Anna Livia's letter from the dungheap, Gross sets about unearthing Joyce's book from its mound of commentaries. But like the hen he leaves only a scratched and unreadable palimpsest. *Finnegan's Wake* has no central myth and no dramatic meaning. We can no more be interested in Earwicker as a *character* than in the Fisher-King of Eliot's *Waste Land*. Joyce gave many useless and confusing clues to his acolytes, and perhaps he is to blame if the lyric quality of his masterpiece is still ignored. But he did once try to convey to Eugene Jolas that the real heroes of his book could only be characterized as 'Time and the river and the mountain'.

One feels that, in the struggle between Joyce and the ordinary reader, Gross has been too eager to take the latter's side. One senses too the effect of recent biographical criticism, in particular of Ellmann. Ellmann's book is so admirably complete that in many ways one can only think of it as a model of what a biography should not be. The scholarship is not used in support of any particular vision of Joyce's work, and the work is made to seem a by-product of other interests. It is, for example, possible to follow Gross in seeing *Dubliners* as a work of satire only if the unassimilated bitterness of this part of Joyce's life (as Ellmann paints it) is allowed to override the settled irony with which the book is written.

In the *Portrait of the Artist*, Stephen Dedalus makes the much quoted pronouncement that 'The artist, like the God of creation, remains within or behind or beyond or above his handiwork, invisible, refined out of existence, indifferent, paring his fingernails'. This echoes the Flaubert of the *Correspondance*, and makes explicit the Flaubertian objectivity which remained part of Joyce's ambition. Now Gross—seeing the book in terms of fantasies which Ellmann has made clear to us—is driven to deny that any objectivity exists. Yet if objectivity is *not* in the book, it should be a reading of the *Portrait* that persuades us of this, not a knowledge of irrelevant biographical material. The confusion comes out in various ways. After discussing the *Portrait*, Gross concludes that, while the first two thirds is completely successful, the book becomes suddenly contestable as Stephen enters his adolescence and his mature personality begins to show. For Stephen is still the undisputed hero of the book, and nothing reminds us that we are not to accept him at his own valuation. But we can hardly do so—he is a 'second-rate aesthete', sterile, arrogant and rather repulsive. Are we then to regard the final sections as ironic? Hardly, Gross argues, for it would be odd to dispatch in such detail so small a victim.

There is something absurd in regarding Stephen as a victim, let alone a 'small' one. Is he any 'smaller' than (the more virtuous) David Copper-field, or the Grüne Heinrich of Keller's romance? It is strange that Gross should have ignored the sensitivity, single-mindedness and social isolation which Joyce is at such pains to portray. These certainly are in the book, and there is irony too; but it is the irony of Flaubert, the irony which '*n'enlève rien au pathétique*'. Joyce followed Flaubert's unwritten precept: never use language that will show you superior to the feelings you are trying to express—let feeling *show* itself. In particular, do not portray the experience of an adolescent in terms of the intellectual and moral framework of adult life. For Joyce there was only one possibility: Stephen's remarkable mental life must reveal itself in its own arch and exquisite accents. The success of the book lies in its tact—a tact which encouraged Joyce to abandon the heroics of *Stephen Hero* and follow more closely the manner of *L'Education Sentimentale*. Stephen's language is both remote and moving; it is the callow intellectualism of an adolescent which has all the precision and single-mindedness characteristic of sincere belief. The mistake comes in thinking that because the *material* of the novel is autobiographical, the language must be the language of the writer himself. But it is no more Joyce's than is the language of Bloom's *monologue intérieur*, or the language of the sickly girl's romance which recounts Gerty MacDowell's experience in *Ulysses*.

14   Sylvia Plath

Winter Trees and *Crossing the Water*, Sylvia Plath (Faber & Faber 1971), from the *Spectator*, 18 December 1971.

IT IS seldom useful to judge a poet's writing in terms of his character, but Sylvia Plath so forces attention on herself that it is difficult to approach her work on other terms. She is present in almost every line, craving attention. Her almost necromantic commerce with nothingness perhaps licenses the reference, in *Winter Trees*, to 'The Courage of Shutting-up', but this is certainly not the best description of her prevailing attitude:

> The courage of the shut mouth, in spite of artillery!
> The line pink and quiet, a worm, basking.
> There are black discs behind it, the discs of outrage,
> And the outrage of a sky, the lined brain of it.
> The discs revolve, they ask to be heard—
>
> Loaded, as they are, with accounts of bastardies.
> Bastardies, usages, desertions and doubleness.
> The needle journeying in its groove,
> Silver beast between two dark canyons,
> A great surgeon, now a tattooist,
>
> Tattooing over and over the same blue grievances,
> The snakes, the babies, the tits
> On mermaids and two-legged dreamgirls.
> The surgeon is quiet, he does not speak.
> He has seen too much death, his hands are full of it.

Why does she signify her sufferings with this figure of the patient surgeon? It seems a kind of cheat, an attempt to mask the obsessive character of her feeling.

But if Sylvia Plath's poetry presents the image of death it is not with alluring accents. Her verse is brutal, and she speaks in it with her own bitter and destructive voice. Unlike Hart Crane, she has no sad protagonist to stand proxy for her; her love of death produces no mellifluous symbolism, only a cluster of images gathered into plain and ugly moods Her tone is seldom far from that of the famous 'Daddy', published six years ago in *Ariel*—a violent ritual exorcism of the father whom she loved and whose death she deeply resented:

You do not do, you do not do
Any more, black shoe
In which I have lived like a foot
For thirty years, poor and white,
Barely daring to breathe or Achoo.

Daddy, I have had to kill you.
You died before I had time—
Marble-heavy, a bag full of God,
Ghastly statue with one grey toe
Big as a Frisco seal

And a head in the freakish Atlantic
Where it pours bean green over blue
In the waters off beautiful Nauset.
I used to pray to recover you.
Ach, du . . .

The language of this poem is wholly characteristic of her later work. Throughout *Ariel* and its newly published companion volume, *Winter Trees*, one finds the same tense rhythms, startling imagery and beautiful control ('Barely daring to breathe or Achoo . . .'). One of the finest features of her later style—the use of multiple metaphors—is here seen at its most effective. At first the poet is a foot, poor and white, trapped in the black shoe of her feelings for her father. But there is no time to assimilate this image of pained submission before a new aspect is presented: the poet does not dare to breathe or sneeze; therefore she must be hiding in the shell of her grievance, fearing punishment. Immediately we discover that it is not she who must be punished, but the dead father whom she has had to kill for a second time. Her phantom father is re-created, not as a black shoe, but 'marble-heavy, a bag full of God.' Again there is no opportunity to absorb the meaning of these images before the father's next appearance as a 'ghastly statue.' As the similes cohere we see something that resembles the Commendatore of *Don Giovanni*, killed once, but now God-like, simultaneously ghost and statue. When the poet addresses the statue with the two poignant lines that end the third stanza, it has already assumed the form of a Colossus, which seems to cast its shadow beneath the surface of a 'freakish' sea. This extraordinary sequence of images does not blunt the final impact: on the contrary, the language is so precise that each word adds a further subtlety of evocation.

Later in the same poem Sylvia Plath seems to identify her own grievance against her German father with that of the Jews against the German race, and at first sight this seems like another piece of grotesque self-aggrandizement, an attempt to validate a subjective resentment by borrowing the credentials of objective suffering. But again the language is too careful to let slip any lies about the poet's feelings; their obsessive quality is merely emphasized: 'With my gypsy ancestress and my weird luck/And my Tarot pack and my Tarot pack/I may be a bit of a Jew.' It is almost as though the poet were playing a part, but playing it so well that her mood has become self-sufficient and acceptable.

This remarkable quality is characteristic of all Sylvia Plath's later writing, and *Winter Trees* contains many fine examples of it. Although the book consists mainly of poems taken from the same batch as *Ariel*, it is by no means a collection of leftovers; the extraordinary accomplishment of Sylvia Plath's later style is manifest in every line. The book finishes with a radio play—'Three Women'—which belongs to the same transitional period as the poems now collected in *Crossing The Water*. Although these poems show a departure towards the freer use of speech-rhythm and a more adventurous juxtaposition of images, they are still written in the careful manner of the early works, with their reminiscences of Eliot and their ruminative style. *Crossing The Water* contains many passages of beautiful verse, and 'Three Women', which is remarkable for its relatively selfless attempt to evoke the moods of three separate personalities, is written in an interesting synthesis of the earlier and later styles.

There are a number of passages approaching closer to the poet's familiar realms of feeling, which adopt the imagery and rhythms of the later work:

> I have had my chances. I have tried and tried.
> I have stitched life into me like a rare organ,
> And walked carefully, precariously, like something rare.

But the verse here, with its measured vowel sounds, is still that of a craftsman. One has the sense of a deliberate striving for effect, a mannered and slightly rhetorical afflatus which is very far from the laconic directness of the poems in *Ariel* and in the rest of *Winter Trees*.

It is difficult to describe the peculiar quality of Sylvia Plath's last poems. Their originality is not simply an originality of mood. Nor does it lie in the brilliance and precision of her language, although in a certain sense Sylvia Plath's descriptive talent was greater than any other she had. Perhaps what is most surprising is the complete avoidance of hysteria. For Sylvia Plath's poetry is never reflective; it contains no sympathy for attitudes that were not her own. Her intelligence sought expression not in judgement but in the lightning clarity of revelation. The poems present a sudden glimpse of things, and, caught in that glimpse, a moment of intense emotion. Her great achievement was to evolve a style that would fit this precarious mode of lyrical expression: the multiple metaphors, the quick rhythms, the mastery of colloquial speech, the extraordinary language, and the direct, unhesitant manner.

In the later poetry we find no attempt to *say* anything. Images enter these later poems as particulars only, without symbolic significance, and however much the poet may borrow the emotional charge from distant and surprising sources (from the imaginary life in ocean depths, from the real and imaginary calamities of modern history) it is never with any hint of an intellectual aim. It is tempting to restore to these poems some vestiges of generality, by interpreting them as Freudian parables, or as complex symbols. But although the poems of *Ariel* and *Winter Trees* invite such an interpretation, they also show how valueless it is. It is not through their coincidence with unconscious wishes that these poems affect us, nor do they have any symbolic force comparable to their overwhelming immediacy of impact. Everything in them is objective, concrete, conscious; we can feel moved by Sylvia Plath's obsessions without feeling any need to share in them.

15   André Breton and Surrealism

Surrealism and Painting, André Breton (Macdonald, 1972) and *Memoirs*, Giorgio de Chirico (Peter Owen, 1972), from the *Spectator*, 16 December 1972.

THE AIM of Surrealism, according to its most articulate apologist, André Breton, was 'to prevent the domination of the symbol by the thing signified.' It was Breton's belief that modern man had found himself in a world of ill-defined and oppressive objects, objects dehumanized in the service of commonplace ideas and materialistic appetites. Art, he supposed, could rescue man from this state of alienation not by 'imitation' (the reproduction of already existing things) but by transformation. Objects must be changed from their habitual forms and remade as symbols; for in order to become visible the world must first become subjective. The accumulated debris of utilitarian matter must be dissolved and held in solution in the consciousness of men.

These ideas—in which a traditional romantic view of the imagination is tinged by the conceptions of Freud and Marx—represent what was serious in Surrealism. Breton was reacting not only against philistine values but also against what he thought of as the swooning defeatism of *fin-de-siècle* poetry and painting, which, with its taste for mere impressions, had allowed material things to dominate the world. For Breton Surrealism presented a direct and serious challenge to materialistic thought. It was a poetry of affirmation and acceptance, whose vision— unlike that of the Symbolists—was directed to the future, not the past.

The present collection consists of a translation of *Le Surréalisme et la Peinture* (1928), one of Breton's most famous writings on art, together with all the pieces of art criticism that Breton wished to preserve at the time (1965) when the French edition of this book went to press. It is now well translated (by Simon Watson Taylor) and beautifully illustrated, with reproductions of almost every painting referred to in the text. The only serious criticism is that the book is far too long. It is precisely in reading Breton's criticism at such length that its weaknesses—and the weaknesses of Surrealism as a whole—are most apparent. Although Breton writes brilliantly, with an astonishing gift for paradox, one soon begins to wish for something more substantial, some real indication of why the work of his friends is so wonderful and the work of everyone else so bad. His strange descriptions are often delightful, but it is doubtful that one can be helped to appreciate the paintings of Victor Brauner (surely one of the most banal of all Surrealists) by Breton's eulogy:

Everything expands, settles again, grows larger. This is the marvellous moment in time when the geometer, his eyes almost closed, walks along the ramparts of Troy and, without either of them knowing it, crosses Helen's path. In the hollow of one's hand, the stars have rescued their courses from the sky. Flame and leaf refashion the form of the heart, the long sought-for quadratix caresses the curves of a lilac blossom.

One would be able to take four hundred pages of this poeticizing if there were any indication that its author was a man of judgement. But a critic who can bestow the same order of praise on Picasso and Dali, on Joan Miro and on Marcel Duchamp, must inevitably awake some suspicion. One looks for reasons to support these strange evaluations, but Breton is disdainful of reasons. He prefers witty paradoxes to genuine ideas. For him originality and surprise have become qualities of such value that the ability to apply standards—and hence the ability to think consistently—has been finally put aside. Surrealism presents itself as something altogether new, but it is unable to say in what its newness consists. Self-consciousness exists here untempered by the consciousness of tradition, and as a result it is impossible to be convinced that the artists and the works which Breton describes really have the importance he attributes to them.

In fairness it must be said that Breton attempts to create an *impression* of standards. *Surrealism and Painting*, for example, contains a long diatribe against de Chirico, who was rejected by the Surrealist school as soon as he turned away from the 'metaphysical' painting of his early years. But one has the impression—from the violence of the denunciation, and the purely abstract terms in which it is couched—that the choice of victim is more or less arbitrary, motivated by external interests. This, not surprisingly, is de Chirico's view. 'All great men are anxious for justice,' he writes, 'and I more so than all of them.' Fortunately most great men are not so naïve as to suppose that justice is achieved through writing memoirs. One can admire the courage with which de Chirico adheres to his amiable and old-fashioned opinions, but despite his many assertions to the contrary one comes away from this book with a sense of the author's smallness of spirit. Breton may have been less consistent than de Chirico, and he was certainly less serious, but he had the sophistication necessary to avoid any merely personal paranoia. His need for enemies was given an objective and rhetorical satisfaction in the founding of a school.

Still, one may wonder how far Breton was successful in this. As a poet and an essayist he is certainly to be respected, but while the poetry of Surrealism represented something genuine, and indeed something more or less traditional, the painting can only strike us now as fatuous and insincere. The poetry of paradox was familiar in France long before

Breton's manifestos. But it is doubtful that paradox can be translated into painting with the same success—certainly not by Dali, Tanguy or Marcel Duchamp. To represent a thing is to represent it as possible: there is no logical absurdity in the fluid watch, or in the table with the head of an angry dog. The supposed 'contradictory' parts of the Surrealist effigy are in fact no more than commonplace entities existing happily in a single space. They remain inactive, sterile, unable to lend to one another the vitality and meaning which they separately lack. In this sense the Surrealists achieved no visual equivalent of metaphor; only a concatenation of unrelated fragments. On the other hand there is genuine absurdity possible in the use of words. When Breton (in *The White-haired Revolver*) describes the seasons as *lumineuses comme l'intérieur d'une pomme dont on a détaché un quartier*, he presents an image that could not be painted (although it could of course be *illustrated*). This is genuine metaphor, and to the extent that it is successful it manages to create something vital from the juxtaposition of incompatible ideas. The real equivalent in painting of this startling use of metaphor is not the work of Dali or Duchamp but rather the Cubism that Breton so much deplored. In Cubism we find the attempt to overthrow normal spatial categories, and thereby bring into a visual relation things that in reality *must* remain apart—the face and the profile of a single head, a vase and its own interior. It is absurd for Breton to assume that Dali and Picasso were engaged in a similar enterprise. Picasso's vision was something finer and more profound than anything that could be captured by the grotesque juxtapositions of Surrealism. In itself Surrealism was visually sterile, as this collection admirably demonstrates. Its products were without visual beauty and relied for their effect on a literary paraphrase, a symbol, or a funny idea (Max Ernst's 'Garden Aeroplane Traps', Brauner's 'Woman into Cat'). Perhaps the most striking example of this is Duchamp's 'Bride Stripped Bare by her Bachelors, Even'; Breton's witty commentary (included in the present collection) is indeed a masterpiece of controlled absurdity, beside which the large glass itself appears as a mindless three-dimensional doodle with no visual character at all. The ideas belong to what is said, and not to what is seen.

Even in literature it is doubtful whether Surrealism can lay claim to the novelty that is sometimes attributed to it. True, the images of the Surrealists are more surprising than those of Baudelaire or Verlaine, but from what does this quality of surprise proceed? From the point of view of logic, Baudelaire's lines

> Vois sur ces canaux
> Dormir les vaisseaux
> Dont l'humeur est vagabonde . . .

offend as much as most of Apollinaire or Reverdy. If they strike us as wholly natural it is surely because the image is precise. The over-whelming effect of '*L'Invitation au voyage*' is an effect of language, and where Baudelaire is concise and original, Breton (in a similar poem) merely extemporizes, to far less effect:

> On me dit que là-bas des plages sont noires
> De la lave allée à la mer
> Et se déroulent au pied d'un immense pic
>   fumant de neige
> Sous un soleil de sérins sauvages . . .

The passage is beautiful, certainly, but surely it is impossible to read it as the work of a man who had broken entirely with the Symbolist tradition. The diction gives the lie to Breton's fanatical futurism. The fact is that the great works of modern French literature had already been written—though not by Lautréamont as the Surrealists fondly imagined—and at its best Surrealist poetry was a refreshing and exuberant return to the urbanity of a previous age.

16   The Japanese Experience

Mishima, John Nathan (Hamish Hamilton, 1975) and Henry Scott Stokes, *The Life and Death of Yukio Mishima* (Peter Owen, 1975); *The Nobility of Failure: tragic heroes in the history of Japan*, Ivan Morris (Secker & Warburg, 1975); and *World Within Walls: Japanese literature of the pre-Modern Era 1600-1867*, Donald Keene (Secker & Warburg, 1977), from the *Times Literary Supplement*, 11 April 1975, 16 January 1976 and 15 April 1977.

I

It is ten years since Kimitake Hiroaka ('Yukio Mishima' as he was known to the world) disembowelled himself in accordance with the ancient custom of *seppuku*, and so continued in death the outrage and scandal that had characterized his entire existence. It is hardly surprising that Mishima's biographers should regard it as their principal task to explain this final grandiloquent gesture. Now that the protests have died away, however, no one can be truly surprised, either by the fact of Mishima's suicide (at least ten other well-known Japanese writers have killed themselves during this century), or by the spectacular way in which he effected it. For Mishima, art took precedence over life, and when at last he turned his attention to the business of living, it was with a dispassionate sense of theatre that he set the stage for his ultimate exit.

Mishima was born a weakling, bred a neurotic, and lived an eccentric and nocturnal existence, writing furiously into the early hours of every morning. By the age of twenty-six he had completed many novels, including *Confessions of a Mask, Thirst for Love,* and the first volume of *Forbidden Colours*, as well as a profusion of stories. He worked extremely hard and, while it is clear that he wrote too much, elevating into literature every passing impulse of imagination, he also laboured over the style, structure and content of his writings in a manner that has no parallel in our own recent fiction.

Through diligent study Mishima established literary roots not only in the Japanese classics—the styles of which he could apparently imitate with great dexterity—but also in the French *fin-de-siècle*. The stylistic reminiscences of nineteenth-century France are more apparent in translation than the Japanese classicism, but perhaps the most striking feature of Mishima's prose is its reflective quality. Mishima wrote thinkingly, and in his best work every sentence, whether narrative or dialogue, is used to express a thought: it is impossible to say where reflection ends and description begins. To that extent, one might say, Mishima resembles Jean Genet, but his superiority over Genet comes from his ability to combine this weighty intellectual idiom with a vivid sense of drama. Genet's characters appear half veiled in a mist of narcissism: the universal 'I' of narration is for Genet not merely a device but, on the contrary, the very substance of his thought. In Mishima, by contrast, for all his ostensible narcissism, there is a generous and passionate interest in character that completely transcends the boundaries of self.

It could not be said of Mishima—as it has been said with some truth of Flaubert and, with a little less truth, of Proust—that his characters are no more than aspects of himself. On the contrary, his choice of dramatic situations is often so surprising that one can hardly understand the feat of imagination that led Mishima to realize them. There are surely few writers in contemporary Europe who could have created the touching Kazu of *After the Banquet*, the Kiyoaki of *Spring Snow*, or the robust Honda of the tetralogy who seems so solidly and yet so sensitively to reflect the reality of bourgeois existence that he might almost be taken for a character of Thomas Mann.

It is true that Mishima's characterization is uneven and that he succeeds with women more often than with men; but, at his best, Mishima was able to present original situations with a depth of insight and a moral seriousness that deserve to be described as classical. Only towards the end of his life when his obsession with the roots of Japanese culture led him towards a self-conscious orientalism at variance with his literary instincts, did Mishima's style give way to the callow self-revelation of which he is so often accused. If a novelist insists on treating reincarnation not merely as a fact but as an observable fact, resuscitating his main protagonist time after time in the interest of some purely abstract idea, then death for him can have no tragic interest. It is not surprising therefore that Mishima's tragic manner seems, at many points in the tetralogy, to be little more than an ornamental preciousness.

It is a pity that neither Henry Scott Stokes in *The Life and Death of Yukio Mishima* nor John Nathan in *Mishima* shows much interest in literature. Mr Scott Stokes, it is true, devotes a section of his book to a discussion of Mishima's writings, but it consists only of lame and rather tedious summaries. Mr Nathan seems to show even less interest in the literature. Inevitably, he discusses the story 'Patriotism', and the other sensational products of Mishima's love of death. Like Mr Scott Stokes, too, he leans heavily on *Confessions of a Mask* for the insight it provides into Mishima's early years. But the interest goes no farther, and what many would regard as the vulgar exhibitionism of Mishima's life is presented as though unredeemed by his literary penitence; in consequence nothing of the writer remains, save the weird antics of a man for whom drama was all.

Mishima's life, as he freely admitted, consisted in the enactment of fantasies which had obsessed him since his early youth, warlike fantasies of death, suffering and stoical resolution. A biographer cannot fail to be interested in the peculiar combination of exhibitionist and morbid Narcissus, the more so since Mishima, who lived in a blaze of publicity, was at pains to hide nothing of his life save that small and endearing part—his marriage—in which he had struggled to achieve a precarious normality. Understandably therefore, Mr Nathan adopts a conventional approach to Mishima, seeing his writing, his patriotism, his love of the warrior ethic, his devotion to beauty in all its forms, and his final suicide, as the several aspects of a single erotic impulse. The result is sober and modestly written, and gives some impression of the distinctive qualities of Mishima's mind. But neither Mr Nathan nor Mr Scott Stokes seem to have much sympathy for Mishima. His conceptions are revealed only in anecdotes, and treated by neither writer as though a serious man might really believe them.

Mr Scott Stokes's interpretation of Mishima's final gesture is indeed a triumph of near-sighted banality, which fails to surprise only because of the many pages of vulgar journalism that prepare one for it. His guess is that Morita, the powerful, young second-in-command of Mishima's private army, was Mishima's lover, and that their mutual suicide was simply a lovers' pact, of a kind once popular in Japan. Mr Scott Stokes was a correspondent for *The Times* in Japan and also, he says, a friend of Mishima (whom Mr Nathan portrays as incapable of genuine friendship). If one is interested in anecdotes his book may be marginally more useful than Mr Nathan's. An interest in Mr Scott Stokes might also be helpful, for the narrative is in fact highly self-centred. Mr Nathan offers a more painless way of learning the relevant details, together with an explanation of Mishima's activities that can at least lay claim to a certain unpretentious common sense. His book is short, well written, and to the point, and these virtues are the more to be esteemed in that few literary biographies now possess them.

The picture of Mishima which emerges from both these biographies is that of a masochistic playboy, who lived in a world of fantasy largely unredeemed by any natural affection. And such a picture is no doubt true to the facts. But in his writings Mishima was vehemently opposed to the 'corrosive' influence of fantasy, and he had conceived of his final suicide as a gesture that would restore him to the world of action.

Although Mishima hated what he saw as the triteness and degeneracy of modern Japan, and although he recognized that his own sense of reality had been dissolved along with all traditional values, he could not rid himself of the hope that his body at least could be turned into an active thing, even if his mind refused to follow it. He therefore imposed on his body a peculiar task. The body was to enact the ideals of the warrior in a world where there are no warriors. But a warrior needs an opponent; the immediacy of the present, the full sense of an objective world, come, Mishima thought, only in the moment of combat. In his search for an opponent Mishima experimented with many imaginary adversaries—the political left, the intelligentsia, literature itself—but he found that they were all too corroded by fantasy to serve as effective combatants. Finally it seemed that only his own body possessed sufficient reality to be worthy of a fight. 'I cherished', he wrote, 'a romantic impulse towards death, and yet at the same time I required a strictly classical body as its vehicle.' Through weightlifting and the traditional martial arts Mishima created what he thought was a suitable body, a body that could be both subject and object of the final combat.

But his act required a dramatic meaning, and for Mishima drama was a public thing. His preparations for suicide took the form of a quasi-political, quasi-religious manifestation of his identity with traditional Japan. Mishima spoke and acted on behalf of emperor worship, vociferously defending the values of the old civilization; he even formed a private army dedicated to the defence of the Emperor in some hypothetical hour of need. In this way he campaigned and proselytized untiringly in the cause of death—of his own death, and of the idea of death—for he wished to restore to his countrymen the consciousness of death which he regarded as a necessary precondition to culture.

This complex of ideas, so shocking to the liberal orthodoxy, did not, of course, gain many converts. But conversion was less a part of Mishima's aim than the dramatic presentation of a moral concept. The elitist and militaristic ideal had to be in the mind of the spectator if he was to understand the ultimate *dénouement*. From the very first, Mishima's final 'action' had a decidedly literary meaning.

It was not only the liberal establishment that condemned Mishima's act. A Japanese classicist complained to Gore Vidal: 'So vulgar. *Seppuku* must be performed according to a precise and elegant ritual, *in private*, not in a general's office and with a dozen witnesses. But then Mishima was entirely Westernized.' Mishima's 'heroism' was not the pure thing he wished it to be, nor did it express his final freedom from a life-long attachment to fantasy. But much of what he had meant to signify in this gesture is true. There cannot be a genuine civilization without a philosophy of death, nor can any merely liberal morality accommodate the feelings aroused in a man by the thought of his own annihilation. Mishima's mask certainly did not hide a hero, but nor, when the mask was lifted, was a fool or a madman revealed in its place.

II

'No sadder proof can be given by a man of his own littleness than dis-belief in great men'—so said Carlyle, who argued that society is founded upon the worship of heroes. If such a view were right, then it would seem that we could reach as full an understanding of the spirit of a foreign race through analysis of its heroes as ever we could through the study of actual behaviour. To understand the hero is to understand a distinctive ideal of human conduct; it is to gain insight into the recognized possibilities, the moral space, as it were, in which the members of a society live out their aspirations. Some such view of the cultural significance of the hero is implicit in Ivan Morris's new book, which recounts in a sequence of loosely connected chapters the stories of the 'failed heroes' of Japan—a class which, according to Morris, has established itself in the popular Japanese consciousness as the type of all virtuous men. Morris argues that the Japanese hero is distinguished from his Western counterpart by a certain genius for failure and that he is revered and loved precisely for his capacity to encounter failure with an unflinching sincerity of purpose and a profound contempt for the material consequences of his resolve.

In Western thought and literature (if we are to accept Professor Morris's view of the matter) the concept of the hero is bound up with the idea of successful action: the Western hero either succeeds directly, or else makes it possible for others to succeed through his sacrifice. If he is defeated it is not by necessity but by chance, and his cause continues to triumph through his downfall, as the cause of Roland triumphed in the vengeance of Charlemagne. The Japanese hero who, on recognizing failure, willingly embraces death does not do so in order to further his cause. Nor does he 'bear witness', in the manner of a Christian martyr, to truths which are made more persuasive through his act of sacrifice. Indeed, it would be wrong to describe the hero's final act in terms of 'sacrifice' at all: there is nothing *beyond* himself for which the hero lays down his life. His life is brought to its end by an inner necessity, by a sense of the impossibility of continuance, and if there is a 'cause' for which the hero has been fighting he dies not in order to benefit that cause but in order to make it manifest. It is thus that the *kamikaze* fighters of the last war saw fit to destroy themselves as defeat overtook their country, and so to manifest their 'purity' of outlook and the imperative nature of the allegiance by which they were bound. In no way did their actions arise from any 'calculation', and only in an intangible sense did they seek to 'benefit' the emperor through what they did. Even the Christian leader Amakusa Shiro died unmindful of success, and owes his popularity to a certain poignant futility that marks him as a true member of his race.

Professor Morris presents portraits of warrior princes and Confucian revolutionaries, of loyal retainers and seekers after power, and attempts to show that it is only against the background of failure that any of them have acquired their heroic status. It is the *mono no aware*—the pathos of mortal things—which it is the hero's task to reveal, and defeat is therefore a necessary means to his moral significance. But while failure is necessary it cannot be sufficient. There is another, perhaps more interesting, aspect to the Japanese hero: he must be possessed of the ability to die correctly, an ability that is the sign of moral education and the manifestation of spiritual grace. While the Christian martyr desires death but does not will it, the Japanese hero wills a death for which he has no desire. The act of *hara kiri*, awakening as it does all the body's natural revulsion against physical injury, symbolizes this conflict between the base desire for survival and the victorious will to die.

It is partly in order to explain and justify the attitudes that make such an act intelligible that Ivan Morris has written the present book. It is dedicated to Mishima, who outspokenly defended the value of suicide and who also committed it under circumstances which would have been no cause for surprise or disapproval had the Japanese ideal of nobility survived more fully the disaster of the Pacific war.

As is apparent from Professor Morris's narrative, the thoughts that motivated Mishima's suicide follow an ancient pattern. Typically the Japanese hero is out of key with his time, traditionalist in inspiration, loyal to his emperor, often a scholar and a literary man anxious to lead his countrymen to an awareness of their moral failings. If Mishima did not succeed in being tragic it is perhaps because the success at which he aimed was too ill-defined and too far from any possible realization, so that his 'failure', when it came, had the aspect of something deliberate and contrived. To be a failure is not easy: it requires skill and judgment, as well as the kind of refinement of outlook that is beyond the reach of the merely successful man.

In this painstaking reconstruction of the lives and values of the failed heroes of Japan, Professor Morris has done a service to Mishima. He has also produced a lively and scholarly work, which will be read with pleasure by all who have a serious interest in Japanese culture. If the book has a fault it is that the author is too much concerned with narrative and not enough with ideas. A more philosophical treatment might have served to distinguish the Japanese hero more sharply from his Western counterpart. As it is the comparison is incomplete. Moreover, Morris considers only the *actual* heroes of Japan; it would have been interesting to find some discussion of the literary hero, and of the concept of failure that we find, for example, in the popular theatre, and in the melodramas of Chikamatsu.

Such speculations might possibly have led Professor Morris to a more persuasive characterization of the heroic motive. It is surely not enough to emphasize the 'sincerity' (*makoto*) of the hero's purpose, as though that alone could provide a description of his state of mind. It is not necessary to disembowel oneself simply in order to show that one is neither an impostor nor a crook.

When the samurai scholar Daidoji Shigesuke (to whose book on the ways of the warrior Professor Morris often alludes) writes that 'one's way of dying can validate one's entire life', he surely meant to recommend the correct way of dying not as a proof of sincerity but as a proof that one attaches to death and suffering a proper value, neither exaggerating their importance nor underestimating it. In fact one finds in the *bushido* ethic something of that idea of 'timely death' which Nietzsche sought to recommend as the basis of all true (i.e., pagan) morality. Nietzsche argued that the man of pure will, the man who was properly identified with the springs of his activity and not at variance with them, must recognize that there is an appropriate time to die, a time beyond which life would be merely a compromise. It was from some such conception that Charmian answered with her dying breath the reproaches of Caesar's servant, declaring that her act was well done, and 'worthy a descendant of the kings of Egypt' (Plutarch). Aristotle argued for a necessary connection between courage and the pursuit of honour, and even the Christian hero Roland expresses the Homeric preference for death over shame. Tacitus writes of the German tribes that men who survived defeat in battles would often put an end to their disgrace by hanging themselves, and we know from our own *Battle of Maldon* that Christianity did not extinguish in our ancestors the imperative will to die when bonds of honour and allegiance required it of them.

It is true that the modern utilitarian orthodoxy finds it difficult to accept such an idea. The utilitarian attempts to found the notion of human good in such concepts as 'benefit' and 'harm', 'pleasure' and 'aversion', 'need' and 'injury'. On such a view it seems difficult to see how death could not be the worst thing that might happen to a man. The idea, common to all great civilizations, that something else—shame, for example, or dishonour—might actually be *worse* than death becomes unintelligible. And really the bafflement that modern Europeans might feel at the Japanese conception of heroic behaviour is no different from the bafflement they must feel at the entire history of their own civilization.

If, then, we are to arrive at a full understanding of what is distinctive in the Japanese hero, besides the peculiar genius for failure which Morris illustrates so well, we ought to describe more fully the motive of the Western hero, and describe the change wrought in that motive by the Christian idea that suicide is a crime, indeed, if we are to follow Dante, a crime worse than murder. Just what state of mind is forbidden by rendering the *act* of suicide criminal? What is the difference between actually killing oneself and merely putting oneself (like Roland) in a situation where one knows one has to die? The distinction is a fine one, but expressive, for all that, of two quite different attitudes to death, and two quite different conceptions of the answerability of a man for the destruction of his mortal frame. In the light of such reflections it has to be admitted that Professor Morris's book poses many questions to which it gives no answer, and however admirable the individual biographies, this work can surely be only the first word on its intellectual theme.

III

During the period of the Tokugawa shoguns (1600-1868), Japan was deliberately cut off from the outside world—hence the title of Donald Keene's history of the literature of this period *World Within Walls*. There were several causes for this experiment in self-sufficiency, the principal one being the disruptive influence of Western trade and religion. It is true that Christianity had not really subverted the standards of popular morality, and had indeed introduced one practice which was greeted by local moralists with undiluted enthusiasm, the practice of crucifixion. None the less, the threat was felt to be a real one, and for the best part of three centuries the ports were closed. This provides one explanation—though not a very convincing one—of the fact that Tokugawa literature is less familiar in the West than the classics of the Heian period (such as the *Tale of Genji* and the *Pillow Book*), or the Nō plays, or the works of recent novelists. But whatever the explanation, it does not lie in the merit of the literature itself.

The Tokugawa period saw the rise and perfection of the haiku—that most Japanese of all poetic forms—as well as the establishment of the puppet theatre and Kabuki. If the self-conscious historicism of its poets and scholars seems stultifying to us, it is perhaps because we have not learnt that art of survival whereby the Japanese have kept a great culture alive through two thousand years of fluctuating fortunes. There is a somewhat crude Marxist view—though not so crude that it does not have its champions among New Left critics—which sees high culture as a part of 'superstructure', rising and declining in obedience to the causality of some economic 'base'. It is always hard to know how to refute such theories, but Japanese culture ought certainly to provide a counter-example. The serious traditions which developed in Japan preserved themselves in relative autonomy, achieving clarity and continuity despite the varied economic and social conditions in which they flourished, and surviving unimpaired even through times of total destitution. Surely, a culture survives because it brings meaning to experience, and it can do that just so long as the language remains alive, and just so long as a historical identity is acknowledged by those who speak it. Indeed, culture is less threatened by economic change than by the invention of some barbarous 'newspeak' from which all sense of history has been purged.

Such a view of culture gains support from the facts recorded by Professor Keene. The intimacy of his acquaintance with Tokugawa literature is as great, no doubt, as that of any Western scholar. Moreover (and for the layman this is the more important feature) Professor Keene possesses a measure of that critical intelligence without which literary history would be merely blind. In the preface he expresses the hope that his book will appeal to a larger audience than the small group of Japanese scholars, for whom, after all, there exist histories enough in Japanese. And his account is sufficiently detailed, and sufficiently vivid, for the layman to find in it not only the interest and enjoyment which Professor Keene intended, but also food for thought about matters which transcend the narrow limits of Oriental scholarship. He writes with clarity and enthusiasm, and awakens a kind of abstract pleasure in the works he discusses. It is true that much of the literature of the period remains untranslated, but Professor Keene has himself done much to remedy that; it is now possible not only to read Bashō and Chikamatsu with enjoyment, but also to understand something of the tradition from which they spring.

The Tokugawa shogunate saw a kind of self-conscious petrification of all traditional institutions. But, despite that, it was a period of literary experiment. A quasi-religious significance attached to the classical literature, to the Nō plays which were performed only at court, and to the *Tale of Genji*, around which a system of occult and largely irrelevant scholarship had arisen, demanding the most extraordinary self-discipline of its initiates. Against the background of such reverence—a reverence which led, for example, to the eventual deification of the haiku poet Bashō—literary experiment acquired a significance that it has seldom achieved in the West. The presence of so many conventions, all of which required a profound consecration to art if they were to be either understood or meaningfully departed from, made possible the formation of an art of pure expression, an art in which the ephemeral and momentary was captured and given objective form. A haikai by Bashō may contain, in the space of seventeen syllables, a revelation of life which is altogether fresh, immediate and universal; the act of communication is the more intense for the constraints with which it is surrounded. It is because of publicly accepted conventions—the restriction to seventeen syllables, the obligatory references to seasons and places, the fixed meaning of certain symbols, the possibility of reading the haikai as the first in a linked sequence, and so on—that so much can pass unsaid. The result is an economy and directness which in our literature have no parallel.

All that must raise the question of how accessible such literature may be to those who are not scholars of Japanese. To take one of Professor Keene's examples, a haikai by Shigeyori reads as follows:

yaa shibaraku
hana ni taishite
kane tsuku koto

Hey there, wait a moment
Before you strike the temple bell
At the cherry blossoms.

An ineffectual poem to those who do not know certain lines of the Nō play *Miidera*, and who are unacquainted with the classical anthology called *Shin Kokinshū*. In the first of these, a madwoman, about to strike the temple bell, is stopped by a priest with the words 'Hey there, wait a minute! What are you, a mad woman, doing striking the bell?' (a speech which, in the original, contains the words of the first line and the third). The *Shin Kokinshū* contains a poem alluded to in the second line, a poem which describes the fall of cherry blossoms at evening while the temple bell is struck. The reader must experience the unity of those two allusions, and so hear the temple bell as a kind of madness, impregnating the flow of nature with unassuageable regret. To those who do not grasp the allusions, the poem reads like any other haikai.

The fact is that the great haiku poets of the period, such as Bashō and Buson, were learned men, pursuing the Chinese ideal of the gentleman scholar (or *bunjin*), developing forms rich in allusion not only to the Japanese classics but also to the Chinese works which influenced them. Their art was one of suggestion and reference, often depending on such recondite details as the Chinese meaning of the written characters—in other words, on an effect that is purely visual, like the shape of 'Easter Wings'. And yet their verse was not strained or pedantic but, on the contrary, fresh and immediate. The art of the haiku depends upon taking everything for granted, and even the best Japanese scholar may miss the essential meaning of a poem. Consider the following haikai by Buson: *otuechi no/fūfu narishi wo/koromagae*. This seems to mean: 'They deserved to be killed, but became husband and wife, and now change their clothes.' But what it really means, according to a Japanese commentator quoted by Professor Keene, is the following:

A young man and woman who should have been put to death by the master of their household for their illicit relations have been spared, thanks to the merciful intercession of the master's wife, and have run off together. They are secretly living as man and wife in a wretched hovel on a back street. Now that they have escaped from the constricting life of service in a great household they remember it as a bad dream. They throw off the padded clothes they were still wearing when they left the household and put on unlined summer kimonos, faded from many washings. Suddenly they feel light and full of joy over their new life. They exchange smiles as a faint breeze blows.

There is no doubt that Buson would have found our English poets long-winded; and there is little doubt that Buson's poetry will appear intolerably cryptic to the English reader, however conversant he may be with the history and culture of Japan.

Now some might hope that at least the prose writing of the period could survive translation and become accessible to the Western reader. For the Tokugawa period saw the production of many tales and novels, including a genuine 'comic epic in prose' in Saikaku's *Life of an Amorous Man*. But such fiction is hardly likely to sustain the interest of readers used to Balzac, Tolstoy and Henry James. The erotic adventures of Saikaku's hero are strung together with little sense of development or resolution, and until the modern era Japanese literature contained virtually no exploratory fiction of the kind which we enjoy. Despite its immense debt to Cervantes and Le Sage, the novel as we know it has its roots in Richardson and Rousseau: it consists in the presentation of individual character and predicament, and involves the exploration of that predicament in terms that are fundamentally moral. The Western novel concerns itself with the peculiarities of individual life, with the pursuit of individual happiness, and, above all, with the exploration of consciousness. In so far as Japanese prose contains such an exploration, it occurs not so much in the picaresque romances of Saikaku and Kiseki as in the travel diaries (the most famous being Bashō's *Narrow Road of Oku*), where the prose is constructed with just the same allusive precision and complexity as the verse which it serves to accompany. And here the exploration of consciousness has moved away from the sphere of the individual. It consists once again in an attempt to achieve an expression that is universal and objective. The feelings belong not to the individual poet but to a landscape, to a race, and to a certain all-pervading religious melancholy which unites the two.

It is this pervasive melancholy—the sense of the 'pity of things' (*mono no aware*)—which is the single most enduring characteristic of Tokugawa literature, and which finds its highest expression in the poetry of Bashō and Buson, and in the poetic narratives which accompany the puppet plays. While the Japanese theatre contains real characters and dramatic situations, the plays exist not for their dramatic development (which is often dictated by convention) but for their touching poetic moments, moments in which the gestures of the puppets and the poetry of the narrative are put to their greatest test. Among the finest of these are the *michiyuki* (the journey narratives) in the plays of Chikamatsu. In these passages one finds again the same abstraction from all that is merely individual, the same love of the frail and the poignant for their own sakes, which are the most striking qualities of the haiku and the waka. One can only regret, therefore, that Professor Keene's discussion of the meaning of the verse forms is so brief, in comparison with his admirable account of the puppet plays and Kabuki. He mentions the doctrine (associated, apparently, with Bashō and his disciple Kyorai) of *fueki ryūkō*—the doctrine of permanence in change. A haikai should be at once a record of an observed moment and a revelation of what is eternal, as in Bashō's most famous verse:

> furuike ya
> kawazu tobikomu
> mizu no oto

> The ancient pond—
> A frog jumps in,
> Sound of water.

A sudden disruption reveals something unchanging in the thing perceived. In this connection, discussing another of Bashō's masterpieces, Keene refers to Eliot's 'moment in and out of time'. But what is the true significance of that moment, and how can we judge that a poem successfully records it? T. S. Eliot subjects the 'moment in and out of time' to an extended poetic examination, which is at the same time both personal and moral. Such examination is impossible within the narrow limits of the haikai. The Western reader therefore stands in need of a serious and independent critical framework in terms of which to approach the poetry.

Professor Keene's criticism does not always gratify that need. Often the best he can say is that the poet really *has* observed, say a narcissus or a butterfly, going on to describe the evocative use of sound and rhythm, and the scholarly reminiscences implicit in the text. But aside from those discussions of technique, his critical musings have a sparse and cryptic quality. His vocabulary is one of association and evocation, rather than of developed significance. While that does not prevent Professor Keene from making frequent and interesting critical judgments, it does make it more difficult for the lay reader to grasp the full importance of the works which he discusses. There is a tendency among Orientalists to shield the works which they study from the analytical rigours of Western criticism. As a result, such arts as that of the haiku are apt to seem to the layman like precious studies in evocation, ripe for dismissal—along with the tea ceremony and the ancient game of 'listening to incense' (described by Ezra Pound in his preface to the Nō plays)—as mere ornament, irrelevant to the feelings of a serious man.

That this is a false view of Japanese literature (and also, for that matter, of the tea ceremony) is evident. Japanese literature was never isolated from life in the way its critics suggest. Chikamatsu's *Love Suicides at Sonezaki*, for example, had an influence comparable to Goethe's *Werther*, and the serious discussion in the puppet plays of the relation between duty and feeling (*giri* and *ninjo*) was made possible precisely by the delineation of ephemeral experiences in which both forces could be seen at work. The fact is that the search for the 'moment in and out of time' is no mere aestheticism, nor is the cult of pathos merely life-negating. These conceptions connect with a specific moral and social order, and that order is as alive in the literature which expresses it as is the bourgeois passion for self-determination in our own nineteenth-century novel. For the Japanese poet the eternal moment is perceived, not through aesthetic isolation, but through moral understanding. Implicit in these elusive perceptions is an intimation of heroic virtue and a sense of a real and active moral order.

It is perhaps unfair to criticize Professor Keene for not producing the kind of philosophy of literature which would make the discussion of those issues possible. But the very excellencies of this book—the clarity of exposition and the honest confrontation with questions of value—lead the reader to hope for something both more critical and more truly historical than he is offered. It seems odd, for example, that Professor Keene allows only a cursory discussion to the Buddhist and Shintoist doctrines which underlie so much of Tokugawa literature. At the end of his book the non-professional reader is still left with the question from which he began: how is it possible to share in the experience of the Japanese poet? And the question becomes more important as Keene's narrative unfolds, and the reader discovers that Japanese poetry is above all the expression of experience, thought and reflection being either implicit in the experience or else wholly irrelevant.

17 The Significance of Dante

The Divine Comedy, translated by C. H. Sisson (Carcanet Press, 1980); translated by Kenneth Mackenzie (Folio Society, 1979); *Dante* by George Holmes (Oxford University Press, 1980); from the *Times Literary Supplement*, 26 September 1980.

IT WOULD be no exaggeration to say that *Four Quartets* owes as much to Dante as to any single writer in Eliot's native tongue. Nor is this an eccentricity; on the contrary, the Dantesque quality of *Four Quartets* is integral to its achievement. Modern poetry grew from the attempt to abandon poetic diction and write of the 'unhappy consciousness' in the language which belongs to it. It reached fruition when that language, uneasy, embarrassed though it was, began to bear the weight of ideas which transcended and measured its uncertainties. It is a stylistic achievement to produce an idiom that is true to the resonances of common experience, while dignified enough to convey such a moral idea. That achievement was Dante's. It was also Eliot's.

When Eliot had acquired his style, he felt obliged to repudiate Milton (perhaps the only great poet to have been a crypto-Italian without also being crypto-Catholic). The reasons that he offered (and which were endorsed by Leavis, and so by a whole generation of critics and writers) were odd, and in some ways unscrupulous. But the motive for the gesture is clear. It was necessary to dissociate Dante and Milton, first as versifiers, secondly as thinkers. The superficial resemblance between them, so often invoked by their nineteenth-century admirers, points in the direction of political and theological commitment. But the Miltonic style is elevated and sublime, unsuited to the poetry of unbelief. By contrast, Dante combines plain speaking and noble sentiment; he never belies either the unhappiness which defines him, or the vision which draws him on. This suggests a model of poetic style suited to the expression of metaphysical desolation. The orderliness of Dante's verse seems to represent an achievement that is stylistic and spiritual at once. It is as though the poet rose to felicity through the purification of sinful speech. So he served as a model for the attempt—variously undertaken by Eliot, Stevens and Pound—to bring order to the experience of unbelief by bringing order to its language.

The stylistic distinction between Milton and Dante needs no comment. But there is a distinction of vision that in part serves to explain it. The power of Milton is a power more muscular than intellectual; his language, abstracted from the spoken tongue, seems, like the Word of

God, to create rather than to record its subject-matter. It sends out a vision into infinite space, which proceeds unimpeded by the preoccupations of mortality. Milton's paradise is human, but without the contingencies of human life: its pathos and beauty stand outside the realm of local emotions. Dante's verse, by contrast, ranges freely through all human experience, and is never so far advanced in abstraction as to lose contact with a particular place and a particular time.

This does not mean that Dante is less universal than Milton. On the contrary, his universality is of a higher order, precisely because the vision stems from and makes room for what is most ephemeral. Dante was unconcerned to be of any time except his own, and he wished to understand his time completely, describing a highly specific historical condition in terms of the eternal truths to which he was a witness. He therefore tried to preserve the particularity of his subject-matter in a language which still moved with the logic of abstract thought.

It is from this peculiarity of vision that there arose the peculiarity of style. Just as he saw the fall of man in terms of the spiritual desolation of his native city, so did he translate the abstractions of Thomist philosophy into a commentary upon his own personal pilgrimage. This reconciling of fragmented experience with a redeeming ideal was an inspiration to Eliot. In his early essay Eliot had praised Dante's ability to turn philosophy into vision. But this praise concealed his own longing, partly fulfilled in *Four Quartets*, to turn vision into philosophical truth.

It is not, then, surprising to find that Dante has become, as it were, a canonical part of English literature. C. H. Sisson's translation into colloquial free verse is testimony to this canonization, and it provides the opportunity to reflect on the contemporary significance of the *bello stile*. (Some idea of Sisson's interest in the aspects of Dante to ..hich I have referred can be gathered from the fact that this phrase is deliberately mistranslated. It becomes, by way of signalling Dante's modernity, 'the exact style'. Exactness, unlike beauty, is a merit in the eyes of unbelief.)

Sisson's translation coincides with that of Kenneth Mackenzie, published by the Folio Society. The second, with its monotonous pentameters, belongs to the nineteenth century, while the first makes a bold and in many ways (despite fine versions by Laurence Binyon and Charles Singleton) unprecedented attempt to unite Dante with his legitimate heirs. It has to be remembered, in considering these translations, that Anglo-Saxon interest in Dante had long preceded the Eliotian revolution in taste. *The Divine Comedy* was translated innumerable times during the last century, and into every available poetical idiom, from Cary's blank verse with the diction of Scott, to the business-like fluency of Longfellow. These translations accompanied the flowering of Dante scholarship in England, which involved one of our great prime ministers (Gladstone), led to the foundation of the Oxford Dante Society, inspired Edward Moore's meticulous *Studies in Dante* and culminated in the

Temple Classics edition of the *Comedy*, which has made succeeding generations familiar with the text and its interpretation. This edition, acting jointly with Dorothy Sayers's insufferable Penguin, has ensured that English readers make serious efforts to read the original. Its succinct and scholarly notes are due largely to the unassuming Rev P. H. Wicksteed, who introduced Ibsen to the English reading public and refuted, in a review of *Das Kapital*, the labour theory of value. It stands as a testimony to the culture and open-mindedness of the Edwardian educated class, and shows an understanding of Dante's theology and politics which are hard to improve upon without writing at considerable length. Were it not for the fact that the Italian text is slightly (but at times significantly) corrupt, and that the scholarship is too succinct for the ill-educated modern reader to bear, this would surely be everyone's preferred edition of the *Comedy*.

It seems to me, therefore, that the best way to become acquainted with Dante is through the Temple Classics edition. There is more to be learned from it than from any short introduction, and there is little in George Holmes's workmanlike volume for the *Past Masters* series which would lead one to recommend it as an alternative. To write an introduction to Dante in some form other than footnotes is indeed far from easy. What is one introducing? The poetry? The life? The philosophy? The criticism? The political doctrine? All these are so worthy of attention in themselves that it is not surprising if an introductory text should have to select among them. Nevertheless it would seem natural to give priority to theology, and this is precisely the realm in which Mr Holmes seems least sure of himself.

He is under the impression that Aristotle did not believe in God, whereas it was in part Aristotle's metaphysical vision of the Deity that inspired Aquinas's and therefore Dante's, philosophy. Holmes prefers to begin from the ideas of courtly love which find embodiment in the figure of Beatrice, and to move on from there to the neo-Platonic cosmology which Dante studied during his years of exile. In other words, he emphasizes the aspect of Dante which most unites him with the poetic orthodoxies of the pre-Renaissance, and, as a result, gives no very vivid impression of his stylistic and visionary achievement. He introduces us elaborately to the problem of Beatrice's reality, acknowledging the while that it hardly matters to an understanding of the poetry whether or not this supreme fiction was also real. He mentions the influence of Cavalcanti, offering the following summary of the *Donna mi Prega*: 'Love is just a powerful emotion for which there is a physical explanation; it doesn't put you in touch with truth or goodness, quite the reverse indeed'. ('I do not hope', wrote Cavalcanti, 'that a man of base heart will understand my meaning'; nevertheless one can venture to say that his meaning was not *that*.)

Holmes argues that the amalgamation of religious and erotic devotion (and their combined representation in the figure of Beatrice) constitutes Dante's originality among medieval poets. But this seems implausible. Surely the assimilation of the two kinds of love is essential to the neo-Platonic doctrines of the soul, and is present, in some form or other, in almost all the literature of courtly love? It seems to be there in the Provençale, in Grandson and Charles d'Orléans, and in Chaucer. Replacing erotic by filial love, the Middle English *Pearl* is a variant which expresses just the same synthesis of earthly and transcendental longing for which Holmes praises Dante.

Still, Holmes is undeniably right to emphasize the centrality of love in Dante's philosophy, and it is important to understand the doctrine of love if we are to assess the merits of any particular translation. It is love which moves the sun and the other stars; it is love which draws the soul towards God, by a *luce intelletual, pien d'amore*; it is erotic love which first afflicts the human soul with the pain of freedom, and it is the presence or absence of love which distinguishes the blessed from the damned. How can one thing have so many effects? It is Dante's distinction to have dramatized that question, and to have embellished his answer to it with an unusual repertory of thought and emotion.

Dante's hidden master was Aristotle, who said that God moves the world as the beloved moves the lover. If Dante's vision has a single meaning, it is contained in that remark. Like Boethius, Dante distinguished the temporal and the eternal aspects of reality: one and the same thing can be seen both in time, and outside time; its aspect, but not its essence, changes with the point of view. Under the aspect of time, human freedom appears subject to Fortune. Under the aspect of eternity it is subject only to the will of God. Freedom, as the divine principle in man, constitutes our essence. But God moves by love, so the exercise of love is also free. Love does not *feel* free: in this world, at least, it appears always to afflict us. Seen from the proper metaphysical height, this compulsion reveals itself to be illusory. The illusion is born of the fact that, in love, a man chooses with his whole soul, and not with some appetitive part of it: therefore he compels himself. Love that is not perverted from its proper trajectory seeks the freedom of another, and this freedom lies in the personality, the quiddity, which makes the other who he is. Love which desires not the quiddity but the generality of the other is not love but lust; it expresses not the freedom but the enslavement of the subject, just as it seeks not the freedom but the enslavement of the beloved.

The mystery of love arises in the following way. The individual is unknowable to the intellect (*individuum est ineffabile*, says the scholastic tag); it is knowable, in time, only to the senses. Individuality is made present only in sensory form, and elicits the choice of love only when so understood. The first impulse of love is therefore sensual, and it has the human body—or more precisely, the human face—as its object. It is the *smile* of Beatrice that leads Dante on through Paradise, and which reveals to him the Love of which she is the refulgence. So erotic love points towards God; but its sensual beginnings contain a temptation. (Without that temptation it could not be free, just as Adam could not have loved God freely had he no means to disobey.) If a man sinks, like Dante, into carnal desire, then his will is perverted from the object of love; he must then pass through the 'refining fire' described in *Purgatorio* (and invoked in *Four Quartets*). When he reaches the reward and fulfilment of love, it is no longer an individual but a universal that he encounters. In this universal, the element of individuality remains: it remains in the smile of Beatrice, which is nobody's smile but hers, even when she is all but absorbed into the light of the Divinity.

One of the most striking of Dante's transformations of this doctrine lies in his political philosophy. Piccarda is one of those whose blessedness, being the fulfilment of an earthly will that wavered in its purpose, lies furthest from the fount of love. In a famous line she describes her contentment: *la sua voluntate è nostra pace*; 'his will is our peace'. There is a condensation in this line which illustrates the thoroughness with which Dante's thought impregnates his idiom. God wills our peace, and this is what pacifies and pleases us (a resonance lost by Cary with 'his will is our tranquility'). More than that. His will and our peace are not two things, but one. In obedience we find fulfilment, because obedience is the highest expression of our freedom and so brings us closest to God. To disobey is to will disharmony and to sever the soul from love. The punishments meted out in Hell are so described that it is the punishments themselves, and not the veil of earthly satisfaction which temporarily concealed them, which their victims are seen inwardly to have desired.

Dante's political vision follows immediately from the thought active in Piccarda's apophthegm. The Church, as God's will in the world, calls to us freely to adopt its yoke and so recognize that its authority binds us not through tyranny but through love. The relation between the Church and its members must be, like the bond of love, one of freedom. But this, too, is a freedom in which the whole soul is engaged. It must therefore be felt, in time, as a kind of ineluctability. The Church cannot impose itself by force without negating the principle of its authority.

It is imperative to distinguish, then, the authority of the Church from the power of worldly princes. The power of a prince is good only to the extent that it freely aligns itself with the Church's spiritual authority: otherwise it is a perverted power and negates the freedom of its subjects. It follows that power and authority must be separable (so as the better to combine); it also follows that power should lie with princes, while for the Church authority alone is enough. In making itself a Princedom, the Church of Rome offended against its mission. Harmony among princes will proceed not from ecclesiastical, but from secular power: hence the need for an Empire separate from the Church. From the height of this political vision Dante surveyed the world of his day and saw the same inadequacy in its political arrangements as he felt in his own personal life; in both was the same estrangement from the will of God.

For Dante, then, love is both the eternal origin and the historical essence of mankind. This is the universal meaning of the *Comedy*. Those who miss the meaning will be impressed not by the sublime vision of *Paradiso* but by those poignant episodes in the *Inferno*—Francesca da Rimini, Count Ugolino, Brunetto Latini—which represented to the Romantic mind the high points of Dante's achievement. There is in Sisson a total dedication to the original that forces his translation away from any romantic reading towards a modernism that is almost bleak in its representation of the underlying view: bleak because behind Sisson's admiration one feels the nagging presence of unbelief. It is a great achievement to have given Dante to the modern reader in such a way that the poem's significance is placed not in its beginning but in its end. Sisson redresses the balance against ages of misreading: but he redresses it with a vengeance, employing verse that is stark, cold, often deliberately uncompelling in its refusal of every rhetorical device. It is impossible not to admire the result, just as it is impossible not to wish that it were otherwise.

Dante's versification and his thought are inseparable: it is partly this that is meant by the 'visionary' quality of the *Comedy*. The translator is faced with the task of holding verse-form and thought together, so that the harmony between the sensuous movement of the one and the argument of the other is preserved. Without this harmony, or rather transparency, between thought and versification, the vision fades into darkness. Sisson's translation brings this problem into focus, as it brings into focus the whole significance of Dante for contemporary verse. There is no doubt that Sisson understands and deeply sympathizes with the doctrines of the *Paradiso*. He expresses them indeed with the greatest clarity. Himself a constitutional theorist of some distinction, and one of the most philosophical poets of our time, Sisson defers quickly to Dante's thought process, translating it into loose rhythms responsive to abstract ideas. Hence the most beautiful moments occur not in the *Inferno*, but in the other two *cantiche*. Here, for example, is the beginning of the great hymn to the Virgin with which the poem ends:

> Virgin mother, daughter of your son,
> Humble and exalted beyond any other creature
> The settled end of the eternal plan,
>
> You are she who made human nature
> So noble, that the maker of it himself
> Did not scorn to have himself made by it.

> In your womb was lit again that love
> By whose warmth, in the eternal peace,
> This flower has germinated as it is.

There is a solemnity in these lines, and a respect for doctrine, that are close to Dante. And whatever there is of clumsiness is explained by that. The phrase 'the maker of it himself/Did not scorn to have himself made by it', is an example. Awkward and unbending in English, it has its justification in its sense. There is no hope that our Anglo-Saxon grammar could encompass the syntactical condensation of '*il suo Fattore/non disdegno di farsi sua fattura*', but the thought is the same—or almost so. 'To have himself made by it' breathes the same open air as the original; 'to make himself made by it', although more true, does not. Sisson's compromise enables us to sense Dante's meaning: which is that no agent but God was active in this mystery.

Nothing in the sound, sense or rhythm of Dante's words deviates from the meaning, or from natural Italian, while each resonance carries the reader further into the heart of a mystery which no words can quite contain. It is impossible to reproach Sisson for having arrived only at the threshold where the meaning makes itself visible. Few translators even get so far. Kenneth Mackenzie's version provides an instructive contrast, employing as it does a monotonous variant of the blank verse made plausible by Cary:

> O Virgin Mother, daughter of your Son,
> Lowly and yet above all creatures raised,
> Predestined goal of the eternal plan,
> You did ennoble human nature so
> That he who made it deigned Himself to be
> Its creature. It was in your womb that Love
> Was kindled once again, beneath the warmth
> This rose has opened in eternal peace.

At first sight this flows more naturally (although after a hundred lines the effect begins to pall). But the sense is lost. Leaving aside the gross implications of 'predestined' ('settled', as Sisson translates it, '*fisso*', in the original: and there is no doubt which of those English words captures the meaning), one has only to think of the overtones of 'creature'. for the speaker of modern English it is impossible to use that word to convey the sense of single agency that Dante expressed. Moreover, it is not that God deigned: he did not disdain; and the rose, which is 'opened' in MacKenzie, is germinated in Dante's peace.

Sisson writes with a pressure of theory at his elbow, and some of this he reveals directly in his somewhat muscle-bound introduction. Dante was similar; his defence of vernacular poetry and his literary self-criticism show him as concerned as any modern poet to demonstrate his up-to-dateness.' Through the defence of the colloquial idiom, and through Eliot's recognition of the significance of this defence, Dante has become for such poets as Sisson what Virgil was for Dante. He provides the model of a live poetic language.

But the achievement of the *dolce stil nuovo* is not only one of clarity: it lends dignity and profundity to the spoken tongue. And if the aim of this attempt is truth, the means is versification. It is through versification alone, and not through fidelity, that Dante's vision can be recaptured, even if the first step in the attempt is to write like Sisson, in a language proper to one's place and time.

What then of rhyme? Sisson dismisses the possibility of imitating *terza rima* on the grounds that he would never dream of using that verse-form in any lengthy poem of his own. 'That', he adds,

> may seem a poor reason, but it is in fact a good one, as anyone will understand who has understood that a translator must write as comes natural to him, in the language of his day and in the kind of verse which belongs to the current development of the language, and of his own technique. The real task is to give the matter of Dante, as one speaks most effectively.

Sisson also thinks, with some reason, that the general differences between Italian and English make the imitation of *terza rima* rather like a clown following a ballet dancer. He cites Cary and Longfellow as proof that one can translate Dante without using rhyme at all. Nevertheless, he keeps the tercet structure. So he must face a question: how far can one move away from Dante's versification and yet preserve his sense?

If Sisson avoids rhyme it is not because it is unnatural to him. One of the longest of his own poems (*The Discarnation*) is written in a rhyme-scheme of Byronic complexity. Nor can he have failed to notice the importance of rhyme in giving expression to the content of the *Divine Comedy*. If you look for the successful episodes in Cary's blank verse you will most likely pick out the vivid moments in the *Inferno*, and the beginning and end of *Purgatorio*, where the imagery has a vast and daring quality suitable for bold treatment. In Dante the web of rhyme persists and persists: it is the force that drives each canto through to its conclusion; it is the refrain that causes every verse to halt. It lends itself equally to the dismal trespassing in Hell, and to the free ascent of the spirit beyond.

To translate the *Paradiso* into blank verse is to leave only a body of doctrine obscured by a metre that denies it. When translators have had it in mind to conserve the status of the *Inferno* as praeludium and to restore the *Paradiso* to its rightful place, they have almost invariably used rhyme as the unit of significance. In 1892 G. L. Shadwell, Provost of Oriel, began his translation of the second two *cantiche*, using a four-line stanza. Thus *Paradiso II*, 142-8 ('*per la natura lieta onde deriva/La virtù misto . . .*') is rendered:

> By the glad nature whence it came
> This mingling doth the mass enflame
>   As in our gladdened sight
>   The pupil flashes bright.
> This is the cause, not dense and rare,
> Which difference makes 'twixt star and star:
>   This the kind source whence come
>   The brightness and the gloom.

The gentle lilt hardly conceals the fact that in this usage rhyme destroys more of the meaning than it restores. The form of the tercet has disappeared—and with it the symbolism of the Trinity. The lines have been shortened into a trot; nothing further from Dante's contemplative movement could be imagined. Most important is that the translation now falls out (or in) as a sequence of unlinked stanzas. Instead of an interwoven chain we have a pile of rings. The verse is held together not by the rhyme but by the sequence of ideas; so that rhyme no longer has a function.

The same objection can be levelled against what G. L. Bickester called, in his translation of 1932, 'English triple rhyme': successive three-line stanzas with rhyming outer lines. Such rhyme, used also by John Ciardi in one of the more vigorous modern versions, again has the effect of breaking more connections than it makes. Still less can we countenance the use of stanzas consisting of an unrhymed first line and a couplet—used in P. Bannerman's disastrous translation of 1850. If the translator is to use rhyme at all he must use *terza rima*. Sisson argues against this course, not only because it is artificial (although, unlike the heroic couplets imposed by Dryden on Virgil and by Pope on Homer, it certainly *is* artificial); but also because *terza rima* imposes a pronounced rhythmic organization. And whatever organization Sisson's translation possesses I do not think that rhythm is the word for it.

Terza rima was Dante's invention. Sisson is not alone in thinking that it requires the abundance of vowel rhymes and feminine endings which Italian (but not English) provides. Boccaccio succeeded in detaching the form from its religious meaning, while still using its catenary character in order to capture the unified compellingness of a vision. Chaucer introduced *terza rima* into English with the *Compleint to His Lady*, but in his own amorous visions he preferred the native forms of English (as in the unlinked stanzas of *The Parliament of Fowls*). Sisson thinks that Shelley's use of *terza rima*, in the *Triumph of Life*, is on the whole successful. I find it difficult to agree: the ten-syllable line seems constantly to be halted by the rhyme scheme. In Dante's more colloquial eleven-syllable rhythm the force of each line carries across into the next, and it is partly this which makes the interweaving so effective. In general, it seems that *terza rima* refuses to accommodate itself to the rhythms of English verse.

Nevertheless, when the fever for Dante translation broke out in country parsonages all over England, the *terza rima* became, the common property of almost every poetaster in the realm. Shelley and Byron had led the way, with translations of fragments. Here is Byron (who fondly thought of himself—see the preface to 'The Prophecy of Dante'—to be the first English writer to use the form) translating a famous passage:

> But one point only wholly us o'erthrew
> When we read the long sigh'd for smile of her
> To be thus kiss'd by such devoted lover,
> He who from me can be divided ne'er
> Kiss'd my mouth, trembling in the act all over:
> Accursed was the book and he who wrote!
> That day no further leaf did we uncover.

In 1843, in what purported to be 'the first attempt to present Dante to the English Reader in the Terza Rima of his own choice', the Rector of Skelton in Cumberland managed the passage yet more stiltedly:

> But one sole moment wrought for our undoing:
> When of the kiss we read, from smile so bright,
> So coveted, that such true-love bore,
> He, from my side who ne'er may disunite,
> Kissed me upon the mouth, trembling all o'er
> The broker of our vows, it was the lay,
> And he who wrote—that day we read no more.

It is not difficult to see the influence of Milton in 'He, from my side who ne'er may disunite': it is precisely such syntactical distortion that modern admirers of Dante abhor. A few years later we have this from C. B. Cayley:

> For when the smile desired in our tale
> Was kissed by such a great and loving one
> This man, who never from my side can fail
> Kissed me all quivering my mouth upon,
> The book, the author, Pander's trade applying,
> That evening we could read no further on.

In none of these versions is there any hint of the urgency of Francesca's memory, or of the utter naturalness of the words which Dante finds for it. The *terza rima* acts as a full stop to every line, squeezing the syntax that precedes it. There is infinitely more flow and simplicity in Cary (published 1814, begun 1805-6):

> . . . But at one point
> Alone we fell. When of that smile we read,
> The wishèd smile, so rapturously kiss'd
> By one so deep in love, then he, who ne'er
> From me shall separate, at once my lips
> All trembling kiss'd. The book and writer both
> Were love's purveyors. In its leaves that day
> We read no more. . . .

Such comparisons lend force to Sisson's contention that *terza rima* is likely to place more constraint on an English writer than his language will bear. They also give rise to an observation that will illustrate the finer shades of meaning that any translator who wishes to be faithful to Dante's philosophy must convey. In all these translations, even in Byron's, not otherwise notable for its fidelity, a conscious or unconscious respect is shown towards the philosophy of love. Francesca remembers reading of the *smile* of Guinevere, desired and kissed by Lancelot. By a fine transition, she then remembers the kissing, not of her smile, but of her mouth; she also remembers Paolo's trembling as he kissed her: '*la bocca mi baciò tutto tremante*'. Much is implied in that transition. The smile of another is the picture of his soul, the announcement of freedom: it is the signal of the divine.

Animals do not smile: at best they grimace. As Milton puts it: 'for smiles from reason flow,/To brute denied, and are of love the food . . .'. Francesca has been aware, through Guinevere, of her own smile, since she has been aware of the freedom of choice that is prompting her (erroneously) to love. Then suddenly her smile, receiving the kiss, becomes a mouth, and the line trembles with the reminiscence of Paolo's passion, and the loss of her freedom. It is important that she attributes this trembling to Paolo: we feel the whole terrible force with which Francesca's self-image is overthrown. In a few natural words her desire and the philosophy which explains it are jointly conveyed.

It is strange to find Sisson mistranslating: 'He who will never be divided from me,/Kissed my mouth, and the two of us were trembling.' One is inclined to respond impatiently to this, on the ground that Sisson is after all unconstrained by rhyme, and allows himself so much latitude with form that he should take none with content. It is also surprising that a translator so steeped in the thought of the *Paradiso* should not have been concerned to capture all the minute ways in which the *Paradiso* is presaged in the verses of the earlier *cantiche*. This is one small instance, and in fairness it must be said that Sisson's few misrepresentations of the 'matter' of Dante are mostly confined to the part—the *Inferno*—where his spirit is least willing to linger. But it leads us to an important question. Precisely what constraints of versification does Sisson, when he varies or underscores a meaning, obey? He would certainly say that if he has dropped the constraint of rhyme this is largely in order to respond effectively to constraints of another kind.

Now the best imitation of Dante's manner in modern English (the Brunetto Latini passage in 'Little Gidding') also dispenses with rhyme, recreating the catenary effect by interwoven masculine and feminine endings:

> So with your own, and pray they be forgiven
>   By others, as I pray you to forgive
>   Both bad and good. Last season's fruit is eaten
> And the fullfed beast shall kick the empty pail.
>   For last year's words belong to last year's language
>   And next year's words await another voice.

If the spirit of Dante is present in these lines it is for reasons other than the superficial resemblance to *terza rima*. The diction has what Eliot discerned in Dante but could not find in Milton: 'the slight alteration which, while it leaves a plain statement a plain statement, has always the maximal, never the minimal alteration of ordinary language.' It seems to me that the discipline of Eliot's lines is the kind of discipline that Sisson is searching for: why else should he negate every movement towards iambic verse, while conserving the tercet structure of the original? That Sisson has Eliot very much in mind is shown in his own occasional reminiscence (*'ch'i'non avrei mai creduto che morte tanta n'avesse disfatta'* comes out as 'so many that I should never have thought/Death had been able to undo so many', the repetition of 'so many' coming, not from Dante, but from *The Waste Land*).

There is one element of discipline in the Eliot that comes directly from Dante: the use of an eleven-syllable line. Sisson rightly points out that Dante is fairly free with his measures, and feels justified in being free himself. (After all, he says, even Dorothy Sayers sometimes stretches to twelve syllables. In fact at one point, *Inf*. XVII. 121, Miss Sayers manages seventeen.) But his freedom is totally unlike Dante's (or Eliot's). It is not a matter of contracting or expanding a received unit of sound, but rather of letting a line complete its impetus according to its own internal movement:

> And just as doves called home to their desire

With stretched and steady wings, back to the nest,
Come through the air because they want to do so;

So, separating from the flock where Dido was,
They came towards us through the malignant air,
So strong was the affection of my cry.

This is Sisson at his best; clear, solemn, and with a firm grasp of English rhythm. (If one complains that the nest ought to be 'sweet'—'*dolce nido*'—this is only because the translation has condemned itself to be judged rather literally.) But the hendecasyllabic movement is accidental; there is no sense of metrical constraint here, such as we find in Eliot.

One cannot help wondering why Sisson is so determined, therefore, to maintain the division into tercets, which follows the original more or less exactly (so that when a tercet drops out one attributes this to oversight). In Eliot the tercets are held together by metre and assonance: at the same time the diction flows through and across them, giving the effect of 'slightly altered' plain statement, with all the high metaphysical dignity that we find in Dante. This kind of ordered flexibility is difficult to maintain, as is apparent from Wallace Stevens's magnificent but repeated failures:

From this the poem springs: that we live in a place
That is not our own and, much more, not ourselves
And hard it is in spite of blazoned days.

Two perfectly Dantesque eleven-syllable lines, suddenly arrested by a characteristic overstatement, which falls of its own accord, and against the movement of the verse, into an iambic pentameter.

It would be unfair to criticize Sisson for not maintaining over many thousand lines the disciplines that Wallace Stevens can hardly sustain for three. But there is a further feature of Eliot's imitation which if copied, would surely have overcome the seeming arbitrariness of many of Sisson's divisions. In every line of Eliot there is a breathing space, a slightly shifting caesura, just as there is in Dante. The caesura forces each line either to complete the movement of the one that precedes, or to begin the movement of the one that follows it:

Second, the conscious impotence/of rage
At human folly/and the laceration
Of laughter/at what ceases to amuse.
And last, the rending pain/of re-enactment
Of all that you have done, and been;/the shame
Of motives late revealed,/and the awareness
Of things ill done/and done to others' harm
Which once you took/for exercise of virtue.

This caesura is an integral part of the catenary effect in Dante. It is also one of the most effective ways of turning 'plain statement' into verse.

Consider the brief description, in the opening canto, of the church of Rome:

> Ed una lupa,/che di tutte brame
>   Sembiava carca/nella sua magrezza
>   E molte gente/fé'già viver grame.

If you translate this literally, you get something like this:

> And a she-wolf, who with every craving ˙
>   Seemed to me over-burdened in her lean-ness
>   And many has she caused to live in sorrow.

All three features of the Dantesque line remain; the eleven-syllable movement, the feminine endings, and the slight caesura. Sisson deliberately avoids them. He also gives a new twist to the meaning:

> And a she-wolf, who seemed, in her thin-ness,
>   To have nothing but excessive appetites,
>   And she has already made many miserable.

After ten or so such tercets I begin to wish for some hesitancy in the verse, something that will stop each line from running itself out. Is it that I have failed to catch some other, more subtle movement, in Sisson's verse, or am I right in thinking that the discipline of Dante can be recalled in more traditional ways? In any event I cannot escape the impression that for many pages this translation is nearer to prose than to verse, and that the division into tercets produces a kind of arbitrariness precisely where Dante made his greatest bid for order. (The caesura is not more respected by Mackenzie, but the monotony of his rhythms and the faintness with which he transcribes the imagery are such that the translation can bear no comparison with Sisson.)

In a recent poem in the *TLS*, Donald Davie (addressing Seamus Heaney) wrote:

>   I think Sisson
>   Got it, don't you?   Plain Dante, plain as a board
>   And if flat, flat.   The abhorrent, the abhorred
>   Ask to be wholly plain.

Dante was never plain, although Sisson often is. Dante achieved harmony between what he thought and what he saw, and what he saw has a meaning that no mere 'plainness' can record. Davie is clearly a romantic: he reads the vision as a vision of Hell, reaching only by a stretch of the intellect towards the light. In Sisson, however, it is Purgatory and Paradise that are described most persuasively. The verse, which limps through the sad plenitudes below, rises with the spirit of the poet. What seems like flatness is not really flatness at all, but a kind of persistent undercurrent of despair. Sisson cannot quite believe in Dante's vision. Therefore he removes from his versification every rhetorical gesture, everything that might imply a self-induced afflatus of emotion. This explains the absence of poetic devices, and the constant refusal to enact any metrical order. Sisson, like Eliot, has seen the significance of Dante for the poetry of unbelief. But instead of using Dante's versification to transcend despair, he reduces it to a wholly new kind of 'plain statement'. Thus his translation is the most sincere, the most modern, and yet in some ways the most distanced from the original that I know.

Architecture

18   Alberti and the Art of the Appropriate

Index Verborum to L. B. Alberti's 'De Re Aedificatoria', Hans-Karl Lücke (Prestel, Munich), from the *Times Literary Supplement*, 16 December 1977

ALBERTI'S *De Re Aedificatoria* was begun in 1443, during the author's second visit to Rome, and not finished until 1452, after extended researches among ruins and libraries, and a labour of thought and invention that is unmatched in the corpus of architectural theory. The first five books deal with matters of construction, location and design, and were finished some two years before the later, more theoretical, books were started. Alberti says of his work that 'the labour was much more than I could have foreseen at the outset; continual difficulties arose at every moment, either in explaining the matter, or in inventing words, or in giving method to the subject, all of which confounded and discouraged me.'

It is perhaps not easy for the modern reader to appreciate the difficulties to which Alberti refers, for his treatise lacks the more obvious signs of creative endeavour. In particular, it lacks the range of examples, the detailed solutions to stylistic and constructional problems, which are characteristic of Alberti's successors, of Serlio, Vignola and Palladio. The treatise may also seem on occasion diffuse and digressionary, a digest of all available classical learning (and this affectation was surely a destructive influence upon much early Renaissance thought). Nevertheless the *De Re Aedificatoria* also exhibits an underlying system, and a determined application of educated intelligence to the most elusive as well as to the most evident of architectural facts. Besides that, it is a work of great descriptive power, in which a Ciceronian style is bent to the task of recording technicalities and aesthetic conceptions that had never been fully treated before.

In this respect, even the modern reader must see how great was Alberti's task. For not only was the technical vocabulary bequeathed by Vitruvius obscure and uncertain in its application: it also proved to be substantially incomplete, even for the description of the Classical Orders, and radically deficient in terms appropriate to the workman and the engineer. Moreover, architecture presents a further and more formidable challenge to intelligent description. Parts, ornaments, structures and surfaces must be described not merely as inanimate blocks of matter but also (if architecture is to be the humane study that Alberti believed it to be) as the components in an articulate and meaningful appearance, as

139

objects of delight and satisfaction, as constituents in the form and scenario of public and private life.

No modern architectural writer has succeeded, as Alberti succeeded, in conveying a full sense of the visual and, so to speak, moral reality of architecture, and of the deep and elusive connection that exists between the questions of how to build and how to live. It is regrettable that his treatise is now read mainly by historians, and that students of architecture are encouraged to derive what little aesthetic education is required of them not from these mature and circumspect reflections but from the naive and hysterical propaganda of Le Corbusier and the Modern Movement. In fact there seems to be no translation of Alberti's text at present available in English. Until recently it was possible to obtain a Tiranti reprint (sketchily annotated by Joseph Rykwert) of Leoni's translation of 1726, itself no more than a rendering of the sixteenth-century Italian translation by Bartoli. Leoni's version is elegant and learned; but it shows no system in its translation of Alberti's philosophical terms, and misrepresents many of the central concepts.

It is fair to say that neither Bartoli nor Leoni had an easy task. Alberti's language was rich and subtle, and while each of his terms was used with a definite and discoverable meaning, he seldom offered definitions even of the most important among them. The labour involved in collating Alberti's terms did not appeal to Bartoli or to any later translator. Now, however, thanks to the as yet unfinished work of Hans-Karl Lücke, an *Index Verborum* is available, which traces every word to its specific context of use and enables the reader to discover for himself the true significance of Alberti's many coinages.

There is a precedent for such an enterprise in Herman Nohl's *Index Vitruvianus* of 1876; but Dr Lücke's work is of greater value than that of his predecessor. By citing not only page references, but also the complete context for each occurrence, he enables the reader not just to know where any word occurs (in itself a pointless piece of knowledge) but also to form a conception of its meaning. The *Index* can therefore be used like a dictionary, but a dictionary which offers implicit rather than explicit definitions. Dr Lücke has collated the various editions and manuscripts, indicating faults, misprints and grammatical slips, and has now published the first two of his three volumes, together with a facsimile of the original Florentine edition of 1485, to the pages of which the dictionary entries refer.

It is to be hoped that this careful work of scholarship will be the occasion of a new and properly argued translation of Alberti's treatise. The Italians already have an elaborate and annotated bilingual edition, but it will be of no more than partial interest to English readers, containing as it does no attempt to arrive at a consistent rendering of Alberti's most important terms.

Because the study of Alberti has been regarded as an almost exclusively art-historical preserve, the unique process of philosophical reflection which his work exhibits has recently had little serious influence. Alberti was not a rigorous thinker, but he was a philosopher in the classically accepted sense of the term, capable of sustained reflection upon complex issues and able to invent concepts with which to describe the most elusive of facts. Yet the *De Re Aedificatoria* has been studied primarily as a historical document, useful for the light that it casts upon Renaissance classicism and upon contemporary attitudes to architecture, but of no more general interest than the many treatises which it engendered.

In his introduction to the Italian edition Paolo Portoghesi even attempts to construe the Treatise as an extension of the earlier Italian work *Della Famiglia* (written roughly at the time of Alberti's first essay in architectural theory, the *Cinque Ordini dell'Architettura*, which he never published). According to such an interpretation, one of the main purposes of the *De Re Aedificatoria* is to describe the external and public embodiment of the private domestic virtues praised in the earlier work, an attempt (as a Marxizing critic might put it) to give objective and symbolic form to urban mercantile values, and so represent a passing social order as a permanent human fact. But whatever we make of that (and reflection suggests that neither the institution of the family nor the classical language of architecture can be so easily circumscribed) the truth is that Alberti's thought is too rich and compelling to be considered only from such an internal point of view, as part of the case history of a remarkable man and a remarkable period. We should read Alberti's work as he intended it: as an extended account of the entire art of building, designed to embrace everything that has to be understood by those who seek to build well.

But there is no doubt that art-historical scholarship, with its compelling conception of the 'Renaissance man', and its all-embracing desire for the discovery of internal connections, has created a distorted picture of Alberti's treatise. A modern reader will know it as a succinct exposition of two or three central aesthetic doctrines, set in a discursive surround of myth, speculation and practical advice, and containing a striking, though not very accurate, account of the Roman Orders. In particular he will be familiar with Alberti's definition of beauty, and with the consequent attempt to separate beauty from ornament. He will also be acquainted with Alberti's Pythagorean reflections on proportion derived from a systematic analogy between architecture and music. And he will see these things as belonging with the centralized 'temple', with the self-conscious paganism, with the profuse respectful reference to every conceivable classical source—fragments of a total attitude of 'Renaissance humanism', the attitude which places man at the centre of the world and derives its idea of perfection from human capacities and the human form.

The picture is an appealing but also a misleading one. Taken in isolation, Alberti's definition of beauty as a harmony resulting from the organic relation of part to part, is presaged in many earlier works (see, for example, Dante, *Convivio*, 1, v). And the Pythagorean theory of proportion is perhaps the most 'medieval' feature of Alberti's thinking, exemplified equally in the systematic dimensions of the Gothic cathedrals, and exerting, through Christian neo-Platonism, a powerful influence on medieval art and literature. In fact, however, the Pythagorean theory does not occupy a truly central place in the philosophy of *De Re Aedificatoria*, despite Alberti's well-known disposition to describe architecture as though it were a kind of music. These mathematical speculations were not designed to show the real meaning of 'proportion', but rather to provide an *explanation* of something that must be described in other terms. The theory that agreeable proportions obey mathematical laws similar to those observed in musical harmony provides what Francesco di Giorgio called the hidden *ragione delle cose*: it does not *describe* what we see, but only explains its effect on us. It follows that we must try to define 'proportion' independently. That was one of the principal aims of Alberti's aesthetic speculations.

A study of Lücke's *Index* reveals that it is impossible to trace Alberti's concept of proportion to any single term (such as *proportio*) or to any group of directly related terms. The discussion of proportion involves the subtle and varied use of a complex vocabulary, of which the most famous term—the *concinnitas* which figures in Alberti's definition of beauty—is far from being the most important one. We find, for example, that the following terms take equal prominence in articulating that central aesthetic idea–*aptus, commodus, decens, dignus, integer, numerus, proprius* and many more—all of which import ideas of what is 'appropriate', 'measured' and 'correct'. These terms are used equally in the description of significant parts. Indeed it is clear that Alberti would not have countenanced any attempt to define proportion abstractly, or to separate it from the sense of appropriate detail. His own version of the Pythagorean theory is not to be understood outside the rules of the classical language which he adumbrated, and even when musical ratios are disobeyed, it is always possible that an apt deployment of detail will restore proportionality to the whole:

> If any wall is of exaggerated height, then attach to it a cornice, or paint it with dividing lines, in order to divide the height into more appropriate spaces *(aptis locis)*. And if a wall be too long, build columns reaching from top to bottom, not set too closely together, but well distanced, so as to obtain convenient points of repose, resulting in the least offensiveness from the excessive length.

It is clear, then, that Alberti regarded proportion in the same way as he regarded beauty, as a quality which could be understood and perceived only through a process of reflection in which the concepts of the 'appropriate' and the 'fitting' play the greatest role. He founded the art of architecture in the idea of a significant visual correspondence among parts. One might say that proportion is exhibited by a building whose parts (judged in terms of their shape and size rather than in terms of their ornamentation) provide adequate visual reason for one another. Our notion of proportion develops in answer to a certain visual application of the question 'Why?'—why this shape, why so tall, so wide, so long? The need to answer such questions led Alberti not in the direction of a mathematical canon of proportion (for that was a metaphysical afterthought) but rather towards a developed architectural language, rooted in a sense of apt and significant detail. The understanding of proportion and the understanding of detail are therefore complementary aspects of a single process of architectural perception.

To understand Alberti's view involves understanding the place of aesthetic reasoning in the activity of design (where design includes anything from the arranging of a dinner-table to the building of a town). Despite the enthusiastic propaganda of utilitarian and functionalist architects, most people recognize that only a very small fragment of practical thought is concerned with function. All our choices are extracted from a chaos of functionally equivalent alternatives, and in all choices which affect, not just present purposes, but also distant aspirations, it is the non-utilitarian residue that is paramount. To build well is to find the appropriate form, and that means the form which answers to what endures, not to what expires. The appropriate form ministers not just to present purposes, but to a sense of ourselves as creatures with identities transcending the sum of present purpose and desire. To find the appropriate form we must look beyond function, to some intimation of long-term satisfactions. And it is arguable that we can find that intimation only in the search for an appropriate and symbolic appearance. The pursuit of such appearances is the pursuit of a certain *style* of life; it is the pursuit of fulfilment not just for this or that desire, but for the self which survives them. Aesthetic education is therefore unavoidable: for it is the means to transform functional calculation into rational choice.

I have put the point in a somewhat Hegelian way, and that is certainly not the way of Alberti, whose cautious and fragmentary observations derive their meaning not from any over-arching system, but from specific concepts and specific habits of thought. It is useful in this respect to consider Alberti's definition of beauty, as a 'harmony *(concinnitas)* of parts, fitted together with just reflection in such a way that nothing could be added, diminished or altered but for the worse'. This definition is often treated as though it were intelligible alone. Alberti clearly did not think so, for he later returns to it, in order to explain the meaning of its constituent terms. *Concinnitas* is the origin of all that is graceful and decorous *(decus)*, and the sense of beauty is no more than a spontaneous application of our knowledge of what is 'appropriate' or 'fitting'; aesthetic reasoning consists in the intellectual structure which those concepts imply.

In its initial form, certainly, Alberti's explanation of beauty appears far from satisfactory. The phrase 'for the worse' naturally invites the question 'worse in what respect?', and if the answer is 'in respect of beauty' then the account is circular. Besides, is the 'organic' conception of beauty that underlies Alberti's definition really so very persuasive? The Doge's Palace in Venice could certainly be altered for the better, by bringing the windows on the lagoon into line (as was sometimes done in early engravings). But it is beautiful for all that.

However, Alberti was referring not to some definable *property* of beauty, but rather to the *sense* of beauty, and the thoughts and perceptions involved in the exercise of that sense. It may be that we *could* alter the Doge's Palace for the better; but to *see* it as beautiful, even in its present state, is to see an adequate correspondence of part to part, a harmony of detail, a visual completion that is *felt* as intrinsically correct.

The concept of beauty is thus absorbed into a certain pattern of reasoning, whose terms are at once intellectual and visual. As Alberti seemed to recognize, definitions in this area are never likely to succeed. What is important is to investigate aesthetic perception, and the reasoning intrinsic to it. And a proper understanding of aesthetic reasoning will put concepts like the 'appropriate' at its intellectual centre. But such concepts elude explicit definition. They seem to bear in themselves the subjectivity of their user, and indeed a philosopher might be tempted to seek for their true meaning, not in the properties of the object, but in the state of mind of the man who observes it. At the same time they contain an intimation of objectivity; as Alberti put it, the aesthetic judgment does not proceed from mere opinion, but from a rational faculty of the mind: *non opinio, verum animis innata quaedam ratio efficiet.*

The sense of beauty, therefore, is not separable from the reasoned discourse through which it is upheld. Once we recognize that, then we must be drawn, as Alberti was drawn, into the acceptance of some settled or 'classical' (by which I do not necessarily mean Greek or Roman) style. For the sense of the apt, appropriate or fitting appearance seeks naturally to root itself in some publicly accepted language of forms, and it is through such a language that we derive the principal basis for critical reflection. To think otherwise is to begin to divorce aesthetic choice from the rest of practical understanding, and so to present it as an isolated and irrational fragment whose significance could never be described. It is to make beauty, as one distinguished modern architect has put it, into a merely 'consequential' thing, a 'product of solving problems correctly'. And nobody with eyes can doubt that for architects to see beauty in such a way is (from the human point of view) usually disastrous.

It is inevitable, then, that Alberti's reflections should lead him towards the acceptance of a certain classical language of architecture, a set of repeatable answers to repeatable problems, a background of settled expectations and flexible rules. As he was well aware, however, the concepts used in describing architecture, while they serve to articulate this reasoned fitting of part to part, possess a detached and fluid quality, seeming to float free from any settled basis for their application. Instead of definitions, therefore, Alberti tried to present a *picture* of the place of reasoning in the judgment of buildings, a picture which shows reason directed not towards theoretical conclusions (such as the conclusions of the engineer), but towards a certain transformation of experience, a sense that a form or structure 'looks right'.

The purpose of such visual reasoning is not to lay down arbitrary laws, but to arrive at a notion of visual significance. The correspondence of part with part which Alberti described is also a correspondence of outer and inner, of building and observer. For the judgment of what is 'fitting' has its origin in us. It serves to transfer to the object the subjective demands of the man who studies it. Aesthetic judgment, and the classical style which he saw as embodying it, were for Alberti the means to effect what every architect should regard as his principal task, which is to work so that people will feel at home with the result, to build an objective and public representation of the movement of human life.

Nevertheless, the absence of explicit definitions and explanations may seem unsatisfactory to the modern reader. Terms like *aptus, decus, concinnitas,* and the mysterious *finitio* (usually associated, it seems, with *collocatio,* to indicate a kind of fine adapting of line to line) are far from self-explanatory. For one thing, the modern reader would wish to know whether these terms are made necessary primarily by the task which Alberti has set himself, of describing not only the construction of buildings but also the appearance which results from it.

But we find that we cannot easily answer such questions. At no point in the *De Re Aedificatoria* do we find a clear separation of terms, or a clear separation of problems, into the aesthetic and the functional. When, for example, Alberti describes the joining of lines and angles as being the most important and difficult of the architect's tasks, it is clear that he is referring to a problem that is at once one of construction and of apt appearance. No true understanding of what he means can be gained until it is seen how closely the two aspects of the problem constrain each other, and how the true solution will be intelligible only as a synthesis (and not a mere concatenation) of its component parts.

For Alberti the idea that there should be architecture on the one hand, conforming to aesthetic standards and setting itself the highest aims, and building on the other, a mere craftsman's activity, of no aesthetic consequence, designed simply to satisfy a function, that idea of a fundamental separation between building as art and building as craft, was wholly inimical to his way of thought. He therefore began his treatise by referring to a single universal art of building, 'which consists in the design *(lineamenta)* and in the structure'. 'The whole force and reason of the design', he continued, 'consist in an exact and correct way of adapting and joining together the lines and angles which serve to define the aspect of the building. It is the property and business of design to appoint to the edifice and all its parts an appropriate place, exact proportion, suitable disposition and harmonious order, in such a way that the form and appearance of the building be entirely implicit in the conception.' (Like many passages of a philosophical nature, this one is confusedly rendered by Leoni.)

Ideas of what is right, appropriate, proper, proportionable, determine from the beginning the direction of his thought. And yet at once he begins to write of the function of walls and apertures, the intricacies of roof construction, the effects of climate, sun and rain, and indeed occupies himself with practical matters throughout the first five books, passing unhesitatingly from the abstractions of the philosopher to the realities of the working engineer. A reading of Dr Lücke's *Index* shows, nevertheless, that the terms expressing notions of the appropriate and proportionable never cease to dominate his argument, and can seldom be tied to a specifically 'aesthetic' sense.

Indeed, it could be said that Alberti did not really recognize the existence of 'aesthetic' terms—each of his many articulations of aesthetic judgment employs terms which derive their meaning from a wider usage, indeed from the whole structure of practical reasoning. Even the *concinnitas* upon which he puts so much aesthetic emphasis had, for him, a significance that was primarily moral. (He had probably derived the term from Cicero's *Orator,* where it denotes a kind of sweetness and persuasiveness of sound, and used it in several early works, in particular in the *Della Famiglia,* to refer to the harmony and grace intrinsic to civilized behaviour.) It is this moral significance that Alberti sought to transfer to the aesthetic sphere. By thus always using terms which take their meaning from a wider usage, he was able to convey the continuity between aesthetic taste and practical reasoning, between the sense of how things should look and the judgment of how they should be.

The point was later made explicit by Daniele Barbaro (the friend for whom Palladio built the Villa at Maser), in his scholarly edition of Vitruvius. In discussing Vitruvius's six aesthetic categories *(ordinatio, dispositio, eurythmia, symmetria, decor, distributio)* Barbaro remarks that 'these terms are general and common and have their definition in the general and common science of metaphysics. But when an artist wants to apply one of these elements to his own profession, then he restricts that universality to the particular and special needs of his own art.' There is the true 'humanist' view of art, the view that the values pursued in art are not peculiar to it, but on the contrary bear an internal relation to the conceptions which determine all our thoughts and feelings.

The whole art of building, therefore, consists in the construction of an intelligible appearance, an appearance which in answering to the demands of the aesthetic sense, harmonizes with the rest of life. Alberti conveyed that view of aesthetic value, without losing sight of the realities of engineering and design. Moreover, his text reveals to us that classicism is not an *accidental* result of seeing aesthetic value in its true significance. The connection is both natural and reasonable.

To have arrived at such a conclusion without distortion or special pleading is a truly great achievement. For Alberti's account of architecture reflects a far deeper and truer understanding of the nature of aesthetic judgment, and of its place in everyday life, than do those of modern theorists, who either elevate function over every other value, or else attempt to attach the aesthetic sense to some clinical ideal of 'proportion' from which all reference to style, detail, ornament and language, in short all reference to anything that enables proportion to be *understood* as an aesthetic aim, has been excised. Used as we are to the megalomaniac rantings of the Modern Movement, to the scornful moralism of its theorists, and the crushing totalitarianism of its practitioners, the mildness and modesty of Alberti's discourse must strike us as truly astounding. It is indeed more like the language of a human being than that of an architect. And yet we know that Alberti was an architect, and also a very good one.

Moreover, the architecture which grew from his conceptions has proved satisfying and intelligible to almost everyone, from the first appearance of his book until the present century. It has flourished in varied circumstances, adapting itself to diverse political orders, religious creeds, economic systems and styles of life, without ever straying beyond the bounds of visual intelligibility. It is one of the greatest problems in architectural aesthetics to uncover the pattern of thought which made the classical tradition possible; now, with the help of Dr Lücke's *Index*, it will at least be possible to understand its finest intellectual flowering.

19   Adrian Stokes

The Image in Form: selected writings of Adrian Stokes, edited by Richard Wollheim (Penguin, 1972), from the *Spectator,* 5 August 1972.

ADRIAN STOKES published *The Quattro Cento* in 1932, and he has followed it with some sixteen slim volumes of ever more complex reflections on art. Both the content and the style of these works are extremely idiosyncratic, and it is hardly surprising that Stokes's influence has been confined to a small circle of initiates. Nonetheless his works are now becoming more widely known, and the present collection of extracts—skilfully selected by Richard Wollheim—is designed to meet this growing interest.

Stokes's criticism is founded on three enduring pre-occupations. First there is a Pater-like aestheticism, a concern for the subjective impressions aroused by art, which Stokes regards as a main task of his prose to capture. Hence the arch and contorted style, in which the grammatical elegance of Ruskin and Pater—from both of whom Stokes takes his inspiration—often gives way to a fulsome and boyish poetcizing ('The marriage of cylinder with square abides. Dressed stone is undressed stone that bathes. The dome feeds the sky . . . In front of Venetian palaces the pliant waters crowd.')

Secondly there is a profound self-absorption, a desire to nurse each fleeting impression and trace its origin, and an almost self-congratulatory pride in his own sensitivity to scenes and objects that others would regard with indifference. This feature, which finds expression in extensive passages of autobiography, does not degenerate into whimsy. For it is given substance by the third, and most striking of Stokes's peculiarities—his penchant for psychoanalysis of Melanie Klein's variety, and the consequent search in every object for its relation to the breast. The Kleinian mythology is invoked to give a more humane, more 'universal' appeal to otherwise private sentiments, and out of his mythology Stokes attempts to develop a complete theory of the creation and understanding of visual art. Art is seen as an instrument in the struggle against fantasy, a struggle on the part of both artist and spectator to overcome envy resentment and guilt, and to find himself once more in the presence of the 'good breast', both accepted and accepting in a world whose value he has measured and whose objectivity he has come to accept.

This doctrine takes a mystical turn in Stokes's writings, so much so that

148

it is not always possible to follow his train of thought, and even the frequent reference to examples ceases to be a help. When in the course of the Kleinian litany a work of art is mentioned it is likely to appear in a quite unrecognizable form, like a dream-apparition of itself, suggestive and disgusting:

> Rembrandt, it seems to me, painted the female nude as the sagging repository of jewels and dirt, of fabulous babies and magical faeces, despoiled yet later repaired and restored, a body often flaccid and creased yet still the desirable source of a scarred bounty: not the bounty of the perfected, stable breast housed in the temple of the integrated psyche that we possess in the rounded forms of classical art, but riches and drabness joined by the infant's interfering envy, sometimes with the character of an oppressive weight or listlessness left by his thefts.

The absurd effect of this passage is no doubt deliberate, and occasionally this kind of critical 'dream-work' can be strangely affecting, as in certain of the remarks on Turner and Giorgione. But more often the reader is puzzled. It is possible to understand the description of Rembrandt, and also to recognize the reference to psychoanalytical doctrines. But how are we to make sense of the suggestion that Rembrandt painted the female nude *as* all this, if we cannot *see* his nudes in this way? What we think of as the profundity in Rembrandt has been described in a manner that bears little relation to the appearance of his paintings. The psychoanalytic fantasies fail to take root in the aesthetic experience, and however hard one studies the paintings, the jewels, the faeces and the babies just obstinately refuse to appear.

However, Stokes aims to be more profound than this suggests. His main purpose is not to describe our experience of art but rather to explain it. He wishes to show why it is so powerful and why it is so valuable. He talks of individual works of art only to use them as examples for general and theoretical conceptions. This is most apparent in his studies of architecture. Architecture is unlike painting in that it does not represent things. If it moves us it is because of what it is, because of the forms, techniques and materials that it employs. How is this possible? This is the kind of question that interests Stokes, and it is perhaps not surprising that in attempting to answer it he comes to lean on the theories of psychoanalysis. Great architecture awakens profound emotions, and Stokes believes that profound emotion is necessarily unconscious emotion: what we know of our deeper feelings is no more than the tip of an iceberg. To discover the *true* effect of architecture is to discover the unconscious origin of the feelings that are awakened by it. If forms and materials are charged with emotion, it is because they remind us of fantasies with which our most elemental passions are linked. If the courtyard by

Laurana at Urbino has an atmosphere of sublime stillness, then it is not a thought of heaven that is responsible for this feeling, but a 'deeper' thought on which the vision of heaven itself is founded, namely the thought of the mother's breast.

If we are able to describe our experience of architecture in such terms, then Stokes seems to think that we will have said something about its importance. The traditional vapourings about peace, harmony and beauty will no longer be essential. Indeed Stokes goes on to draw vast but not wholly surprising conclusions about the value of art: art is a therapy for the disintegrated ego. But what do we gain by thinking of visual art in this way? For all his intelligence Stokes is unable to give more than very general sketches of the feelings aroused by architecture. The house is a womb; it is 'our upright bodies built cell by cell;' a ledge is the foot, the knee and the brow. The smooth wall is a source of health, being the 'good breast' that we wish to appropriate as a source of our own goodness; the wall pierced with apertures is the 'bad breast' that we have torn open with our vengeful teeth; and so on. The building as a whole transmutes our frenzied longing for 'part-objects' by presenting an image of the whole— the loved and hated attributes united in a single object. And so beauty is 'a sense of wholeness.'

Such a description of the effects of architecture tells us nothing that we wished to know. It is a description of the unconscious sources of our feelings towards art and even if it were both meaningful and true, it would still be irrelevant to our enjoyment of individual works. If we wish to know why Laurana's courtyard awakens such powerful feelings, then it does not help to be told of some emotion of which we are unaware, and which is in any case inspired by every great work of architecture. We do not wish to be told of some emotion that is so general that it becomes detached from the particular building that interests us. The fact is that Stokes has not explained the *appreciation* of architecture at all. For if the unconscious impulses to which he refers are the true source of our enjoyment, why should we ever wish to visit a building that we had not seen before? Why should we not remain content with what we already had? The fact is that the emotions aroused by buildings are conscious, even though they may be difficult to describe.

It is for this reason that the constant tendency of Stokes's writing is to penetrate beyond works of art, to the materials and methods out of which they are formed. In particular he has much to say about the love of stone—why stone and particular ways of treating stone should have acquired the importance that they have. The predilection for dichotomies that he derives from Kleinian psychology encourages him to reconstruct one of the classical distinctions in the theory of sculpture— the distinction between carving and modelling. Each of these he equates with a separate attitude to stone (and, at a further remove, with a separate psychological 'position' towards the mother). The details of this theory are more interesting; nor is it the only successful part of Stokes's enterprise. In his study of Michelangelo, for example, and in his remarks on Donatello, he writes lucidly and elegantly, the psychoanalytic obsession is played over in a lower key, and the argument is easy to follow.

But all too often Stokes's sensitive perceptions remain crushed beneath an immovable apparatus of psychoanalytical theory. Freud set the precedent for this kind of discussion of art in his study of Leonardo. Since then there have been Freudian and Jungian analyses of everything from Sophocles to Wagner. And naturally art, like any other human product, is open to this kind of interpretation. But where do the conclusions of analysis make contact with our conscious enjoyment of art? Perhaps there is an answer to this question, but until it is produced the work of a writer like Stokes—who combines an extreme subjectivity of response with an allegiance to one of the most eccentric schools of psychoanalysis—will be impossible to evaluate.

20   Buckminster Fuller

From *Cambridge Review*, 10 June 1977.

THE RELIGION of Progress, which still survives in the popular imagination and in the minds of architects, is a strange one, having neither form nor ceremony, and requiring of its believers little besides a deep distrust of custom and a faith in things to come. It encourages belief both in 'history' and in 'evolution', yet its liturgy derives not so much from Marx and Spencer as from popular science, H. G. Wells, and *Boys' Own* magazine. Despite this amateurish quality, Progressivism is strikingly fanatical: no action performed in its name can be wrong, and no one opposed to it can be heard with respect. Should a believer be thwarted—as Le Corbusier was thwarted in his plans for the enlightened demolition of Paris, Stockholm and Algiers—this shows only that he was 'born before his time', it being in any case a sin to be born after one's time and of little merit to be exactly contemporaneous with it. Like all the saints of Progress, Le Corbusier possessed an infectious optimism and a childlike tenacity of purpose. In the world of architecture his crazed scribblings now have the character of sacred texts. The same is true of the most comic of all progressive thinkers, the inventor, architect, engineer, poet, philosopher, scientist and 'world-redesigner', Buckminster Fuller ('Bucky' as he is known in the architectural world).

Taking advantage of the discoveries of modern science (in particular of the magical formula, variously interpreted according to need and circumstance, $E = mc^2$), Fuller has consecrated his life to his fellow men, conferring on them, to their inestimable advantage, the dymaxion house (some examples of which exist), the geodesic dome (to be found at international exhibitions and in the Garden of Scroope Terrace, Cambridge), and the World Town Plan (which has yet to be realized). For these inventions Fuller was awarded the RIBA's gold medal in the year of grace 1968. His generous devotion to mankind is, he assures us, inescapably forced upon him. An exhaustive study of the first thirty-two years of his life revealed to him that

> I was positively effective in producing wealth only when I was dedicated to others. Further . . . observation then showed that the larger the number for whom I worked the more positively effective I became. Thus it became obvious . . . that if I worked for all humanity I would be optimally effective.

Having come to that conclusion Fuller had no option but to draw attention to himself in every available way. And the euphoria which he has expressed through his 'world redesigning stratagems' is matched only by that of others' belief in him. He has designed domes for exhibitions, campuses, and private back-gardens; he has often travelled around the world, lecturing and demonstrating his inventions; he has held chairs at many institutions, including the Charles Eliot Norton Chair of Poetry at Harvard; he has inaugurated on Cyprus (in the company of the World Academy of Art and Science and Archbishop Makarios) the 'World Man Territory Trusteeship', and indeed, in every fantasy that he contrives he seems never short of an audience. Nevertheless, Fuller still finds cause to regret the absence of that total commitment to Progress, and the Future and himself which history requires of us. As he puts it, in the poetic vein for which he is so famous:

> Reflex-conditioned society, facing exclusively towards its past, backs up into its future, often bumping its rump painfully but uncomprehendingly against the wealth coffers of its future years' vastly multiplying capability to favourably control its own ecological evolution and the latter's *freedom-multiplying* devices. (Fuller's italics).

But if the world has been slow to realize Fuller's plans for it, the plans themselves have been accepted in many quarters as having an authority equivalent to divine revelation. 'I seek', he declares, 'to reform the environment instead of trying to reform men'. He has therefore redesigned the world (or 'spaceship earth' as he prefers to call it) in the form of a single town, which will carry its human contents in a perfectly controlled environment through the ceaseless whirl of the cosmos, untroubled by crime or revolution, undarkened by superstition, history or guilt. In his own words, he has designed:

> ... a mechanized human container service, purveying to you a controlled atmosphere of seventeen cubic feet of air per minute per person, free of toxic or disagreeable odours and dust, at a dry bulb temperature of 74 degrees Fahrenheit, relative humidity 45%, wet bulb temperature of 60.5 degrees Fahrenheit, dew point 51.3 degrees Fahrenheit, vapour pressure 0.01869 pounds per square inch, with reasonable plus or minus controls, with a noise level below the audible threshold, and with every essential refreshing and resting and sensing (illumination etc.) device necessary to your happy wellbeing ready to hand.

In this brave new world there will be no need for law courts and policemen; as he puts it: '... if you don't play ball, the service is "shut off" — engineering simplicity replacing legal complexity'. Everybody can communicate with everyone else by means of a 'portable radio transceiver set', and all men will participate in the 'complete set of ever-advancing

standard-of-living conditions, whether you be speeding, poised, lingering or dwelling, upon the service of the dry land, the high seas, the steam-
ing tropic, on the fly-teeming Arctic tundra, on floating ice, high in the
sky, on a mountain top, under the sea, or within the depths of the earth'.
Each man's dwelling is to be collapsible and transportable, and the individual will carry along with it his 'personal luggage, tool kit, files and display miscellany'. Anything not comprehended in that 'will be
expediently deposited in, or loaned or donated to, vaults or public
collections without loss of access on the one hand and with increased
public enjoyment on the other, while at the same time freeing the individual to enjoy his world-girdling freedom of motion and poise'. And so
on. Lest anyone should fear that he might be beset in such an arrangement by some crippling nostalgia for a chaotic and disordered way of
things, he need not fear for his sanity. Fuller reassures us that 'the degree
of probability of the inherent sanity in the individual is proportional to
the degree of maintenance of inherent sanitation in the environment', so
that a dependence on religion, for example, can be rendered quite
unnecessary by 'shower baths, sulfa compounds, steri-lamps, radio-
summoned air ambulances and scientifically cooperative blood banks'.
As for the human yearning for a sense of history (revealed, apparently, by
the continuing sale of Bibles and World Almanacs), this will be better
satisfied in the future world, for everyone will have access to
computerized data-banks containing all historical facts.

It is clear that the naivety of all this goes beyond what is strictly
required by the religion of Progress. It is worth reflecting, therefore, on
why Fuller's works should have been taken so seriously, why Reyner
Banham, for example, should have described Fuller's writings as 'one of
the great mind-changing documents of the century'. It can hardly be the
titles of Fuller's works that have commended them to the purveyors of
fashion, titles as clumsy and unmeaning as 'No More Second-hand God',
and 'Seven Chains to the Moon'. Nor does the pseudo-scientific rhetoric
count for very much. It requires little knowledge of physics to recognize
the muddle in the view that Einstein 'chose speed as an absolute' and
'identified the universe with absolute energy E'. This is how Fuller
expressed Einstein's criterion of simultaneity (which determines the constancy of the speed of light), and his law of conservation (which determines the constancy of mass-energy in physical change). Fuller's half-
comprehended speculations arise from a sense of the absolute value of
energy, speed, and change; and he imagines that modern physics somehow confirms this sense, and misreads it accordingly. But it is doubtful
that anyone, even if he be so entirely bewildered by technicalities as to
think that his 'mind' is being 'changed' by Fuller's jargon, will take
seriously the idea of man's 'trend towards an ever-increasing mastery of
the affairs of energy or absolute speed', a trend which enables Fuller to
plot the curve of all man's future movements:

... Such a curve (to be employed for politico-economic navigation) would identify any point in man's affairs upon the over-all curve of transition from the limbo of absolute ignorance of universe towards (and only towards) absolute knowledge and mastery of universe, the universe identified by Einstein as absolute energy—'E'.

Such passages reveal how little there is in Fuller's writings of serious understanding, and how much of half-digested jargon, picked up from the 'frontiers' of science, and used to express a Panglossian optimism that is fundamentally hostile to critical thought. It is hard to imagine what extremes of gullibility would be necessary to feel a 'mind-changing' force in that.

There is, however, a more important idea to which Fuller's pioneering spirit leads him, an idea which perhaps only Americans have been able to experience, as it has to be experienced, with the full force of moral revelation. Indeed, if someone with a mind like Fuller's could be said to have an intellectual ancestry, it is to be found in that tradition which began with Walt Whitman's 'Song of Myself', and which holds on to the dream of a New World in the face of all opposing experience by postulating the 'Self' and its 'liberation' as the true end of man. This view of things is something more than mere individualism. In Whitman and Ginsberg it has an hysterical quality, like the wild joy of a child, which suggests that in the midst of all this 'liberation' there is an unconscious yearning for a strong parental hand. Fuller's writings exhibit the same hysterical megalomania, divorced from the poetic expression which makes it not merely infectious but also plausible. Fuller's world will be packed with 'freedom multiplying devices'; on it, man will be free (as the cant expression has it) to 'realize his potentialities'. And the whole rhetorical force of Fuller's pseudo-scientistic invocations is to give euphoric expression to that liberationist ideal.

Now, the notion of an ideal freedom in which no history, society, or custom is presupposed—a freedom of the pure unencumbered Self—is of course one of the most powerful among received ideas. It has been appropriated not only by the advocates of 'existential psychotherapy' and 'authentic choice' but also by forward-looking clergymen, educationalists, and even certain sections of the Tory party. The incoherence of the idea has often been commented upon. One cannot sever a man from the historical forces which have shaped his identity—placing him in a world of endless random movement, with no sense of place, time, history or custom—one cannot do that and still expect him to have a 'self' to be 'liberated', still expect him to be the kind of creature for whom freedom is a value and not a source of fear. The incoherence of the idea lies not so much in its conception of freedom, as in the naive presuppositions about the 'Self' on which it is based. The self is a social product, and to remove all hardship and opposition, all need of fellowship and custom, is to bring about not self-freedom but self-dissipation. And in the megalomania of Whitman and Ginsberg one sees, of course, not the liberation of the self, but its dissolution into unmeaning fragments.

In considering Fuller, however, it is not so much the incoherence of the ideal which is at issue, as its blatant contradiction with the underlying plan. It requires little insight to see through Fuller's mask of 'liberation' to an absolutist and totalitarian ambition, an ambition which recognizes no serious opponent, having placed history on its side. Being identified with 'progress', Fuller can ignore all those who attempt to stand in his way: rival ideas are simply outdated, unscientific and reactionary. It is this thought which gives to the ethic of progress its peculiar charm, its quasi-religious authority free from the discipline of humility which other religions demand. In Fuller's world there is no real freedom, only a perpetual hallucination of freedom, meted out daily by the central authorities to those who agree to 'play ball'.

Of course, the cult of Fuller is essentially ephemeral; there are signs that it has already entered its decline. The geodesic dome at Scroope Terrace—for all its ostensible purposefulness—now has the dusty abandoned air of a shrine to forgotten gods. The World Town Plan has encountered difficulties; Fuller himself has retired to a Professorial sinecure at the University of Illinois, and his books are now more often to be seen on the unexplored shelves of expensive polytechnics than in the hands of university dons. But it is precisely through his ephemeral nature that Fuller hoped to make his most lasting contribution to science. In 1917 he decided, as he put it, to 'contribute to the scientific documentation of the emergent realization of the *era of accelerating-acceleration of progressive ephemeralization*'. (B.F.'s italics). He therefore constructed a chronological inventory of all references to himself. His motive was of course not passionate egomania, but the same desire to serve mankind and science that has motivated all his other work. To prove his good faith he even presented the 'Dymaxion Chronofile' to the Southern Illinois University, who now house it in a special room. In 1967 it comprised 250 volumes containing about 80,000 letters. A copy of the present article will be sent to the librarian, in order to encourage his teleologic preoccupations. I use the word 'teleologic' in the sense given to it by the poet, scientist, engineer, mathematician, designer and first-hand god Buckminster Fuller, namely:

> the subjective-to-objective, intermittent, only-spontaneous, borderline-conscious, and within-self communicating system that distills equatable principles—characterizing relative behaviour patterns—from our pluralities of matching experiences; and reintegrates selections from those net generalized principles into unique experimental control patterns—physically detached from self—as instruments. . . .

21 Morality and Architecture

Morality and Architecture, David Watkin (Clarendon Press, 1977) and *The Rise of Architectural History,* from *Encounter,* November 1978, and the *Cambridge Review,* 1981.

I

DAVID WATKIN's *Morality and Architecture* has derived a certain *succès de scandale,* not from its underlying conceptions (familiar already in the work of Sir Karl Popper, Geoffrey Scott, and Sir Herbert Butterfield) but from its striking historical perspective. With rare insight and directness, Watkin describes the single spiritual force which leads from the moralism of Pugin and Viollet-le-Duc, through the hysteria of Giedion, Taut and Le Corbusier, to the recent crusade against every style of architecture that rejects the forms of the Modern Movement, and hence 'the spirit of the age', the *Zeitgeist,* which is supposed to have required them.

The book is short, sharp and to the point, singling out, as principal object of attack, Sir Nikolaus Pevsner (whom the author also praises for the many aspects of his work that do not require the didactic commitment of *Pioneers of Modern Design*). Those of Watkin's critics who seem unable to grasp the proper nature of intellectual debate have construed the discussion on a personal level. But Watkin's victims are subject to no personal abuse, being criticized, and sometimes ridiculed, only when their writings seem ridiculous or wrong. Of course, to know that Reyner Banham and Charles Jencks have condemned the book, while Osbert Lancaster and John Betjeman have praised it, is already to have a fairly clear idea of its ideological tone. Watkin has a steady aim, and an inquisitorial style, and these will prove highly offensive to those for whom the ravings of Le Corbusier constitute a serious mode of architectural reflection, as well as to many more sensible men, for whom the stylistic changes of the 1920s and '30s seemed to be the necessary outcome of changes in the eye, mind and soul of 20th-century man.

Nevertheless, *Morality and Architecture* should not be read as an attack on the Modern Movement. The author is concerned not with modern architecture, but with the apologetic of which it has stood in need. Watkin discusses the handful of doctrines through which the Modern Movement has been able to convert itself from an aesthetic enterprise into a moral and political crusade. He argues that the ideology of the move-

157

ment has been largely materialistic, secular, and egalitarian; it has been against style, ornament, excess, and grandeur; it has been in favour of the collectivity against personal imagination, of historical force against individual will, of the socialist millennium against privilege, patronage and class. (And all this is explicitly reaffirmed by one of Watkin's angry modernist critics—Kenneth Campbell, former housing architect to the London County Council and Greater London Council—in the *Architectural Review* for February 1978.) Nevertheles, in seeking to translate that ideology into architectural form, the Modern Movement has relied on arguments that were used as much by Pugin in his polemics on behalf of a 'Christian' architecture, as by the eggheads of the Bauhaus, for whom cleanliness and not godliness had to be first in a builder's thoughts. For 150 years the same collection of fallacies has been invoked to provide each succeeding style, or lack of style, with an appropriate dressing of necessity.

Watkin writes at a considerable distance from the ideological conflicts of the '20s and '30s, and he can no more be blamed than the rest of his generation if he fails to admire the baggage of egalitarianism placed on the public market in those years. Nor can he be blamed if he rejects the attitude that has sought for progress and novelty in everything, even in art, which, because it values not novelty but originality, is necessarily among the most backward-looking of human enterprises. The tone of *Morality and Architecture* will come as no surprise to any member of the generation that has witnessed universal desecration in the name of progress, justice, and artistic truth. Why, then, should Sir John Betjeman call Watkin's tract 'a brave and lonely book'? Certainly there have been reviewers whose hostility might seem to justify the remark. Reyner Banham (*Times Literary Supplement*, 17 February 1978) attributes to Watkin the kind of vindictiveness 'of which only Christians seem capable' (a view which sheds surprising light on Banham's own religious views), while Richard Wollheim (*Architectural Review*, February 1978) regards the welcome given to *Morality and Architecture* as yet one more sign of the poverty of architectural theory, resolving his seemingly ambivalent and circumlocutory review on a sudden note of passionate distaste. But these reactions—while being those of an established intelligentsia—are untypical. The book has indeed been welcomed, and sometimes with an enthusiasm as intemperate as Banham's and Wollheim's abuse. It is somewhat odd, therefore, that neither side has seen fit to discuss the central argument.

Watkin asserts that a long tradition of fallacious reasoning has not only obscured the true nature of aesthetic judgment, but also has made possible the wholesale subjection of architectural values to the exigencies of moral or political thinking, often by practical men, for whom thinking of any kind is a mistake. (And if Watkin singles out Pevsner as his principal target, it is surely because Pevsner is a thinker, and not just a jobbing builder with an eye for the market.) Architecture, Watkin claims, is an autonomous enterprise, in which individual taste and cultural tradition are the major legitimate guides; the attempt to reduce architecture to a by-product of social need, or of historical force, or of the *Zeitgeist;* the attempt to see it only as a moral or political instrument—all these are ways of denying to architecture its essential nature as a decorative art.

As a diagnosis of a curious episode in intellectual history, *Morality and Architecture* is persuasive and highly entertaining. But some of its admirers, grateful for a book ʰthat pours scorn on the gibberish of modernism, have sought for more in Watkin's pages than the historical vision which they contain. Thus Paul Johnson, writing in The *Daily Telegraph* (17 December 1977), declares that 'all sensible and sensitive people know that modern architecture is bad and horrible, almost without exception. Mr Watkin explains why.' But how can fallacies in the theory of modern architecture explain the disaster of its practice, when the same fallacies were invoked in support of the highly successful styles of the Gothic revival? Watkin's opponents have also taken him to be writing, not of the history of architectural dogma, but rather of the relation between theory and practice. Much of Wollheim's antipathy rests on the assumption that Watkin is out of sympathy with the stylistic changes of the '20s, and that he has no sense—as Wollheim puts it—of the 'tiredness' of styles. But surely the first of these accusations is entirely irrelevant, even for someone who can muster the kind of sympathy for the 'international style' that Wollheim intimates.

The second of Wollheim's accusations is, however, more interesting, in that it betrays a lingering attachment to one of the theories that Watkin attacks, the theory that an architect is compelled to be 'of his time' in some way beyond the mere fact of living in it. Styles suddenly become 'tired', and hence unavailable to the architect who wishes to maintain his status as a modern man. The trouble with such a view is not that it is false, but rather, as Watkin points out, that there is no way in which an artist can be seriously influenced by it. Suppose the Gothic style really was 'tired' when Pugin, Butterfield and their predecessors revived it. Should that have deterred them? And should it deter the builders at Bury St Edmunds and Lancing College? Moreover, how can we say that the classical tradition was 'tired' when the Modern Movement set out to destroy it? It is certainly not exhaustion that we witness in the exuberant classicism of the Edwardians, in the proud city palaces of Fleet Street and Piccadilly. We may see bad taste here, but we can see no exhaustion comparable to the dismal emptiness of the *ville radieuse* and all that it engendered. Something is wrong if we see only 'tiredness' in the Edwardian style, and 'freshness and youth' in the sterile forms that were engineered to replace it.

But to the point: sensible and sensitive men no more say that *all* modern architecture is horrible than that all preceding architecture was good. The trouble is that in architecture the rewards are vast and multifarious, and the desire to obtain will always exceed the power to justify. The enthusiasm that surrounded the death of style in architecture made it inevitable that there should be no serious consideration given to the arguments of those who had signed its death warrant. As Watkin's polemic shows, the question of the nature of architecture is rich and complex; at the same time, every unscrupulous intellectual trick has been used to simplify it, so as to represent the 'international' style as historically, socially, politically, morally and technologically necessary.

It becomes apparent that for 150 years stylistic changes have sought to justify themselves, and to justify themselves in identical, or closely related, terms. Besides establishing this important historical conclusion, Watkin also hints at his own aesthetic position, a position which involves a defence of the autonomy of aesthetic values. In a brief and unfriendly review (*RIBA Journal*, February 1978), Lord Esher pointed out that the case for the autonomy of architecture had been effectively put by Geoffrey Scott (in *The Architecture of Humanism*, a finely written book that deserved to have more influence on the thought of the '20s than the *Zeitgeist* would permit). However, this similarity with Scott ought not to be regarded as a defect; the doctrine of the autonomy of aesthetic values is essentially rhetorical, a question of emphasis. It must be put afresh for every generation in the language most suited to the time. Modern students of architecture will be grateful for a renewed statement of the position, a statement that chooses as its principal target, not the romanticism of the late Gothic Revival, but the more deadly spirit of comprehensive development, urban renewal, the technological revolution, and, as its crowning aesthetic embodiment, the Festival of Britain.

But their gratitude will also go to show that the arguments are not all on the side of Scott and Watkin. If you hate those things, then it *is* partly because of their moral and political meaning; the ugliness of the Smithsons' project at the Elephant and Castle is not separable from the contemptuous conception of life's value that it conveys. It is important, therefore, to try to see behind the high-toned irony with which Watkin presents his opponents' dogmas to the real intellectual issues upon which he too must take a stand.

So far as I can see, there are two issues, intimately connected. First, there is the issue which focuses on the term 'historicism' (used one way by Popper, another by Pevsner); secondly there is the issue just mentioned, the autonomy of aesthetic values. In discussing the first of these, Watkin persuasively argues that the Hegelian view of history, which has been so important an instrument of architectural criticism, has been also applied as a rule of practice, in which sphere it is strictly nonsensical.

Giedion, Pevsner, and many others have all argued that the spirit of the age, being compelled by all that preceded it and propelled towards its *Aufhebung* in the world to come, must dictate the forms of architecture, making it impossible, retrograde or dishonest to build in the manner of the past. That view relies on a discredited notion of history. It is also necessarily selective. (How, Watkin asks, do we *know* that Gropius was essential and Lutyens only accidental to the spirit of the time which fostered both of them?). Moreover, the view has the stunning consequence that all Western architecture, from the Romans to the Edwardians could not, or should not, have happened.

Nevertheless, for all its exaggeration, the Hegelian view of history has a legitimate critical use. (It would now be difficult to discard the Hegelian distinction between Renaissance and Baroque, however much one may wish to qualify it.) Perhaps Watkin, like Popper and Gombrich, does not sufficiently appreciate this fact, or sufficiently acknowledge its intellectual implications. But for Watkin the really obnoxious feature of the view is not the possibility of its legislative (as opposed to its critical) employment, but its almost inevitable degeneration into 'progressivism'—into the view that the movement of history is necessarily *forward,* from worse to better. Following Sir Herbert Butterfield, Watkin castigates this outlook as the 'Whig view of history.' The concept is a crude one, partly because of the crudeness of what it describes, but also because discussion of these issues requires more serious consideration of what 'better' and 'worse' consist in than was ever to be heard in the Smoking Room of the Reform Club (incidentally, one of London's greatest, and most thoroughly backward-looking, classical buildings). As a rhetorical instrument, Butterfield's label is effective, but blunt; Watkin's ironical tone would have benefited, perhaps, from the use of something finer. Applied to the doctrines of national and international socialism, as these became entangled with the apologetic of modern architecture, the 'Whig view of history' begins to obscure as much as it clarifies. Can we really believe that the mad rationalism of the Jacobins, the evolutionism of Spencer, the dialectical materialism of Engels and Lenin are all adequately subsumed under a label invented to ridicule an English aristocratic faction? This is not to reject the truth of what Watkin means, but rather the over-schematic way in which he displays it.

More importantly, there are attitudes which no one could describe as 'progressivist' and yet which cannot be characterized in terms of the parochial conceptions of Whiggery. Consider the architects of the Italian Renaissance. They worked within and towards a tradition, with their minds firmly fixed on a classical ideal. At the same time they worked in a spirit of improvement, a spirit to which Hegelians have rightly attributed a world-historical significance, compelled towards a new architecture by self-conscious spiritual change. The Renaissance architect did not articulate this change as we (with hindsight) would articulate it, and it is true, as Watkin points out, that the distinction between the Renaissance and the Medieval attitude to building has often been grossly exaggerated. Nevertheless, one could not characterize Brunelleschi's artistic intention if one did not recognize that his style was seen as an improvement, consonant with the social, moral and intellectual changes among which it was conceived. Clearly, criticism of such a style will require sharper distinctions than that between, on the one hand, the Whig view of history, and, on the other, the respect for tradition, custom and individual will.

As Watkin demonstrates, the *Zeitgeist* enthusiasts of our time, in so far as they have inspired and justified the forms of modern architecture, have usually done so out of strong political convictions. Watkin refers to these convictions dismissively and briefly, using the word 'collectivist' many times, and always as though it had a clear political meaning. Since the reference to these political attitudes is not intended to preface any full analysis of them (Watkin's contention being that politics is one thing, architecture another), the argument comes to rest on the second major assumption, the assumption of the autonomy of aesthetic values.

One of the many virtues of Watkin's book is that it shows how difficult it is either to affirm or to deny this assumption, particularly when considering the useful and decorative arts. How far can one separate those aesthetic values which Watkin assigns to 'taste', 'tradition', and 'the way it looks' from the moral, political and functional considerations which animate the architect and his public? Watkin argues pithily against what Scott called 'the ethical fallacy', and against every other view which seeks to explain architecture away, as a means to an end, or as a byproduct of some independent force or interest. Wisely, however, he refrains from providing an aesthetic theory of his own. Scott's attempt—a messy concoction out of bygone psychology—provides the weakest chapter in his brilliant essay. But Scott's failure is a necessary result of the obscurity in the doctrine of aesthetic autonomy, a doctrine whose value will always be more rhetorical than intellectual. While Watkin is right to insist that one cannot pass from moral maxims to clear aesthetic rules, he cannot be right if he thinks that there is *no* connection between these things. How else can one explain his own (and Paul Johnson's) anger at the Modern Movement? The reader is left, then, with an intellectual puzzle, and Watkin's effective dismissal of a tradition of nonsense still does not solve the puzzle which served to generate it.

The lesson of Watkin's book deserves to be absorbed, not only by students of architecture, but by everyone interested in the *Zeitgeist* in its surprising most recent form. Here is a young man writing intelligently and perceptively about architectural theory; and the spirit which he expresses is high-toned and élitist, as contemptuous of fashion as it is respectful towards 'tradition and the individual talent.' If this is the *Zeitgeist*, then the established pundits of architectural theory must look forward to an early overthrow. And I doubt that many will mind.

II

In *The Rise of Architectural History*, David Watkin presents a succinct and scholarly survey of the history of the history of architecture, from its beginnings in the writings of the baroque architect J. B. Fischer von Erlach, to its most recent manifestations, in Anglo-Saxon universities, in conservation societies, in private connoisseurship and public allegiance to the National Trust. The subject is vast, and could be treated shortly in one of two ways: either as an independent essay in cultural history (of which architectural history is a part), tracing main currents and demonstrating their spiritual unity; or as an annotated catalogue of writings, guiding the reader to a literature that is left to speak for itself. Dr Watkin adopts the second method, although he enlivens his *bibliographie raisonnée* with interesting, sometimes curious, and usually pertinent observations. The author of *Morality and Architecture* here appears in conciliatory guise. He does not permit himself the rhetorical verve and irreverence of the previous work, writing instead as though his quarrel with the moralists of modernism were over, and the time were come to take an Olympian stance. His erudition must surely convince his opponents that they, like himself, can be seen from a standpoint above and beyond their passing quarrel, and, were Watkin as wise an historian as he is an able critic and polemicist, this book, by transcending their quarrel, would also resolve it. However, its bibliographical character forbids the perspective from which this or any other controversy can be viewed with either clarity or detachment. There are rewarding passages of exegesis and genuine historical insights. But the mass of compressed detail makes it hard to identify quite what the subject is which this book chronicles, and which Watkin professes.

The best chapters deal with the early attempts at architectural history in Germany and France. Here the landscape is clear, and the traveller's vision unencumbered. By the time we are in England and the nineteenth century, we are forced to run through the unpatterned suburbia of architectural polemic, with the occasional glimpse of a spire or portico to guide us. When at last we confront the great intellectual edifice of Ruskin we are hurried onwards, not because Watkin under-estimates Ruskin's genius, but because there are other writers crowding into consciousness who may not merit three stars, but perhaps ought to be granted one or two. Scholars will be grateful, for it is as important that architectural history should be noted down and documented, as it is that historical buildings, however minor, should be accurately surveyed. For Watkin, indeed, the analogy is especially apt. As he shows, the rise of architectural history in England has been contemporaneous with the rise of conservation. And the values of each of those activities have profoundly polluted those of the other, so introducing into English architectural history a spirit that is at once amateurish and aggrieved. By a miraculous transformation this spirit can express itself in profound observation of detail and high moral seriousness. So it was with Ruskin. It can also find its level among the cranks and pamphleteers of the tourist classes. But whatever the similarities, there is the greatest intellectual difference between these two phenomena, a difference that history, but not bibliography, can reveal.

It is curious that there should be an academic subject called architectural history, originating in the idiosyncrasies to which Watkin draws our attention and now held in such great intellectual esteem. What made this possible? Watkin writes vividly of Hegel and historicism; and his fervent hostility to the idea of the *Zeitgeist* must inevitably awaken some residual sympathy towards it. While Watkin is right in condemning the use of this concept by the apologists of bad architecture, his own frankness of expression makes it abundantly clear that he has no rival concept to offer with which to provide either an explanation or an excuse for his subject. As he recognizes, without the German tradition of *Kulturgeschichte,* and the Hegelian philosophy which inspired it, his subject would be as formless as it was in Pugin's time—say—or 'Women's Studies' is today. Architectural history cannot now be studied except in the terms laid down for it by Burckhardt, Wölfflin and Wittkower. One may retain the passion of Ruskin, but only on condition that one subjects it to the discipline of which the Warburg Library is the living symbol. This discipline is deferred to in everything that is now written on the history of architecture, and is conveyed in large doses to the ordinary citizen, as he staggers about the countryside with his Pevsner in his hand. The old English eccentricities survive. But even fashion-mongers in the style of Charles Jencks prefer to call themselves 'cultural historians'. How else, after all, can they play the game of 'style' and 'period'? 'Post-modernism' (the latest label) could never have been considered to be either a significant style or a significant period, were it not for the Hegelian supposition that what is happening in architecture exhibits some deep connection with what is happening everywhere.

Having demonstrated that it was the Germans who brought order to our native insolence, Watkin leaves us with an intellectual problem. How can there *be* such a subject as architectural history? Is it a branch of history? Or a branch of criticism? Or both? The myth of the *Zeitgeist* has caused as much confusion in the theory of architecture as disaster in its practice. But what happens to Watkin's subject when you take that myth away?

Architectural history becomes an intellectual discipline only when it is granted some capacity to abstract from particulars. Otherwise a student of the subject would be better employed with a sketchbook than with an historical text. This abstraction can proceed in one of two ways: according to style or according to period. The first method introduces classifications like 'mannerism', 'baroque', 'neo-classicism'; the second introduces 'medieval', 'Renaissance' and 'Post-industrial'. The master-thought of German idealism is that, with insight, the classifications generated by the first method will coincide with those generated by the second. And this will provide our test of a genuine, as opposed to an arbitrary, class. The class will be genuine since it will have the power to *explain* something. To describe a building as baroque will be to tell us *why* it looks as it does, and not just *that* it does. Hence, if there is a method, a discipline, a practice, that can train the eye and the mind in such classifications, there will be a true subject of architectural history. Otherwise, there may be chronology, there may be criticism, there may be anecdote, but there will be nothing that deserves the name of history.

Moreover, the classifications of the architectural historian aim at, even if they do not always achieve, a certain generality. 'Mannerism' seems intellectually respectable to the extent that it identifies, first a common property of more than one artist, secondly, a common property of more than one art. The intellectual imperialism of *Kulturgeschichte* attempted to establish these conceptual beachheads in all territories at once. It failed to demonstrate that Mozart's music should be described as 'rococo'. But it succeeded triumphantly with its distinction between Renaissance and Baroque, generating historical and critical insights that no student of architecture can now ignore.

The form of stylistic and historical analysis introduced by Winckelmann and theorized by Hegel is therefore still the basis of architectural history. We may try to separate the description of style from the description of period, but we soon find that it is very difficult to do this without losing all ability to describe the 'spirit' which is common to both, and the primary object of our intellectual interest. If we concede this then we concede too that architectural history has no true autonomy: at best it forms part of that larger discipline—art history—which, Watkin rightly observes, is one of the most remarkable creations of modern education.

Humanities, like sciences, may arise overnight and disappear on the morrow. How is it that this one, which takes so many of its credentials from an outrageous metaphysical doctrine, has managed not only to survive but also to establish itself as one of the most respectable of university subjects? I feel that there ought to be an answer to this question, and am grateful to Watkin for raising it so vividly. Had he said more about the pedagogic influences bequeathed by Aby Warburg to our nation, then he might have cast more light on it. One may admire the elegance of

Summerson and the passion of Blomfield, but it is towards Germany that one must turn for a solution to the problem of art history. Watkin accords cursory treatment to Riegl and Dvořák. Nevertheless it is they who gave a theoretical basis to stylistic analysis, and so tried to build on land that bridge between art-history and philosophy which Hegel had projected, rainbow-like, in the heavens. Perhaps, in a sequel to the present work, Watkin will deal with these thinkers more thoroughly, and find cause to mention the great Hans Sedlmayer more than once.

Meanwhile this book is to be enjoyed for what it is: a detailed survey of the English tradition in architectural history, written with a frankness and range that command considerable respect. One may entertain intellectual doubts about the methods of architectural history. And one may question whether it has a history of its own. But Watkin reveals its chronicle, and proves that the subject exists. He shows that it has become part of the consciousness as much of the ordinary cultivated amateur as of the practising architect, causing gloom in the one as it gives confidence to the other.

22 Marxism in Architecture

Theories and History of Architecture, Manfredo Tafuri (Granada, 1980),
from the *Times Literary Supplement*, 25 July 1980.

Manfredo Tafuri's *Theories and History of Architecture* is similar in style,
thought and outlook to the author's widely known *Architecture and
Utopia*, and is likely to have a similar success. Manfredo Tafuri is the
model of the new Italian 'metaprofessor'. He speaks not language but
'metalanguage'; he has no methods, only 'methodologies'; he discusses
not questions but their 'parameters', and even when engaged in architectural analysis, he refers not to the illustrations provided, but to
others, related to them by unknowable chains of association. He utters
propositions in order to withdraw from them, and casts over the whole
subject a veil of fashionable pedantry, turning problem to 'problematic',
and solution to ideological stance. In this way Professor Tafuri conceals
almost everything about his beliefs, except that, whatever *you* think, *he*
thinks something meta. The one thing he professes openly is Marxism, to
be understood in the 'strict' sense which is becoming obligatory in the
Italian academy. I do not suppose you would get your legs shot off if you
tried to teach architecture to Italians without professing Marxism. But it
is unlikely that you would become head of the school of architectural
history in Venice. This is not to question Tafuri's sincerity. It may be that
the one commitment which he expresses unhesitatingly is also the one
about which he feels convinced. But I doubt it, since his incidental
exposition of Marxist thought is as unclear as his exposition of everything else. And it is difficult to think that a man believes sincerely that
which he has taken so little trouble to understand.

Consider the following introductory remark, which leads us directly to
the main theme (as I understand it) of Tafuri's book:

> . . . *just as it is not possible to found a Political Economy based on class, so
> one cannot 'anticipate' a class architecture (an architecture 'for a
> liberated society'); what is possible is the class criticism of architecture.*
(Tafuri's italics)

This, Tafuri assures us, is the expression of a 'strict—but sectarian and
partial—Marxist point of view'. 'Just as'; just as what? Marx argued that
the science of 'Political Economy', as he found it, assumed the permanence and the autonomy of exchange-value, and thus represented as a
part of 'human nature' the transient economic structure which had
created the bourgeois class. *Perhaps* that is what Tafuri means. But then:

167

'so'. So what? To 'anticipate' (is that the same as to anticipate?) a class architecture is presumably to say what architecture would be generated by, or suited to, the dominance of a particular class. You can easily do that. It was done with minute exactitude by Palladio, and also, less systematically, by the Russian constructivists. Even if you think the enterprise presents problems, what have they to do with the 'demystification' of 'bourgeois' political economy? The 'just as' and the 'so' seem to have no intellectual relation. Perhaps that relation could be established; but it is thought, and not contiguity on the page, that would achieve this. What, moreover, is this 'class criticism' that Tafuri seeks to introduce into architecture?

Is he going to tell us, in the manner of Viollet-le-Duc, how the Gothic style was more suited to collective activity, the Romanesque to the dominance of priests? Is he going to give us the familiar observations about the aristocratic character of Palladianism, the individualistic, and therefore, bourgeois, nature of the bow-fronted house? I looked in his book for such things, but did not find them. His angry protestations of Marxist affiliation (which would be interesting if he could carry them through into the criticism of architecture) seem to get lost precisely in the application to architectural thought and practice (I mean praxis) which he claims to unfold. Eventually all we have is a general rejection (or acceptance, depending on which sentence you happen to read) of architectural 'ideology'.

One of the few times that Marx writes in a manner relevant to the criticism of architecture (in the '18th Brumaire'), he speaks of the dignifying role of classicism in the French Revolution, arguing that this reference to ancient forms was part of the bravura of the new order. You find the same kind of classicism in Schinkel; you also find it (or a version of it) in Albert Speer. Here it is commonly described as 'ideology', and regarded as an attempt to falsify, rather than to dignify, the perception of the present. I myself do not see the difference: neo-classicism is a stylistic and social phenomenon that occurs and recurs. It can be used in the service of revolution or of reaction. It can generate bad architecture and good architecture. But, if it has a common spiritual essence, then this must remain the same in all these applications.

For a certain kind of Marxist that is impossible. Hence, I suppose, the difficulty Tafuri has in discovering whether he believes anything definite about architectural ideology.

There is an important enterprise represented by the attempt to find a Marxist 'method' in architectural criticism. In Italy the motive for this attempt is obscured, since it is also the protestation which earns you respectability. But the intellectual task can be detached from its social origins. We all recognize the increasing importance of a sense of history in the practice of architecture. And 'history' is one of the things for which

Marxism offers a theory. Tafuri takes up Pevsner's concept of 'historicism', in order to describe the adoption of a style that is motivated not by a sense of intrinsic fittingness, but by the association with some favoured and pre-existing social order. He points out that the practice of building in past forms and with past embellishments is not a single phenomenon. It can consist in random architectural 'quotation', as in the classical references of Rudolph, Rauch, and Philip Johnson. Or it can consist in a thoroughgoing attempt to adopt the style of another age, as in the High Victorian Gothic.

In either case, you might argue (and it seems to me that Tafuri does at least suggest this point, although argument is not quite the right word for his manner) this 'historicism' belongs to 'ideology'—to that part of the system of architectural values which is concerned with the false representation of the present social world. And in contrast, you might point to those styles which, through refusing this game of reference, are more properly at one with their time. These styles, through being free of 'historicism', achieve 'historicity'; that is to say, by making a conscious identification with the present, they restore to architecture the historical nature that is its own. Historicism is the attempt to represent as natural and eternal what is in fact transient and socially determined. The style which truly represents the historical nature of architecture is the style which does not conceal the economic or social reality from which it grows.

Now the problem about French neoclassicism, conveniently answered for Tafuri by Marx, is constantly resurging. According to Marx there are revolutionary epochs in history, when the transition from one economic order to another generates the overthrow of all social institutions, from religious belief down to architectural style. And yet the odd fact seems to be that these revolutions have been accompanied by the most backward-looking of architectural idioms. The renaissance style of Florence is an example of this. It involves the attempt to revive something that is represented as the 'eternal truth' about form and detail in architecture. Tafuri has a great interest in showing that this revival was not *really* a revival, but something else. For this was an architecture which, belonging to social revolution, reveals its own 'historicity', perceiving truth in crisis.

Here is a task for the critic of architecture which is also historical: it involves re-describing the Florentine Renaissance at the deepest level, both as social phenomenon and as stylistic experiment. As Tafuri puts it, this is possible only for the historian who tries to 'historicize' his criticism. The present 'crisis of aesthetics' can be solved, we are informed, only through a 'strongly historicist attitude, able to determine . . .' Before saying what this historicist attitude is able to determine, it is important to remind the reader of the task in hand, which is to inject into the description of architecture a method that will separate 'ideology' from its opposite. I cannot see that there could be Marxist criticism which did not involve *at least* that attempt. But what Tafuri *says* that the 'historicist' attitude will determine is, 'each successive time and with an eye to the future, a horizon for the study of aesthetic problems that is constantly variable and determined by the concrete experience of art's unforeseeable changes'. In other words, speaking honestly, nothing at all. (An 'eye to the future' determined by the experience of 'unfore-seeable changes'? A 'horizon' for the study of 'problems'?) So how do we describe the architecture of Brunelleschi?

There seem to be at least the following three possibilities. We could say that Brunelleschi's architecture *is* 'ideological', concerned with resusci-tating a past 'language' (the word that Tafuri always favours when he really means 'style'), in the interests of concealing and consolidating some new economic order. Or we could say that it is a revolutionary idiom which breaks through the veil of ideology to reveal architectural truth. Or else it is that third thing which Marx mentions, the flamboyant Romanism of the revolutionary, who uses the past only to hearten the present.

Most of us would choose the second view, and I think that Tafuri wants to do so too, since it is the view that enables him to describe Brunelleschi's architecture as *true* to its history (since it is true to itself). This is a property which it shares with the architecture of Gropius and the Modern Movement (in its 'heroic' stage). But Tafuri is aware that the Marxist reference is now in danger of dropping out of consideration alto-gether. For you can now say that Brunelleschi simply discovered eternal architectural values, and also (although it is infinitely less plausible) that Gropius did the same. Hence there really is an architectural essence, of which the classical style partakes, and which is valid for all places and times, independently of the particular social context that gave rise to it. In other words, you have become (abhorred word) a 'neo-classicist', who believes in a trans-historical reality that unites the forms of architecture with enduring features of human nature, and who regards the relation of those forms to any socio-economic 'base' as irrelevant to understanding them.

Tafuri wriggles for a while on this point and comes up with an ingenious answer. 'We have mentioned . . .', he writes, 'the constant mis-understanding of the meanings piled up on architecture in the course of history. But we must also specify that this "misunderstanding" is not only constant but also the only way available to approach architectural reality.' In other words, the only way to understand architecture is to misunderstand it. Tafuri illustrates this interesting doctrine with a dis-course on a drawing by Francesco di Giorgio, not reproduced in the book, but available, for those interested, in the Codice Saluzziano in Turin. (This is characteristic; just as most of the examples discussed are not illustrated, so are most of the 'illustrations' not discussed.)

At the end of the book we learn that the only purpose with any 'historical sense' is to 'find out what architecture is, as *a discipline historically conditioned and institutionally functional, first, to the "progress" of the pre-capitalist bourgeoisie and, later, to the new perspectives of capitalist "Zivilisation"* '. This sounds more like a coherent programme; and one to which Marxism might have something important to contribute. But even if we deck it out with all the 'methodologies' which Tafuri's wide (perhaps one should say 'scattered') reading has brought to his attention, I fail to see its *critical* value.

Let us leave aside the bizarre idea of a 'pre-capitalist bourgeoisie' (which implies the existence of a bourgeoisie in the absence of exchange- and surplus-value). What would result from seeing architecture in this way? Of course architecture is historically conditioned: so is everything human. And of course it may have a functional significance in relation to the social order in which it was conceived. But this functional signifi-cance belongs alike to the beautiful and to the ugly, to the skilled and the unskilled, to the harmonious and the ill-proportioned. It belongs to every style and every lack of it. Hence all the *critical* differences seem to be an-nihilated by the quest for historical function. What we begin to see are not the important features of architecture, but the unimportant accidents that belong to its every manifestation. It is not surprising if such a 'method' is pedantic and uninteresting. We do not know how it will help us to understand (or misunderstand) architecture, any more (to use Tafuri's favourite analogy) than we could be helped to understand language by observing its 'functional' role in consolidating the interests of a ruling class.

There *is* a real significance to architecture, but it is doubtful that we can approach it by separating what is ideology from what is not. That process will, if the Marxist is right, give us the reality of economics, but it will often give us the unreality of those cultural products which exist in the realm of ideas. Architecture bears (let us suppose) the same relation as every other cultural entity to the economic 'base' which determines it, but it is not *this* relation which interests us when we try to understand a building. On the contrary. A man who looked for the economic deter-minants of every building and every street would have fallen out of com-munication with architecture. He would be like the man who looked for the physiological basis of every facial expression, for the anatomical causes of every feeling, who saw the skull beneath the skin. Such a man would miss what is there, namely, the human nature that exists in the surface of things and which is invisible, because non-existent, in the depths.

If we are to take the concept of ideology seriously (and Tafuri is adamant that he uses the term in a strict Marxian sense), then we must give a criterion which will distinguish what is ideology from what is not.

In the case of a belief the criterion *might* be this: a belief is ideological when the *full* explanation of a man's holding it lies in its ability to secure his economic position, by concealing social reality. Otherwise it is not. The best guarantee that a belief is *not* ideological is that it is held because it is *true*.

The problem with architecture is that it is not a language and does not have the primary function of conveying truths. (Think of a man who walks down a street nodding at each house as he passes it with the words 'True' or 'False', offering arguments to one and accepting useful counsel from another. He too would be out of communication with architecture.) So what now becomes of our criterion of ideology? We might try this: a building is ideological if it *expresses* something which bolsters the economic position of, by concealing social reality from, the man to whom it appeals. But who is this man? The builder? The client? The spectator? Is 'ideology' a permanent feature of a building, or just part of the explanation of its quondam popularity? Must a building be ideological even to those who can both identify with, and also see through, the act of concealment? Such questions go unanswered in Tafuri's work. Furthermore, we might ask how a building could ever, on this account, *not* be ideological. Everything that has been built was built because it appealed to someone who had the power to build. If the Marxist is right, the building must therefore have offered no direct affront to the economic order which conferred that power. So it must have expressed a picture which confirmed and consolidated the position of the builder. But every order that is not classless is also (we are told) unjust. If it is part of human nature (as it is) to abhor injustice, then this 'picture' could not have revealed (and in that sense must have concealed) the injustice of the order which it served. So all buildings are or have been ideological. Or is there an alternative?

Even if we can pursue those speculations to some point of rest (or at least of exhaustion), we will not have said much that is relevant to the criticism of architecture. It is a known fact that the most beautiful buildings keep their beauty despite radical changes in economic circumstances. The economic order of modern Italy is unlike that of the Venetian Republic, yet even Professor Tafuri, who feels no great sympathy for either, is presumably not entirely antipathetic to the architecture of that town. This is an architecture developed over many centuries and in many styles, in an active spirit of conservation and renewal, with its own internal traditions, yet seemingly unconstrained by the economic upheavals of the Adriatic. (Why did Sangallo urge the city council to restore the Doge's palace in the Gothic and not in the contemporary classical style? Why did the Venetian cresting survive for century after century, throughout every stylistic revolution?) If we think that architecture is or ought to be understood in terms of some distinction between the ideological and the 'pure', then not only do we fail really to explain these facts, but our whole interest in architecture becomes topsy-turvy, just as our interest in each other would be topsy-turvy if we lost the sense of a common human nature and saw every gesture in historical terms.

Tafuri objects to something he calls 'operative criticism' (typified, apparently, by Giedion), saying that it is 'an ideological criticism (we always use the term ideological in its Marxian sense): it substitutes ready-made judgments of value (prepared for immediate use) for analytical rigour'. By this criterion every value by which men live is ideological. Except for the existentialist, values *are* ready-made, prepared for immediate use. This is what makes them useful to us, not as members of social classes, but simply as human beings. It is useful that we do not substitute analytical rigour (what would this mean?) for the immediate perception of the horror of murder, for the prompt response to an insult, to an injustice, to an act of tyranny or violence. Mercifully most people do not go around thinking analytically about these responses. They arise out of our common human nature, and it is of no interest that someone may wish, for didactic purposes of his own, to describe them as ideological. It is to this common human nature that architecture addresses itself, and with which, if it is successful, it belongs.

23 Architecture of the Horizontal

A talk broadcast by BBC Radio 3 in (August/September) 1980, and printed in *PN Review*, *23*, 1981.

Imagine a modern factory. In all probability you will envisage an oblong building, with a flat roof supported on steel girders, standing unconnected to its surroundings in a field of concrete. You will not expect the windows to be placed in any particular position, nor will you imagine anything significant by way of a door. The typical modern office block is taller, squarer, finished off with a grey-green veneer of glass. It is striated like a chest of drawers, with the divisions between the storeys marked by metallic lines. It rises from the middle of streets and houses, but, as a rule, belongs to no particular street, and makes concessions to no discernible plan. Its angles dig into the surrounding town, and all the way up to its flattened summit it spreads itself in long horizontal wedges of glass. If asked to envisage a modern apartment building, you will probably imagine something more like the factory in its setting, more like the office block in appearance. It will be greyer than any office, drabber, with smaller windows interspersed by slabs of discoloured rendering. But, the horizontal divisions will be just as clearly visible, partly because each floor is an exact replica of the one beneath it, differing, if at all, only in the colours of the drapery. And, as with the factory, the whole block will be surrounded by a clearing, this time of muddy grass. In none of the three cases are you likely to expect any clear relation to a street, or to any other building.

It is fashionable to criticize modern architecture, and the so-called 'modern movement' which made it respectable. But in many ways the criticisms say little that is relevant to the three archetypes that I have described. The modern movement of Le Corbusier, the Bauhaus, and Mies van der Rohe, was an intellectual affair. It was interested less in building types, than in single projects, to be appreciated for their unique aesthetic appeal; if people complain about this movement, it is not because of what it produced, because it produced hardly anything. It is because of what it thought. But architecture is not like painting or poetry: it does not preoccupy itself with the unique and the sublime. Its primary concern is with the mundane and the repeatable. It is, in other words, a vernacular art, and its principal examples are types or patterns that can be reproduced whenever required. I have described three of the modern types, and I like none of them. But it does not seem to me that we can understand what is wrong with them by attacking, either the polemics of twentieth century architects, or the stylistic experiments of the Bauhaus and the 1920s. To find what is wrong with them, we must study the vernacular element: we must concentrate on what is common, repeatable, and according to type.

In all three cases we find a regularity of ground-plan. The building rises on a single geometrical base: a square, a rectangle, sometimes (but rarely) a circle. This means that such buildings do not fit easily together. They can be placed side by side, but it is not easy to join them or fit them into an existing space.

To build them you require not a space but a *site*. Which means that in each case you need to clear the ground for them. In the case of the factory and the block of flats the clearing is bigger than the building which sits in it. In the case of the office, the building and its clearing are identical in shape and size. But either way, it is the environment and not the building which must be made to fit.

It is also difficult to insert such buildings into streets. They appear in our town centres like strangers at a gathering. Either they stand behind a little clearing and refuse to align themselves, or else they shuffle forwards and stare blankly and meaninglessly into space.

I have referred to regularity of ground plan, the need for clearance, and the denial of the street. But there is a feature of the three archetypes which is far more important, and which to some extent explains the others. These buildings are constructed entirely from horizontal planes. In each case, whether there be one storey or a hundred, the building is organized according to a two dimensional plan. The office block and the apartment building are stacked up in layers like angel cakes. In each case, the ground plan is taken as the principle of construction for the building as a whole, so the plan must be regular, symmetrical, and indefinitely repeatable. This leads to the layered effect, and to what we might call the horizontal style. The characteristics of the horizontal style are these: the disposition of windows is arbitrary, so long as they are horizontally aligned. The divisions between storeys are marked, not by mouldings, plinths or any other decorative detail, but simply by the transition from one layer to the next. The entrance bears only an arbitrary relation to the windows; the roof is flat, and masonry appears merely to fill the gaps between the layers.

This emphasis on the horizontal leads to the dissolution of the façade. A building constructed solely from horizontal layers cannot have a façade. It has neither back, nor front, nor sides. It faces in no particular direction, and even if all the windows happen to be gathered on one wall, this will not give that wall the character of a face. A building faces things only when it contains some principle of upward movement, some vertical tension. Without vertical tension it is nothing but a striated heap. Now buildings bear relations to their neighbours only if they have façades.

Otherwise they can be as high as you like, and yet will always remain glassy-eyed and expressionless. They may be placed beside their neighbours but will remain incapable of the dialogue that could bring them together. This I think, is why the horizontal archetypes, even when aligned, never seem to form themselves into streets. And if you introduce them into existing streets, you begin to destroy the order that is there. It is no accident that, under the impact of the new building types, the streets and squares of our towns seem to be crumbling away. This is a logical consequence of the horizontal style.

It has been usual to explain the rise of the horizontal in terms of factors outside the architect's control. For example in terms of technical innovations, such as steel frames, reinforced concrete, pre-cast elements. And these technical innovations are described as a kind of overwhelming economic force, compelling the architect, the builder, the client and the public purse alike. They permit cheaper ways of building, vaster projects, greater economy of space. Social and economic pressures inevitably lead to their employment. And you cannot use new materials without accepting the aesthetic consequences. As Le Corbusier put it, in 1923: 'Reinforced concrete has brought a revolution in the aesthetics of construction . . . suppressing the roof and replacing it by terraces . . . with accent running not from top to bottom, but horizontally, from left to right.'

For many years people have found this kind of explanation convincing, whether or not they have also joined in Le Corbusier's praise of the thing explained. But I find it far from convincing, and indeed pernicious in its underlying assumptions. On the one hand, steel frames and reinforced concrete are far from cheap. They require a great outlay in engineering plant, and become economical only when large projects are being considered. On the other hand, people have learned to think in terms of large projects partly in order to justify the use of the new techniques. There has been no real necessity for the works of clearance and redevelopment that have ruined our inner cities; it is simply that planners have been seduced by the mythology of the new materials. Most people are now well aware of this.

Neither is it true that the new materials require the horizontal style. They had been used in American cities since the end of the nineteenth century, in structures which unashamedly adopted or modified the vertical traditions. The Woolworth building in Manhattan has a steel skeleton, filled with precast sections in a Gothic design; the Chrysler building rises on a steel frame, culminating in a decorative Aztec pinnacle of polished alloy that draws together the upward movement of the window frames. It was no change of technique that led to the layered boxes which now surround and obscure those buildings. It seems, then, that the new materials have been neither necessary in themselves, nor sufficient alone to generate the horizontal style.

It is a sound principle, in the explanation of human things, to look first for human agency. The laws of economics are unknown to us, and as often happens with unknown things, we begin to think of them as peculiarly powerful. We suppose that they can provide the *real* reason for things which in fact need no explanation. This prejudice in favour of economic explanations, even when they cannot be formulated, is the ruin of politics. It is also the ruin of architecture. For it causes us to forget the most important fact, which is that buildings are the product of human choice and labour, and that a corruption in style is nothing less than a corruption in the choice which adopts it. Vernacular architecture used to be the province of the small builder. He worked from a pattern book, building according to principles of received wisdom that he saw no necessity to change. Gradually the architect has begun to replace the builder as the principal agent in vernacular construction. And it is to the education of the modern architect that we should trace the rise of the horizontal style.

Architects used to be needed primarily for public monuments, country houses and the occasional church. The principal learning required of them was stylistic. And to acquire that learning the architect had to be able to draw, not plans, but buildings. He had to know the visible relations among parts of an Order, the requirements of style, down to such fine details as the changing aspect of a skyline, or the effect of shadow on the various mouldings and window frames. He learned these things with a sketchbook. For if you learn to draw something then you also learn to see it.

Such an architect inevitably acquired an interest in elevations and façades, these being the things which strike the observer. So he had to discipline his architecture in accordance with that interest. It is not difficult to see what form his discipline had to take, and why it led to the familiar classical, neo-classical and neo-Gothic styles. When we stand before something and try to make sense of its visual aspect, then we project on to it a sense of our own bodily posture. We try to see the object as itself standing in a recognizable posture before us. That means seeing it from top and bottom. If we also see it from side to side, it is because we have already understood the many vertical movements. An architect who is taught to draw what he sees will require principles of vertical organization, and without some discipline of the vertical he will be unable to construct an intelligible façade.

His modern colleague is trained in a different school, designed to make him indispensable to the vernacular builder. He is brought up at the drawing board, in the study of ground-plans. And a ground-plan will look satisfying only if it exhibits horizontal order. No other form of order can be contained in it. So verticals have to look after themselves. Unfortunately, this is possible. It is made possible by the technique of axonometric drawing, which involves projecting a plan into three dimensions by joining the angles of identical planes. This technique was originally used to *analyse* buildings. It is now used to *construct* them. Its use permits an architect to project a horizontal plan into an elevation, without expending any further thought on how the thing will look. The elevation can have no character of its own. It simply reiterates in layers the horizontal plan which generates it. The elevation is without vertical organization, and without intelligible posture.

Vertical organization requires vertical discipline. Such a discipline once existed; it was familiar to architects and, through pattern books, to builders. The classical Orders provided its intellectual basis, modified in accordance with developing problems of design, and with inevitable changes of taste.

An Order consists of a particular kind of vertical organization, based on the unit of the column. To understand an Order you have to understand the relations between base, column, architrave and frieze, and you must concentrate especially on the points of transition between them. It is here that shadows must be made, in order to create the fall of light necessary to vertical harmony. So it is at the points of transition that mouldings and ornaments occur.

But it takes some training of the eye to see how all this works. Only gradually do you come to realize that in studying the fall of light on a moulding, you are studying, not just an isolated detail, but the whole organization of which it forms a part. You are discovering something which geometry alone cannot teach you: namely, the vertical posture of an architectural form. You can then learn how to spread this posture from side to side. You will eventually learn how to construct a satisfactory façade even in the most constricted space. Such vertical discipline encourages the street over the site as the unit of development. It encourages a flexibility of ground-plan, and a diversity of form. It leads to habits of building that are not just different in quality, but different in kind, from those exemplified in the archetypes from which I began. The tyranny of the horizontal arises not from economic necessity, but from visual ignorance. It arises because architects are taught to study plans first and elevations afterwards. People have lost sight of the fact that, to understand an elevation, you have first to perceive the complex biographies of ascending and descending lines.

Architects have at last begun to distrust the horizontal style; and have sought to discipline it in accordance with a new aesthetic. You find an example of this aesthetic in the National Theatre. Another example is projected in the New British Library, designed to lie down beside the matronly verticals of St Pancras on the Euston Road. The architect of the National Theatre, Sir Denys Lasdun, has made a conscious effort to re-create, through the language of horizontals, some of the values associated with the traditional façade. The result is a peculiar stylistic phenomenon which we might call horizontal baroque. The classical façade is dissolved, and reconstituted as a series of planes, cantilevered out into platforms. Seen from below these present in their lower surfaces the same upward accumulation of detail as the classical façade. They also cast shadows which spread across the surface of the building. But as we recede, this effect of façade gradually disintegrates. Once again we notice the striations, this time more reminiscent of a stereo set than of a chest of drawers. The construction is still horizontal; but the layers are detached from each other and displaced. They seem to float on some transparent fluid that pours between them. The building offers an even firmer negation to the idea of a street than is offered by our vernacular archetypes. It would indeed be inconceivable without the vast clearing that surrounds it. It is argued that the transparency of such a building recreates the lost human significance, and so justifies the horizontal style. It reveals the activity of people inside the building, and so fills the prospect with life. As for the street, perhaps our desire for such a thing should be discounted. Perhaps, after all, it is only a form of nostalgia for styles of human commerce that are no longer possible. In which case, the dissolution of the façade, and the free horizontal, will represent the true ideal for architecture in our time.

I remain sceptical. A façade gives a building an independent posture. Its meaning is not merely borrowed from the activity which it displays. The visible commotion of its inmates no more gives humanity to a building than the wriggle of worms gives vitality to a corpse. It is not this that we seek when we ask for life in a building. We seek an expression, a way of facing us. Nor can we assume that this demand for life and expression is an accident. We expect buildings to stand and look at us, because *we* stand to look at *them*. I could be more persuaded by the horizontal style if I thought that the vertical posture of people was an accident, or if I thought it was an accident that people stand up to converse together. The horizontal style would be a part of the human world only if all our public activities took place on stretchers.

Culture and Anarchy

24 Radical Therapy

From *Cambridge Review*, 13 May 1977.

A man might see all the patches of colour which make up a painted portrait and yet not see the face which it contains, even though no feature of the painting has escaped his attention. He sees all the details, but not the *portrait*. There is a way of understanding what he sees, and a way of responding to it, which for some reason has eluded him. Analogously, a scientist may observe in another all the workings of a human organism, and avail himself of a complete account of the organism's structure and behaviour. And yet he may fail to see the person whom this organism embodies. And just as the detailed scrutiny of coloured patches militates against the understanding of the portrait, so, it might be suggested, does the clinical objectivity of the scientific observer damage his understanding of the person. Our ability to observe and understand the mind of another is of a piece with our disposition to treat him not as an organism only, but as a person. In adopting a scientific 'objectivity' it may be that we cease to treat him in that way; and if that is so it follows that a scientific approach to the mental life of human beings must falsify what it pretends to study.

Such a thought, variously expressed and variously embellished, has many adherents among contemporary psychologists and philosophers. It is possible that it is as old as Aristotle; in any case it was reborn in the philosophy of Kant, found support in the works of Hegel, and achieved a distinctive utterance in the writings of the phenomenologists and Sartre. It was the language of Sartre which R. D. Laing borrowed in giving renewed expression to the thought, and his resulting description of the phenomenology of mental illness was vivid and compelling. Laing suggested as one of the origins of 'schizophrenia' (to borrow for the moment a classification which he would reject) precisely that sense of 'ontological insecurity' which comes from seeing oneself not as a person, but as an organism, mechanism or thing. The striking consequence of this diagnosis was the rejection (or rather subversion) of accepted ways of treating the mentally ill. The philosophy which dwells on the distinction between seeing a man as a person and seeing him as a thing *might* have been used in the defence of hospital treatment. It might have been held that we take a clinical and objective attitude to another precisely when his behaviour makes personal understanding impossible. (For the distinguishing mark of mental, as opposed to physical, illness is that it affects the potential of its victim to be understood and treated as a person.) On such a view,

183

clinical treatment is a consequence of mental breakdown. It does not deprive the patient of his freedom, for his freedom is already lost. The master thought of Laingian psychology (and the thought which explains much of its emotional appeal) consists in the reversal of that doctrine. It is the patient who *becomes* an object because the clinical scientist treats him so. The patient has not lost his freedom: it has been stolen from him by the clinical refusal to treat him as a person. And it is from this refusal that his 'ontological insecurity'—and therefore what others might regard as his 'illness'—arises.

Had Laing written nothing after *The Divided Self,* the accusation of charlatanism which lies so evidently against his principal followers could not be extended to him. All the same, the seeds of intellectual dishonesty are already there in that hasty inversion of accepted causality. The trick has by now a considerable history, beginning with Marx's idea of 'mystification', according to which the true causality of social phenomena is always 'hidden' in the interests of an established order. Perhaps its boldest product, and the one most disrespectful of anything that might be thought of as scientific truth, is Foucault's *Histoire de la Folie*, a book from which the later excesses of Laingian psychiatry derive much of their inspiration. Like Foucault, Laing could not rest content with accusing clinical practice of creating the behaviour which it purports to 'cure'. For it is necessary to explain how the patient arrived in the clinic in the first place. By a predictable stroke, both Laing and Foucault hit on the family—especially the 'bourgeois' family—as the culprit. The patient, in the later writings of Laing, is presented as an innocent victim of a life-long process of depersonalization. When the family has reduced him to the object which it requires him to be, he is then handed over to the clinic, so that the process can continue in a controlled environment adapted perfectly to the systematic destruction of the self.

It is because it lends itself to that paranoid vision of institutional treatment that 'existential' psychology has achieved its success. By a deft juggling with the rhetoric of subversion, Laing's followers have turned an innocent philosophical claim into a quasi-political dogma. There is certainly nothing in the original insights of *The Divided Self* to necessitate the stance of *The Politics of Experience,* or *The Politics of the Family,* with their obsessive fixation upon the familiar objects of radical discontent—upon the family, the bourgeoisie, capitalism, the established moral order, upon morality itself. But, because of these later works, and because of his association with Cooper and Esterson, Laing has acquired a following out of all proportion to his medical achievement. He has, in effect, given rise to a 'radical critique' of psychological medicine. This critique can best be understood from the works of the Radical Therapist Collective, a body which has produced what can only be described as the most inspoken attack ever to have been made on the social consequences of Western Capitalism. Among its paranoid convictions the following is by no means the most remarkable: 'Most therapists are men; most patients women. Therapy thus reinforces and exemplifies the sexist practices of this society . . .'

By such astonishing mental contortions, the Collective is able to see the work of Laing and his followers as justifying a 'total revolution' to end the 'system' of which schizophrenia (by which it means both the symptoms of the victim and the attitudes involved in so classifying them) is the principal sign. This 'total revolution' will involve many radical changes: 'Third-world, female and gay organizing; the setting up of counter-institutions . . .' and so on. Lest the idealism of the Collective should be doubted, it is worth quoting a paragraph from one of its reports (a report resulting from a 'Workshop' on the Rights of Children, in Berkeley, 1970):

> Our revolutionary children are entrusted with the responsibility for rediscovering the true human nature, perverted by thousands of years of racism, capitalism, so-called communism, sexism, nationalism and false religion. Forced limitation of their experience, in the name of protection and love, has always been a central part of reactionary repression, especially for the bourgeois class. The destruction of human potential for love by repression in childhood must end now.

It would be unjust to reproach Laing with the absurdities of his disciples—though his failure to disown them is of a piece with the messianic image in which he now rejoices. Nonetheless, the difference between that paragraph and the thoughts expressed in Laing's recent autobiography are not so very great—not so great that they could not be explained by an evident difference in intellectual gifts. The posturings of the Radical Therapist Collective exemplify a moral vision to which Laing himself subscribes, and which finds expression also in the work of Esterson, Cooper and (to some extent) Szasz: the vision that the mental patient is essentially innocent, and that someone, somewhere, is to blame for what he suffers. It is not just that the victim of mental illness cannot be reproached for his condition. It would hardly be novel to suggest such a thing, since the whole purpose of the classification 'mentally ill' is to remove the victim from the sphere of moral disapproval. According to the Laingian, the classification incorporates a deeper, unspoken charge, a charge that goes beyond morality to the very roots of personal existence. A charge of covert 'criminality' is involved, and it is in respect of this covert 'criminality' that the victim of mental illness is profoundly innocent and his accusers profoundly to blame. Dealing in spiritual profundities it is hardly surprising that the theory begins to describe the innocence of the insane as saintly—as a kind of absolute discharge from original sin. This arises through the manipulation of certain dogmas, among which the following are particularly notable:

1　'All that is certain about "mental illness" is that some people assert that other people have it.' (Morton Schatzman; 'Madness and Morals' in Joseph Berke, ed., *Counter-culture: The Creation of an Alternative Society*). The diagnostician is therefore necessarily an aggressor, being prepared to assert something which has terrible consequences for his patient, and for which there can never be adequate grounds.

2　The characteristic psychiatric case is 'opposed to a normality which is intimately related to the major value orientations of Western society.' (B. Kaplan, in Kaplan, ed., *The Inner World of Mental Illness*). In other words the inmate of the clinic is a dissenter, speaking with a 'radical voice'; and what he says is repugnant to the established moral order. (Cf. Foucault).

3　'The mental hospital system serves . . . to promote certain values and performances, and to suppress others.' (Thomas Szasz in *Ideology and Insanity*). The institutionalization of the insane is therefore an attempt to silence their 'subversive' thoughts and attitudes.

4　Hence the concept of mental illness is really that of a 'crime', of a re-prehensible rejection of the values implicit in the established social order. It is an invented concept, whereby 'bourgeois' society attempts to sup-press those manifestations of free spontaneous life which it cannot bear. 'If A and B are incongruent, the mind police (psychiatrists) are called in. A crime (illness) is diagnosed. An arrest is made and the patient taken into custody (hospitalization). Interviews and investigations follow. A con-fession may be obtained (patient admits he is ill, displays insight). He is convicted either way. The sentence is passed (therapy is recommended). He serves his time, comes out, and obeys the law in future.' (Laing, *The Politics of the Family*).

5　But the real culprit here is the society which sets up the repressive institutions of bourgeois life: 'families, schools, churches are the slaughterhouses of our children; colleges and other places are the kitchens. As adults in marriage and business, we eat the product.' (*The Politics of the Family*).

6　Hence, in so far as there is 'disorder' in the behaviour of the 'schizo-phrenic' it is the result, and not the cause, of the 'aggression' of others. The 'schizophrenic' is really nothing more than the 'scapegoat' for the 'burdens of guilt and hatred' which others force on him. (Aaron Esterson, *The Leaves of Spring*, p. 297). In this the angelic nature of the 'schizo-phrenic' lies.

7　The principal instrument of aggression is the family—in particular, the bourgeois family, which is 'paternalistic' and 'authoritarian', demanding the submission of all to a tyrannical father. (Foucault, *Histoire de la Folie*). The family is therefore bound to generate the 'hatred' of which the schizophrenic is the innocent scapegoat.

8   It follows that the schizophrenic, far from being ill, is a creature of remarkable 'purity', attempting to maintain a stance of total rebellion against a cruel and repressive social order. Society, in order to punish him, forces him into a particular 'existential position' or 'double-bind', from which he cannot easily escape. He is cast into the role of a thing, and the procedure of the clinic is to make him accept that role, and come to recognize that he can re-acquire a self only by accepting the values which he had tried to reject. This covert plot of bourgeois society, being ideological, is necessarily self-confirming. There is no way in which the schizophrenic can establish the validity of his posture in the face of an over-mastering 'normality' which he is unable to oppose. (See Thomas Szasz, *Ideology and Insanity.*)

Of course, there is no suggestion that these 'insights' of the Laingians are hard-won. On the contrary, they are each the outcome of a sleight of hand, whereby evidence is reinterpreted in order to support the desired conclusion, and no thought is considered which is not already clothed in the language of radical dissent. No one could really believe, for example, that there is *nothing* certain about mental illness other than the use of the label, or that the voice of insanity is always, or even typically, a voice of 'dissent'. The idea that people of perfectly 'normal' and conformist moral outlook might find themselves unable to live, that they might ask for help, and seek to be hospitalized (often in the face of opposition from hospital authorities) simply has no place in this web of fantasies. The paranoid vision of the hospital as a prison, and of the schizophrenic as a scapegoat, nourishes itself on evidence too slender to be significant. There is a sleight of hand involved even in the very method of 'phenomenological' psychiatry. For phenomenology, being the study of the self, presupposes that there is a self to be studied. To describe the experience of the schizophrenic in phenomenological language is automatically to describe it as though it were the experience of someone who is largely sane. A genuine breakdown of the self would simply elude phenomenological description altogether. By constantly presupposing that such description is possible, and that it is the sole means of access to the true position of his patient, the Laingian psychiatrist assumes from the start the conclusion which he pretends to establish, the conclusion that psychosis is always amenable to personal reaction.

When we come to the propositions about the 'bourgeois family' we have left the realm of clinical observation altogether, and entered that of French intellectual rhetoric, the rhetoric of *Saint Genet*, of *l'Histoire de la Folie*, and of the 'structuralist' criticism of Roland Barthes. Here one is required to be mesmerized into some sense of an intrinsic connection between 'bourgeois', 'family', 'paternalistic' and 'authoritarian'. Historical facts—such as that the aristocratic family is more paternalistic, the peasant family more authoritarian, than the family known as 'bourgeois'; or that the middle class has an ability to dispense with the family which has never been shown by those classes which are normally thought of as economically 'beneath' it, and consequently that the family has only ever seemed dispensable in those societies which are dominated by the ideology of bourgeois individualism—such facts are naturally to be kept out of mind.

Now, the bourgeois family is certainly different from other families. For example, it tends to include only one or two generations. It is likely to be individualistic, inward looking, conscious of its existence as a social unit. The child's affections are narrowly focussed on father and mother, rarely spread out over grandparents, servants and cousins. There tend to be few children, and therefore fewer competitors in the pursuit of love. A certain individualistic intensity attaches to primary affections when they develop in such a milieu. The child learns to play the game of personality, and to establish with his parents relations that are ridden with conflicts and yet also indestructible. This has always been of great interest to psychologists, most of whom have felt that there is a certain presumption in dismissing the entire arrangement as a psychological disaster. So let us consider how the Laingian psychiatrist considers that the bourgeois child is to be 'liberated' from the mental torments of his situation; how he is to obtain that psychological freedom which the family denies. Consider this representative passage from Aaron Esterson:

> Since his aim is to facilitate existential change already implicitly present, it follows that the scientist should not try to impose on the emerging pattern his conceptions or preconceptions. He must allow it to unfold according to the laws proper to itself. A psychoanalyst, for instance, must not seek to impose on the analysand his idea of what the other should or should not be. There is no question of seeing it as his task to teach the other to conform to society or to any particular morality. He is there to learn from and to help the other discover and actualize his own existential possibilities, whatever they may be, and wherever they may take him, whether they are specific talents or general human possibilities like the capacity to make heterosexual love. (*The Leaves of Spring*, pp. 248-9)

Freedom, therefore, is the 'actualization' of 'existential possibilities'. The process of liberation culminates in this discovery (or 'actualization') of a self—a self that had otherwise been stunted or extinct. There is no suggestion that some existential possibilities (for example, that the patient might murder Dr Esterson) should be discouraged. The patient must not be made to conform to 'any particular morality'—for example, the morality of Christ, or Buddha, or Hitler, or Charles Manson. He can shop around, until he hits on the right way of 'actualizing' the 'possibilities' that are already intrinsic in him. But that is precisely the individualistic notion of personal fulfilment—the notion represented at its best in the bourgeois family. Laingian psychiatry goes one step further in the same direction, suggesting that a man may achieve his freedom alone, in indifference to social standards and constraints.

It is in fact somewhat remarkable that a doctrine which officially recognizes the self as a social product, and the self-image as an internalization of social activity, should take that view. Not only the process of recovery, but its end result, are described in terms that are internal to the individual. He must simply 'actualize' his 'possibilities'. The clinical process should be one of self-determination and self-discovery, in which the individual is answerable to no one but himself, and need accept no morality that is not of his own devising. But of course, there is a paradox involved in recognizing the self as a social product while at the same time attempting to give it a 'freedom' that is purely individual. Marx pointed out that it is part of the 'false consciousness' of the bourgeoisie that it cloaks its sterile individualism with this empty concept of freedom. If one asks what 'freedom' consists in, one obtains only incoherent and negative replies: freedom is doing what you want to, or rather 'actualizing your possibilities', and therefore doing what you *really* want to, that is, so long as you don't murder, or steal, or perhaps you *can* steal—at any rate sexual intercourse is permitted, at least, so long as there is no danger of harm to another, or at least . . . What emerges is either incoherence, or precisely that 'particular code of morality' which the psychologist was supposed to avoid.

There is a concept which Freud wisely placed at the heart of psychoanalytic thought and practice, and which Laingian psychiatry has ignored at the cost of its coherence: the concept of reconciliation. The Laingian vision is essentially paranoid: it sees the world in terms of an irreconcilable struggle between 'us' and 'them', and the cure of the mentally ill as a sort of internal (or for the Radical Therapist Collective, even an external) victory over 'them'. It has no place for the idea of reconciliation, since it recognizes the validity of nothing outside himself with which the individual can be reconciled. Indeed, to recognize an 'objective', 'public', 'established', or 'external' validity would be to abandon the picture of the essential innocence of the mentally ill.

The Laingian argues that a therapist should assist the ego to re-assert its potentiality. The idea of the ego as a product of accepted customs, institutions, attitudes and practices is an idea which the theory purports to recognize at the outset but also to reject at the end. Sometimes, surely, the ego can discard the social morality which created it only by an act of suicide: if that is what innocence consists in, then innocence cannot be desired. As soon as the psychotherapist recognizes that his patient might have a need to be reconciled—with the father, the conscience, the moral order, with God—and that his patient might be suffering precisely

because of that need, then he must reject the idea of an 'essential' innocence, and with it, the whole structure of received ideas with which
Laingian psychiatry has embellished itself. It is the ideal of conflict, guilt
and reconciliation, which has enabled bourgeois individualism to put on a
brave and appealing face. To remove that ideal in obedience to the
Laingian imperative is to destroy what is valuable in bourgeois society
while retaining what is not. Without it there is nothing but the 'dust and
powder of individuality' which Burke lamented, a fragmentation of all
serious moral values, and the sickly sentimentality about the sufferings of
others which, present everywhere in the writings of the Laingians, serves
only to mask a fundamental lack of sympathy for whoever is healthy,
successful or strong. The Laingian vision is as far from being truly anti-
bourgeois as any other theory which depends upon radical fashions for its
appeal: its cant words ('existential', 'dialectics', 'liberation', 'realization'), its facile doctrines, and above all its unscrupulous sentimentaliza-
tion of individual experience, adapt it perfectly for the market in cut-
price ideas; while its flimsy ideal of an 'inner' purity fosters that sublime
illusion of the middle classes, the illusion of an individual, united with no
social order, who has nothing to lose but his mental chains.

25   A Note on Foucault

Madness and Civilization and *The Order of Things*, Michel Foucault (Tavistock, 1967, 1970), from the *Spectator*, 9 October 1971.

In the earlier work, now reissued, *Madness and Civilization*, Foucault attempts to describe the place which civilization, since the Renaissance, has offered to madness. He traces the confinement of madmen to its origins in the seventeenth century, associating this confinement with the ethic of work and the rise of the middle classes. Foucault thinks that, as an historian, he should be concerned not with the origins of events but with their deeper significance. He reduces every object of historical study to an epi-phenomenon—a by-product and manifestation of what he calls the 'experience' that compels it. Thus he says, not that the economic re-organization of urban society *brought about* confinement, but that 'it was in a certain experience of labour that the indissolubly economic and moral demand for confinement was formulated.'

The madman is 'other' in the classical age because he points to the limits of the prevailing ethic, and alienates himself from its demands. But through confinement madness is subjected to the rule of reason: the madman now lives under the jurisdiction of those who are sane, confined by their laws and instructed by their sense of what is right. The resource of reason in this close encounter is to reveal to madness its own 'truth.' To lack reason is, for classical thought, to become an animal. The madman must therefore be made to enact the part of an animal; he is used as a beast of burden, and by this confrontation with his own 'truth' is finally made whole. Each successive age finds a similar 'truth' through which the experience of madness can be transcended into sanity. But Foucault suggests that the stock of these truths is now exhausted. The book ends with a satanistic encomium of madness, in which Foucault appeals to the gods of the modern French Olympus—Goya, de Sade, Hölderlin, Nerval, Van Gogh, Artaud and Nietzsche—to testify to this exhaustion. Banal as it is, this encomium gains no substance from the studies that precede it.

It was clear to the eighteenth century, according to Foucault, that while madness was able to express itself, it had no language in which to do so besides that which reason could provide. The only phenomenology of madness lies in sanity. Surely then, the eighteenth century had at least one sound intuition about the nature of unreason? The province of language and the province of reason are coextensive, and if madness contains its own 'truths,' as Foucault claims, these are essentially inexpressible. How then can we rightly imagine a 'language' of unreason, a language in which the truths of madness are expressed and to which we must now attune our ears? The idea of such a language is the idea of an endless delirious monologue, which neither the man of reason nor the madman himself can understand. Such a language, even if it could exist, would bear no resemblance to the remorseless logic of *The Twilight of the Idols*, or to the precise symbolism of *Les Chimères*. Foucault's heroes would have been unable to use this language, even in their final madness, and if we can understand them it is without its aid.

For the nineteenth century, according to Foucault, the experience of 'unreason' characteristic of the classical period becomes dissociated: madness is confined within a moral intuition, and the fantasy of an unceasing monologue of madness, in a language inaccessible to reason, is forgotten. This idea is to be resuscitated, however, at the beginning of the twentieth century, in the Freudian theory of unconscious thought-processes that determine the behaviour of the irrational man. In the nineteenth century madness has become a threat to the whole structure of bourgeois life, and the madman, while superficially innocent, is profoundly guilty in his failure to submit to familiar norms. The greatest offence of madness is against the 'bourgeois family' as Foucault calls it, and it is the 'experience' of this family that dictates the paternalistic structure of the asylums. The ethos of judgement and reprobation in the asylum leads to a new attitude to madness—madness is at last *observed*. It is no longer thought that the madman has anything to *say:* he is an anomaly in the world of action, responsible only for his visible behaviour.

In the asylum the man of reason is presented as an adult, and madness as an incessant attack against the Father. The madman must be brought to recognize his error, and reveal to the Father his consciousness of guilt. Thus there is a natural transition from the 'confession in crisis' characteristic of the asylum to the Freudian dialogue, in which the analyst listens to and translates the language of unreason, but in which madness is still forced to see itself as a disobedience and a transgression. Finally, Foucault intimates, it is because psychoanalysis has refused to suppress the family structure as the only one through which madness can be seen or known that its introduction of a dialogue with madness leads to no understanding of the voices of unreason.

But this facile association of the words 'bourgeois' and 'family' has no historical justification, nor indeed is it clear that the bourgeois family has always had the most paternalistic or authoritarian structure, as families go. By this association Foucault is able to suggest that the family structure is as dispensable as the particular social structure which gives precedence to the bourgeoisie—which is surely both historically and logically a simple fallacy. If the family is always with us, is it surprising that it leaves its traces in the psychological deformities of those who are deranged?

How can this fact be used as a measure either of the value of family life or of the truth of any particular conception of mental illness?

The Order of Things (a translation of *Les Mots et Les Choses*) goes one stage further in every direction than the earlier work: the sources are more recondite, the ideas more obscure and the argument more difficult to follow. It is subtitled 'an archaeology of the human sciences' and concludes with the view that 'man' is a recent invention, doomed to disappear. It is only since the Renaissance that the fact of being a *man* (rather than, say, a farmer, a soldier or a nobleman) has been given the special significance we now attribute to it. The sciences which have taken man as their object are recent inventions, already outmoded as forms of knowledge. The idea of man is as fragile and transient as any other idea in the history of human knowledge, and must give way under the impulse of a new 'experience' of the world to something we cannot name.

But are Foucault's theories really as ambitious and surprising as he makes them sound, and are the facts on which they are based so difficult to unearth? We are told for example, that the Renaissance saw the world in terms of resemblance, but that later this *'episteme'* was replaced by another, that of 'identity and difference.' But every application of a concept can be described as the discovery of a resemblance. How then, can resemblance cease to be a fundamental form of human knowledge? And how can it be replaced by identity and difference, with which it is interdefinable? These logical difficulties lie at the heart of Foucault's theory, and however brilliant the rhetoric, they cannot be thought away.

26 Jacques Lacan

Jacques Lacan, Anika Lemaire (Routledge & Kegan Paul, 1977); *The Four Fundamental Concepts of Psycho-analysis,* Jacques Lacan (Hogarth Press and the Institute of Psycho-analysis, 1977); *Ecrits: a selection,* Jacques Lacan (Tavistock, 1977); and *Le Séminaire: le moi dans la théorie de Freud et dans la technique de la psychanalyse,* Jacques Lacan (Seuil, Paris, 1978), from the *Times Literary Supplement,* 11 August 1978.

Does Jacques Lacan exist (ex-sist)? Twenty-four volumes of his *Séminaires* have been promised by the Editions du Seuil; some have already appeared, and are being translated. His writings *(Ecrits)* are available *(ob-tenables)* in both French and English. The *Séminaires,* however, give more evidence of in-sistence than of ex-sistence. The style is choked, bombastic, and arcane; and the books read like a parody of French intellectual manners. Despite the credence given to Dr Lacan's ex-sistence by the gullible, it is easier to understand these volumes as fiction than as cold statement of fact. The portrait is of a mind pursued by delusions of grandeur, from time to time imagining itself as a kind of reincarnation of Freud, rambling from theme to theme and from symbol to symbol with little connecting thread other than the all-pervasive 'I' of paranoia. The irony is heavy, and indeed the portrait seems far too emphatic to be real. It is not hard to discern the satirical intention underlying Dr Lacan's 'theories', or to appreciate the imitative skill with which they are expressed:

> Today then I must keep to the wager to which I committed myself in choosing the terrain in which the *object a* is most evanescent in its function of symbolizing the central lack of desire, which I have always indicated in a univocal way by the algorithm $(-\phi)$. I don't know whether you can see the blackboard, but as usual I have marked out a few reference points. *The object a in the field of vision is the gaze.* After which, enclosed in a chain bracket, I have written:

> $$(\textit{in nature}$$
> $$($$
> $$(\textit{as} = (-\phi)$$

> *(The Four Fundamental Concepts)*

One can almost hear the squeak of laughter which accompanies that final jab at the blackboard. The tone of rectitude and unassailability which pervades these volumes reminds one of Dr Schreber; but

Schreber's frankness is absent, as is his clarity. The ruminations cover most topics of French intellectual fashion—Saussurian linguistics, Freud, Marx and Hegel, Lautréamont and the surrealists—and are pervaded by incomprehensible mathematical devices (usually called, in defiance of any mathematical meaning, 'functions' or 'algorithms.')

It is important to explain how this anonymous satire should have been taken seriously. Miss Lemaire's worthless study (which reiterates in Lacanian jargon a message that can be expressed in no other way) has been 'translated' (if that is the word) into five separate languages. Moreover, the Parisian intellectual establishment, which has perfected the manufacture of intellectual commodities so far as to secure a permanent balance of consumption in its favour, seems determined to sustain the Lacanian myth. There is good reason. Foucault has conquered the realm of social thought, and Barthes the realm of literature. To extend the method into the jungle of psychoanalysis is to capture all that fashion acknowledges in the studies called 'humane'. Consequently each of the Trinity is sustained by the acclaim accorded to his fellows. It is true that some of the more outrageous of its prophets have fallen into disrepute, and now reside, far from the intellectual excitement of the Centre Pompidou, purveying their mantic gibberish to wandering scholars. But in Paris the fetishism of the intellectual commodity prevails, and requires this Trinity to sustain it. If Dr Lacan does not ex-sist, it is still necessary to in-vent him.

The most appealing feature of Lacan's incantation is the alchemical transformation which it effects in the science of linguistics (a science which appeals as much to those who do not understand it as to those who do). The attraction of alchemy needs no comment: it is the attraction of a science which requires not learning but initiation, a science, therefore, in which the wholly ignorant might claim expertise. The attraction of linguistics—in particular of that general science of signs foretold by Saussure—is that it gives the illusion of 'method' to the ancient skills of prophecy and interpretation. It is hardly surprising, therefore, if the alchemy of linguistics (which has nothing to do with the science of linguistics) should lie at the centre of the modern Hermetic art. And it is this art that is satirized by the creator of Lacan. In one of the imaginary 'écrits' (called 'The Agency of the Letter in the Unconscious of Reason since Freud') we find something called an 'algorithm' and attributed to Saussure:

> To pinpoint the emergence of linguistic science we may say that, as in the case of all sciences in the modern sense, it is contained in the constitutive moment of an algorithm that is its foundation. This algorithm is the following:

$$\frac{S}{s}$$

which is read as: the signifier over the signified, 'over' corresponding to the bar separating the two stages.

The sentence which opens this passage has that self-confident manner proper to the charlatan: this is how science *must* be. The allusion to Hegel adds further authority: Dr Lacan has transcended science (which is only a 'moment' of consciousness) and reached some superior position from which science itself can be surveyed. Against the background of these certainties the gross misuse of the term 'algorithm' therefore strikes a note of resounding comedy.

The satire is sustained over many pages. When Saussure placed that innocent-seeming line between the sign representing language and the sign representing world, he meant that the science of linguistics must study the relation between the two. Dr Lacan proceeds to convert the bar into a kind of mathematical symbol. (This is the true Hermetic impulse, neatly captured in a single phrase.) Having reduced all language to this 'formula' Lacan looks for a way of reading it. His first attempts are hesitant:

> If the algorithm S/s with its bar is appropriate, access from one to the other cannot in any case have a signification. For in so far as it is itself only pure function of the signifier, the algorithm can reveal only the structure of a signifier in this transfer.

Our hero gathers confidence, however, when he notices that *barre* is an anagram of *arbre*: 'Let us take our word "tree" . . . and see how it crosses the bar of the Saussurian algorithm' (*arbre - cadavre?*). Eventually, he decides to interpret the bar as a sign of division, so that the 'S' and the '*s*' become quasi-numerical symbols. From this point on he can declare himself in terms which—while they necessitate a reinterpretation of the entire fields of linguistics, arithmetic and classical algebra—provide him with a perfect symbol of intellectual omnipotence:

> What we have been able to develop concerning the effects of the signifier on the signified suggests its transformation into:

$$f(S)\frac{t}{s}$$

> We have shown the effects not only of the elements of the horizontal signifying chain, but also of its vertical dependencies in the signified, divided into two fundamental structures called metonymy and metaphor. We can symbolize them by, first:

$$f(S \ldots S')S \cong S(-)s$$

> that is to say, the metonymic structure, indicating that it is the con-

nection between signifier and signifier that permits the elision in which the signifier installs the lack-of-being in the object relation using the value of 'reference back' possessed by signification in order to invest it with the desire aimed at the very lack it supports. . . .

I quote at length in order to exemplify the style. Well might the reader puzzle over such passages: is the '*f*' *really* a function sign? Is the bar really a sign of division, the '=' of approximate equality, the 'S . . . *s*' of a mathematical series? At first these questions may be submerged in the hilarious flow of the prose. But we soon find that we must answer them in the affirmative. All meaning has indeed been reduced to an equation and, in the solution of this equation, the signified is found to be identical with the square root of minus ego:

$$\frac{S \quad (\text{signifier})}{s \quad (\text{signified})} = s \text{ (the statement)},$$

$$\text{with } S = (-I), \text{produces } s = \sqrt{-I}.$$

(*Ecrits,* page 317)

Thus we prove that Lacan's absence may be squared into meaning, and that the distance between the object (=a) and the existent (=e) is after all no greater than that between Freud and Fraud.

The writer's dead-pan tone can be gathered from the extracts. Whether this is the most effective way to satirize intellectual fashion may be doubted. Nevertheless, there is something highly persuasive in the implications that the obsession with symbols is no more than an elaborate form of narcissism, and that this obsession leads by compelling steps to the emergence of an all-embracing intellectual hubris. As the hero declares: 'There is no further need to have recourse to the outworn notion of primordial masochism in order to understand the reason for the repetitive games in which subjectivity brings together mastery of its dereliction and the birth of the symbol.'

With twenty-four volumes promised there is a clear danger that the comedy will wear thin. Even the dialogue contained in *Le Moi dans la théorie de Freud et dans la technique de la psychanalyse* begins to pall after 300 pages, although every reader will enjoy the scene in which Dr Lacan encounters Octave Mannoni, in single combat, and which ends with the hero standing over the sobbing form of his rival and addressing an imaginary crowd: 'Je vous demande de ne pas procéder comme a procédé Mannoni. Faites-le au hasard. Manifestez votre inertie symbolique.' Aware of the danger inherent in over-zealous irony, the writer tries to retain the reader's attention by constant reference to a certain 'theory' of Dr Lacan's (a theory which was overlooked when first delivered, but which is clearly meant to represent the hero's contribution to the life of the outside world—an intellectual equivalent of Dr Schreber's activities as judge). This is the theory of the 'mirror stage'. In addition to its dramatic significance, as a rationalization of the hero's narcissism, it is also worth discussing for its own sake, since it is the only aspect of Lacan that can be made intelligible in an idiom that is not his own.

The theory arises from a comparison between the Freudian and Hegelian concepts of the self. The Freudian theory, which construes the self in terms of conflicts first experienced in an infant world, is superficially not unlike the impressive parable of the master and slave, through which Hegel illustrates the 'I want' of infancy launched on its dialectical process towards self-as-other in the mature adult man. Lacan has a comic way of expressing the move from 'pure subject' to 'objective spirit': it is the first 'Ah ha!' of the infant staring in a glass. But there is no need to represent the transition so naively. Hegel construed it in terms that were at the same time logical and historical. The parable of the master and slave shows what self-consciousness is; but it also shows how it arises. (The being of self is also its becoming). The to and fro of power between conflicting wills has its resolution in society, in the recognition of the other as end in himself, and hence in the recognition of self and other as bound in a common law. It is only at that stage, the stage of the fully political being, that the truth of the infantile cry is enacted.

The similarity with Freud derives from two features, from the location of the primitive force in infantile desire, and from the recognition of the self as a social product, as an inner representation of external laws. But can the analogy be taken further? The unintelligible rhapsody that follows Dr Lacan's 'Ah ha!' is clearly meant to invite our scepticism. Nevertheless he regards the comparison as central to his intellectual enterprise, which is, to put it crudely, to show the truth and validity of everything in Freud, and the ultimate identity of doctrine between Lacan and his master. (An identity which is not concealed but only deepened by the borrowings from sciences not sanctioned by Freud.)

In fact the comparison with Hegel is incompatible with such an enterprise: one must again suspect the author of an ironical intention. The essence of Hegel's theory is this: that the truth or reality of the infantile experience (of the primitive 'I want') can be understood only in terms of the mature realization towards which it aspires. The infant's gestures of desire are fierce, but unformed. Their nature resides in their *telos*, and that *telos* is not available to the infant consciousness. It consists, rather, in the mature forms of human life and society. It is to those forms that one must look in order to describe the *reality* of the infant's desire. That theory is the exact opposite of Freud's, who wished to see in infantile experience the paradigm (what Hegel would call the 'truth') of all later emotion. What the adult is *really* doing, says Freud, is enacting an infantile jealousy. What the child is *really* doing, says Hegel, is making an inarticulate gesture towards the bond of society. No two attitudes could be more opposed. For Hegel, we must understand the child in terms of the adult; nothing other than moral confusion comes from the attempt to understand the adult in terms of the child.

Freudolatry is in decline, and this portrait of a hysterical disciple can only serve to discredit it. Throughout the *Séminaires* the tone of evangelical fervour and morbid self-involvement endures unabated; the only respite lies in the passages of staccato dialogue where Dr Lacan fights off his questioners and foes. But what is the content of Lacan's theory? As the author demonstrates, the view of the unconscious as a 'language' is worthless until supplemented by a proper theory of language. Without that addition, it means no more than that the un-conscious is susceptible of interpretation (a view as ancient as civilization itself, and common property to all whose interest lies in the creation of myth). In effect, Lacan is shown to add nothing to Freud; the same theories, and even the same examples, lie unchanged beneath the ruffled surface of his prose.

The author's instinct is surely sound. Devotees of Freudian analysis dislike scepticism, greeting it as it was greeted by Freud, who, presented with a dream which seemed to refute his wish-fulfilment theory, replied: 'No: your dream is an expression of the unconscious wish to refute my theory.' It is uncharacteristic of a Freudian to engage in anything so low as collecting evidence or elucidating concepts. Is it not significant that, in general, the examples discussed are still those of Anna O., of the Rat Man, of Little Hans? These examples have the relation, not of instances to theory, but of parables to dogma. Lacan's return to Freud is like that of a fundamentalist to the gospel, and his delusions, like Dr Schreber's, take on a form that is more religious than scientific. In so representing his central character, the author of these volumes has — for all his clumsy irony—captured a truth about the appeal of psychoanalysis (what Wittgenstein called its 'charm'). We are dealing, not with a science, but with a religion, a religion in which the self and its past are given the redeeming attributes of God and Eternity.

27 The Ideology of the Market

From *Cambridge Review*, 29 June 1979.

MRS THATCHER is in office, and her ideas in office with her. It would be unjust to look for system in those ideas. Conservatives have always represented themselves as enemies of system, people who see and confront the true complexity of social arrangements. The conservative, we have been told, is a realist, with no over-mastering ideal in the interest of which to sacrifice his common-sense or to propagate falsehood. At the same time, he is a political animal, and must needs have some sense of the common good, and a desire for the policies which would further it. No more than his rivals, therefore, can he dispense with the ideas from which policies are justified.

When Mrs Thatcher and Sir Keith Joseph established the Centre for Policy Studies they made it clear that they, at least, were anxious to discover the intellectual content of their beliefs, and to translate that content into practice. Throughout the recent campaign, Mrs Thatcher has tirelessly displayed her intellectual conviction, and her willingness to enter into every pertinent battle of ideas. It is very important to her that her views should be intellectually persuasive, and she is ready to reward those who find them so. It is hardly surprising, therefore, if the Centre for Policy Studies is now presided over by one of the renegades who abandoned the left-wing camp in the cause of Freedom. And no doubt the Centre will long continue to be associated with that cause.

But matters are more complicated than the appointment suggests. In its own words, the Centre aims 'to secure fuller understanding of the methods available to improve the standard of living, the quality of life and the freedom of choice of the British People, with particular attention to social market policies'. That is an aim of some generality, and indeed obscurity. The last phrase means one thing when 'social' qualifies 'policies', another when it qualifies 'market'. The second meaning can hardly be intended. It is unlike conservatism to reflect on the market in societies with a view to exchanging ours for some newer model. But the first meaning suggests that the Centre is aware that the state of the 'market' has social implications, and that those implications should be taken into account in formulating policy. One recognizes an old Tory theme: that the value of social order is higher than that of the market economy, and indeed, that the value of any economic policy is to be measured not in its own terms, but in terms of the social arrangement which it serves. But it is clear from the remainder of the declaration that this old-fashioned protectionism is very far from the Centre's interests.

There are three things that the Centre seeks to improve: the standard of living, the quality of life, and the freedom of choice of the British people. The first of these suggests a tangible political objective. It has an 'index' to measure it, and can be seen to rise or fall in relation to preceding periods, or to the situation abroad. It is measured in terms of the availability to the common person of those things he might be expected to desire: food, clothes, housing, cars, radios, refrigerators—in short the 'commodities' which circulate in the 'market'. It is no part of the conception of a 'standard of living' to distinguish those things which are naturally desired from those which are desired only because they are declared desirable. Nor does it distinguish the desires which stem from need or interest, from those which pander to whim. This is important, for in so far as we have a conception of the second goal—the 'quality of life'— it is only because we have a conception of the real interests of those who pursue it. Improving the quality of life may not be compatible with raising the quantity of something else. In particular, it may not be compatible with raising the quantity of all available commodities. Moreover it is precisely this 'quality of life' that is invoked when the third goal is (as it must be) put aside or qualified. Addictive drugs are outlawed: that is a real infringement of freedom, but a necessary support to actual interests, and to the 'quality of life' which stems from their satisfaction.

It seems, then, that the three goals that we are asked to consider may not be compatible. The question arises, which of them takes precedence? 'The quality of life' has usually been put aside as a notion too nebulous to generate policy. If we turn to the actual pronouncements of Mrs Thatcher and Sir Keith Joseph we find, in fact, a politic oscillation of emphasis, between the commonsensical goal of the 'standard of living', and the noble ideal of 'freedom'. It is not unusual to suggest that these two, at least, can be combined to form an ideology. Sir Keith Joseph, for example, has been anxious to impress on the British public that a free market is an essential condition of prosperity, and that the freedom of the market is no more than a consequence of that higher and more generalized freedom which is the Englishman's birthright. He has spoken of the merchant and the industrialist as 'wealth creators', who must be given again their freedom to invest, to speculate, to engage in enterprises the rewards or losses of which will not be automatically confiscated or sustained by a vigilant sovereign state.

Until recently Tories have looked upon these libertarian doctrines with scepticism and occasional distaste. But libertarian economics has increased its sophistication since the days of Adam Smith. In the works of Hayek we find the *homo economicus* of John Stuart Mill dressed in the respectable cloth of constitution. He has become a moderate traditionalist, a cautious individualist, a well-meaning benevolent Tory with the grace and authority to hide the invisible hand that guides him. From the Institute of Economic Affairs this newly civilized being has taken his first steps towards Central Office, assuring the curious bystander that the invisible hand of self-interest is after all a sound constitutional device, introduced by the Conservative Party precisely in order to safeguard our liberties, uphold our traditions, and reveal to the world the benefits of Western democracy. As for the 'quality of life'—this is not so much a goal as a consequence of other goals. Time alone will see us obtain it.

Despite the air of intellectual conviction which surrounds the new economic man, it is doubtful that he could convince someone who did not already accept—as Mrs Thatcher and her Cabinet accept—that the 'market' is a natural and inevitable arrangement. Marxists would dismiss as an ideological fiction the view that capitalists are 'wealth-creators'. Wealth is created, they would say, by productive forces, of which labour is the principal constituent. 'Capital' denotes, not a productive force, but an economic arrangement, through which productive tones operate. It is not just false, but a category mistake, to suppose that capital creates wealth. 'Capital' is the name of an economic system. That system may permit the creation of wealth but it may also prevent it. As Marx puts it, capital may (at some stage) prove a 'fetter' on the forces of production. To take an example. The rule of the 'market' implies that men become redundant as technology improves. To protect themselves they withdraw their labour, offering it again only on condition that new technology is not introduced. A perfectly sensible move, in which the law of the market finds blameless enactment. So imagine that some alternative arrangement exists, in which the introduction of new technology is not hampered by the operation of that law, for the simple reason that no one is in a position to contract away his labour power, and no one else in a position to hire him. It is on behalf of that new arrangement, says the socialist, that he is struggling. The real intellectual issue is therefore this: is such an arrangement possible? Or are we condemned to that old arrangement wherein capital must appear to be (although of course this is only an ideological mirage) the actual creator of wealth?

But suppose we grant that there is no alternative arrangement, and that the 'market' (which is but another name for capitalism) is the natural and inevitable form which all production must take. It may nevertheless be true that there is a real limit to which the standard of living can be raised. For capitalism is impossible without wage-labour, and wage-labour will always lay down security of employment as one of its terms, whether or not unemployment is essential to economic growth. Hence if freedom involves freedom of contract, freedom might entail a falling standard of living. Whether it does so is an issue of great complexity, and one that requires us to ask ourselves again precisely what this conservative 'freedom' amounts to.

Consider education. For a long time it has been thought (for no very clear reason) that education is a good thing, in fact such a good thing that it should be the responsibility of government to ensure, not only its universal availability, but also its universal actuality. The attempt by socialists to force all parents to send their children to comprehensive schools was simply an extension of an accepted principle, the principle that the state has a duty to provide schools, and the citizen a duty to attend them. The Conservative, in answer to this problem, calls upon the ideal of 'freedom'. Parents should have freedom to choose some alternative arrangement, in particular the arrangement which the labour government sought to destroy. But the principle remains the same. The state compels parents to educate their children, and dictates the ways in which they may do so. It may look as though a widening of choices has been achieved. But the effect is only temporary. The parents of intelligent children actually prefer to send them to grammar schools, if grammar schools exist. All competing comprehensives, with their better pupils removed from them, must therefore return to the status of the 'Secondary Modern'. The only new choice made available by this process is one that no sensible parent desired—the choice to send their child to a worse school than he might otherwise have attended. There is neither increase in freedom, nor loss of freedom. The question concerns the imposition of rival educational systems, and the real argument for that imposition must lie, to put it crudely, in the 'quality of life' which thereby emerges.

But this brings us back to the idea without which the 'quality of life' is a meaningless slogan—the idea of a real interest. Marxists have argued that a man's real interests may not coincide with his desires, for the reason that many of his desires are imposed on him, or extorted from him, by arrangements which damage his humanity, and which it is in his interest to change. Consider the desire to immerse oneself in pornographic or gory spectacles. Such a desire is fostered precisely by the possibility of its fulfilment, and to fulfil the desire is no more in a man's interest than to possess it. One who argues in that way (as anyone but the most fixated liberal must argue) sees nothing wrong in a restrictive law of censorship. Such a law interferes with 'freedom', just as does the law of drugs. But what concerns us is the quality of life, of which freedom is no more than a small and qualified component. Someone might likewise argue (in the spirit of the Marxian who sees a connection between 'fetishism' and alienation) that the endless pursuit of commodities runs counter to a real interest. Once again the pursuit compels the desire, and in fulfilment breeds dissatisfaction. If that is so, then the goal of the 'quality of life' may be incompatible not only with the reckless pursuit of freedom, but also with the increased standard of living which all our politicians promise us.

No doubt there are forms of 'bourgeois ideology' that do not generate these contradictions. But the ability of this form to create puzzlement is especially remarkable. Not only are the three goals in conflict among themselves; they are also in conflict with accepted Conservative policy. Consider again the market in labour. A man offers money, another offers labour; the first needs labour, the second needs money. In what sense is the ensuing contract free? It will be free only if neither side is constrained to enter it. Ideal freedom occurs when the labourer has the option to contract with no one. (A situation which would be secured only by a state that distributes dole to everyone, whether they choose to seek work or no.) No one wishes for that freedom. The desire for endless leisure is an unnatural one, and exists only in the mind of someone who sees vividly how to fulfil it. What substitute freedom are we then to offer to the working man? The freedom to work for another employer whenever he should choose? But this is not something that he wants. On the contrary, he wants to keep *this* employer, and *this* employment, but on terms that are to his greater advantage. Hence his dependence on the Union, which has as its aim not the contractual freedom of its members, but rather the restriction of that freedom, in the interests of bargaining power. And it seeks bargaining power so as to further the 'standard of living' of its members. In the struggle between Conservatives and Trade Unionists we find that the second are motivated by one of the goals that the Conservative professes to advance, while the first offers nothing in return but the 'freedom' which no Unionist desires. The value over which they might agree—that of the 'quality of life'—has been forgotten in the fruitless conflict between the other two.

If political issues of this kind are to become clear, then it seems that the Conservative leadership should cease to multiply goals beyond necessity. And the vaguer the goals the better. In the all-embracing ideal of the 'quality of life' our *homo economicus* is finally submerged. In his place we find the citizen, whose fulfilment lies not in the pursuit of self-interest, but in the condition of society.

28   The Ideology of Human Rights

From the *Times Literary Supplement*, 14 March 1980.

CLASSICAL Marxism pledged itself to the abolition of the nation-state, and hid this pledge in a prediction. The local and historical allegiances which compose a nation, together with the constitutional devices which consolidate them, were described as 'superstructure', serving to protect and endorse a transient phase of economic development. As soon as nationhood 'fetters' economic development, then it must crumble away. The final resolution of history will be classless, placeless, timeless, international.

If the government of one nation can persuade the people of another to believe that doctrine, then it acquires superior power. It attracts attention away from local allegiances towards a cause which claims to transcend and replace them. The cause in question—'international socialism'—is not only an ideal, but also (it is supposed) an ineluctable reality, the outcome of impersonal forces which no one can resist with impunity or for long. The doctrine does not need to be proved; it can usually support itself negatively, by emphasizing the local grievances which generate the desire to believe in a timeless and placeless ideal. Its victims will rarely ask themselves what foreign interest chooses thus to beguile them. If there is an interest at work, it will seem to be their own.

It is fairly obvious that ever since Lenin converted the concept of imperialism to his uses, Russian foreign policy has advanced behind this internationalist doctrine. In most cases the advance has been to the detriment of that loose association of nations described, out of a Spenglerian sense of its destiny, as 'the West'. America, as the principal power among these nations, has perforce been their principal spokesman. But until recently American foreign policy lacked a convenient international doctrine behind which to conceal the pursuit of power. Striving for a nationhood of its own, America could hardly propose the removal of the nationhood of others as a universal ambition. Under the Monroe doctrine American ideology licensed the interference in the affairs of other peoples only negatively: it was permitted to assist the attempts of any people to cast off the colonial oppression from which America itself was newly free. The aim of emancipating a nation from colonial power may often be right and sensible. But it is coherent only when the nation has acquired an existence apart from the power which colonized it. It would be absurd to assist the citizens of Shepherd's Bush in a struggle for 'liberation'. Shepherd's Bush does not, and never did, constitute a political entity, and has no consciousness of itself as such. Nor can it rise up from the midst of the United Kingdom and declare its historical right to self-government, or in any other way make show of its political self-consciousness as a fact to be reckoned with. Legitimacy is an elaborate artifact, requiring constitution, custom, usage and history.

The Monroe doctrine presupposes such a historical legitimacy to which to lend support against those who would usurp it. It must therefore prove an ineffectual screen for international policy towards peoples whose sense of their national identity is confused, fragmented or nonexistent. What, such peoples may ask, are we being helped towards, when there is no identity which is naturally ours? The internationalist doctrine of Marxism provides a kind of answer; and it is one that hides, for a while, the interests of those who advance behind it.

Recently Western foreign policy has had to be as ubiquitous as the foreign policy of Russia. It has therefore stood in need of a doctrine which is as positive and international as the predictions of Marxism, and also as immediate in its appeal. President Carter, in identifying this doctrine as that of 'human rights', merely draws upon a fundamental strand in all American political consciousness; it is therefore rare for his followers to inquire what the doctrine means. But it is pertinent to ask, since our destiny depends upon it, whether this doctrine can at least conceal our interests from those against whom we need to advance them.

The doctrine that there are 'human' (which is to say 'universal') rights has its antecedents in medieval theories of natural law, according to which there are principles of justice which preside over the affairs of men independently of the local practices which have achieved the status of law. Authority is useless without power, but the Church gave enactment to the authority of natural law, by exerting international influence. Right and might did not diverge; moreover, each seemed to stem from a single divine origin, so that the first neither concealed nor distorted the second. The question whose interest was advanced by the observance of natural law did arise, but it never led to the rejection of the doctrine. When sovereigns were able to break from Rome it was because they had acquired national churches, and a common law which enshrined those principles of natural justice that had formerly been the property of an international Church. Such sovereigns appeared to be constrained, not by an external power, but by the internal conditions of their legitimacy. And still the name 'natural law' was used to denote the authority which interceded between sovereign and subject.

The subsequent history of 'natural justice' and 'natural rights' is complex but familiar. What was once owed as an obligation to God came to be thought of as a generalized obligation to humanity. But 'humanity' names no sovereign power; only the hope that men might live without one. So the authority of these 'natural rights' is an unhappy one; when right lacks power to substantiate it, its allegiance will begin to slip away. In the end only brave men may stand by it, in a spirit of tragic self-sacrifice.

Nevertheless, it is from the conception of 'natural rights' that the current American internationalism gains its credentials. 'Human rights' are rights which belong to all people, whatever local arrangements should constrain them. In upholding such rights America tries to put its authority behind a doctrine that will capture the support of every citizen everywhere, and which will not presuppose any particular economic order—such as capitalism—as its precondition. But because American power is hesitant, qualified by the same sense of justice that informs its ideology, the upholders of 'human rights' will lack international protection. It is impossible to arm them, to send troops to their rescue, or to excite them to insurrection as the Marxist may reasonably do in the name of his international ideal. So the doctrine is of little practical avail against its rival.

It could also be doubted that the doctrine is coherent. Perhaps it is; perhaps it is not; I do not know. Bentham described it as 'nonsense on stilts', but the authority is perhaps not a very persuasive one. Sometimes, reflecting on all that was meant by the 'natural law' of the scholastics, and on that 'sense of justice' which seems so real in the breach and yet so indescribable in the observance, I think that there is truth in the doctrine. But then, if there are rights, there must also be obligations. Whose? Against whom are these rights being claimed? And what is being given in return for them? We find ourselves in the depth of philosophical controversy, trying to uphold that there are rights which ought to be granted to each citizen by every sovereign power, irrespective of history, constitution and local complexity, and (so it would seem) irrespective of any right which the sovereign power can claim in return. To know whether this doctrine is coherent, we should have to examine again the questions discussed so inconclusively by Locke, Rousseau and Hegel: we should have to embark on efforts of abstraction which have defied the capacities of the greatest philosophers, and must inevitably escape the understanding of the common citizen, be he as intelligent as they.

We should not be surprised to find, therefore, that 'human rights' tend to become a cause of action only in the minds of people who have the historical consciousness through which to understand their local meaning. In the absence of that consciousness, the doctrine is felt merely as a kind of generalized anti-authoritarianism, a licence to the individual to take no notice of obligations towards the state, and to ascribe legitimacy to almost any gesture of rebellion. The children of the Iranian middle classes who were sent to America for their education absorbed from the idea of 'human rights' only the ability to forswear allegiance to established power. The influence of their 'education' spread to their contemporaries at home, and was easily incorporated into old habits of vengeance. Young Iranians, having learnt how to disguise barbarity behind the Western dignity of 'student', proceeded to invade the 'natural rights' of the only American citizens weak enough to fall victim to them. And there is no arguing with them. Islamic law has always vested the exercise of criminal justice in the sovereign and so dispenses quite easily with a doctrine of what is 'natural' irrespective of place and time. It need make no room for the 'human rights' which, propagated by American liberalism, served merely to instruct the violators of right in the arts of injustice. Rebellion which has vengeance and not natural justice as its aim is a local affair, indifferent to the large metaphysical questions of the rights of man. The ideology of 'human rights' fails, and with it the foreign policy that sought to advance behind it.

The case should be compared with that of Eastern Europe, where traditional forms of law, surviving as custom, as memory, and as reality in the church's renewed temporal power, give support to the idea of an authority that mediates between citizen and sovereign. The doctrine of 'human rights' begins now to refer to something specific and cogent— not, indeed, to any universal ideal, but rather to old habits of allegiance and constitution towards which history has generated independent respect. The so-called 'dissident' in Czechoslovakia is no more univer- salist in his attachments than the Iranian fanatic. He seeks to find, in the constitution of his country, a regard for that process of law to which his sense of historical identity directs him. If he speaks of 'human rights' it is because his loyalty is being required by an arrangement which promises certain privileges in return, privileges which can be understood in terms of the great tradition of European sovereignty. Such privileges are inti- mately bound up with complex local customs. They have indeed been overlaid and qualified by a Draconian law of sedition, and this law seems to be understood neither by those who enacted nor by those who apply it. But the old privileges persist in the memory, being part of the sense of place, time and nationhood without which there could be no serious alle- giance to the Czechoslovakian state. It is this historical content which makes 'human rights' intelligible, and so enables the citizen to feel instinctively when his rights are being denied. What suffers in that denial is not the citizen's 'natural' freedom (which would be nasty, brutish and short), but the more concrete, qualified freedom which is the condition of national identity. The cause of 'human rights', while it involves a clear appeal to justice, becomes a part of patriotism, inseparable from the love of tradition, language, custom and history which internationalism seeks to dissolve. But in that case, once again, the ideology of 'human rights' provides legitimacy to no ubiquitous foreign policy, becoming absorbed into loyalties which are immovably local and self-regarding. The nation survives as the principal object of affection and despair, and no new allegiance is formed to replace it.

Many of the places where foreign policy really matters are characterized by civil bonds which are both extremely local (scarcely deserving the name of nationhood), and extremely atavistic, having never transcribed themselves into constitution, sovereignty or law. It is hardly likely that the doctrine of 'natural rights', redolent as it is of Western constitutionalism and the traditions of Roman law, will provide the inspiration to people seeking to 'emerge' out of timelessness into history. But it is likely that Marxism, which speaks the language of might and not of right, will at least be understood by them. Paradoxically enough, it is by reaching towards that 'higher' form of timelessness promised by the Marxist that Africans often begin to envisage themselves as constrained by interests that are both local, and also internationally recognized. In other words, this peculiar form of internationalism can catalyse a developing sense of nationhood. We must not be surprised, then, if the nationalism of emergent peoples throws in its lot with Marxism and not with the doctrine of 'human rights'. Our power, having adopted an ideology that retards its exercise, seems fragile beside that of Russia. The Russians disguise foreign policy behind a theory which, however internationalist in its ultimate meaning, is understood by its victims as the sanction of a budding nationalism, and hence becomes an object of all the allegiances which matter to them most.

29 Poetry and Politics

From *PN Review* 17, 7, iii, 1980.

THERE are many ways of enjoying poetry, and many ways of destroying enjoyment through a misplaced didacticism. However, despite Wilde's doctrine that all art is absolutely useless, despite all those conceptions, from Kant to modern expressionism, which have tended to the views that art is 'without purpose', a form of 'play', an activity of 'intuition' divorced from conceptual or instructive aims, it is no more possible now than it has ever been to think of poetry as bearing pleasurable but slight relation to the world. We should beware of taking the many theories that declare the 'uselessness' of poetry too literally. If poetry is useless, it is in the way that friendly conversation is useless; which is to say that it has no purpose besides itself. Friendship is valuable; so too is the conversation through which it finds enactment. But the value of friendship is not an aim which determines every moment of a conversation.

In like manner, art has a value, but this value generates no purpose to be pursued in every artistic gesture. The purposelessness of art is external, like the purposelessness of words in a conversation. But art is as *significant* as conversation, and owes its significance to the absence of an external use. The difference between poetry and propaganda is like the difference between polite conversation and the bargaining which precedes a contract. Bargaining contains its polite components, but these vanish with the failure of the purpose. They are embellishments, indispensable only because of an ideal of human association created not in contract, but in conversation, where individual purposes are dissolved in the human nature which transcends them.

Those comments might seem obvious, but they lead to a puzzling question. Poetry, unlike conversation, is entirely one-sided, commanding the attention of a reader to whom it allows no reply. Perhaps it is essential to aesthetic endeavour that it has this one-sided, unreciprocal character. Not that the reader is a recipient of impressions to which he makes no imaginative addition; on the contrary. But his reaction, however vigorous or violent, must be consequent upon something else, which is the perception of an aesthetic content. By 'aesthetic content' I mean everything that is involved in understanding a poem: everything which it 'puts across'. And, paradoxical though it may seem, it is the one-sided character of aesthetic activity—the seemingly passive role of the audience—which leads people to think that this 'content' defines a new, more subtle, and yet inescapable purpose for poetry, a purpose which must be understood in political terms. The captive audience is the victim of his captor. His reactions can be commanded, controlled, abused and reformed, in the interests of conceptions which, if they are not political, are not so only by neglected opportunity.

But surely a poem is *not* propaganda, or if it tries to be, it will not be good poetry? Someone who says that has a *theory* about the way to appreciate art, a theory which says that our attitude to art must be 'disinterested', 'distanced', or whatever. Beauty, he says, is apparent only to the man who adopts the 'aesthetic' stance, and this requires the kind of disengagement which propaganda seeks to destroy. But that theory is inadequate. Bertholt Brecht, in the *Messingkauf Dialogues*, is not the only one to have made the obvious retort, that you can keep your 'disinterest': it will not interest *me*. I shall tell you of some new ways of reading poetry and watching plays. I shall cultivate in you the effect of alienation, whereby what is familiar is displayed as strange—and try to remain politically distanced from *that*! And I shall use techniques which you would have otherwise called 'art'. Let 'aesthetic response' and the 'beauty' which is its object be as irrelevant as you like, as nice, as refined as you care to make them. But don't expect me to be very interested in the result. I have other and better uses for this 'art' of yours, and if you think that those uses denature poetry and theatre and turn them into something else, well, it is the something else that I am looking for. Let's just give it another name; not poetry but potery. It is potery that I shall make, and potery, if I have my way, that you shall read.

The battle is not just about words: it is about the nature of the institution of art. We shall have to keep an open mind—more open than Brecht's ever was—if we are to bring this contest to a resolution. The example of conversation serves to remind us that value and purpose may diverge: but it does not deter the hardened activist, who wishes, in Walter Benjamin's words, to 'politicize art'. On the contrary, it tells him how best to go about it: pretend that it's all in a friendly spirit, and then sock it to them.

Like words in conversation, poetry may be true or false. There is an absurd doctrine that denounces truth as irrelevant to poetry, seeking to erect an ideal of 'truthfulness' or 'sincerity' in its stead. But if we forgo our interest in truth, we forgo too our interest in understanding. First, there is literal truth:

> Which whoso list look back to former ages,
>   And call to count the things that then were done,
> Shall find, that all the works of those wise sages,
>   And brave exploits which great heroes won,
>   In love were either ended or begun:

Not wholly true perhaps; but without the 'ring of truth' such lines would be poetically empty and dramatically meaningless. Secondly there are the more poetic usages, of metaphor and simile: 'Our tongues recant like beaten weather vanes.' (Hart Crane.) Our response is 'yes' or 'no'; not 'how pretty', or 'how odd'. Suppose the poet had said 'Our tongues decant like eaten leather veins.' You don't know what it means, because you don't know how it could be true or apt (and aptness is truth to airy thinness beat). Finally, there is the truth of experience:

> ... when I have hung
> Above the raven's nest, by knots of grass
> And half-inch fissures in the slippery rock
> But ill-sustained, and almost, so it seemed,
> Suspended by the blast which blew amain,
> Shouldering the naked crag . . .

Now it seems that the true has become the lifelike. An experience is being expressed, in language designed to capture its immediacy (and that is the purpose of rhythm, metre, and accent). Truth is important, but it is not didactic truth. No abstract idea is offered, no proposition set up for proof or refutation; we have only an experience, and truth is truth to *that*. How much politics can you squeeze out of such a poetic intention?

Our concession that poetry can be understood only by someone with an interest in truth has not taken us far. So let us consider two examples notorious for their political 'stance' (I choose that word, because it would be begging all questions to use a clearer one): Marvell's 'Horatian Ode', and Yeats's 'A Prayer for my Daughter'. Both end on a note of abstract conviction, Marvell telling us that 'The same arts that did gain/A power, must it maintain', a thought which if true makes nonsense of the humanitarian pretensions of revolution, Yeats offering us a thought of rare sophistication (some may say, sophisticality): 'How but in custom and in ceremony/Are innocence and beauty born?'. It is clear that Marvell does not intend us to remain indifferent to the truth of his concluding lines. On the contrary, the preceding verses bear a relation to them which might best be described as 'persuasive'. A literary critic who remained ignorant of this would miss the aesthetic content of the verse. Consider the famous description of King Charles's execution:

> He nothing common did or mean
> Upon that memorable scene,
> But with his keener eye
> The axe's edge did try.

This nothing 'common' invites us to compare Charles's conduct with that of the 'Commons' who tried him. And the ambiguity of 'mean' makes clear both the poverty of what is 'common', and the fact that Charles neither did, nor 'meant', in the Anglo-Saxon sense of the word, any common thing: his spirit, which is the locus of 'meaning', was displayed as uncommon, lacking in commonality, on the scene which he made memorable. The force of 'mean', carried through to 'scene', now qualifies the very graces which constitute Charles's virtue: they are scenic virtues. He is tragic indeed, but an actor nonetheless, and it is only in such a 'scene' that his virtue can be apparent—it is not, like Cromwell's, the virtue of resolution, but rather that of display. Yet legitimacy lies more in display (custom, ceremony) than in resolution. The internal rhyme carries the 'meaning' of Charles's spirit through to the 'keenness' of his eye, which is the spirit's outward form, and so back to the 'trial' which Charles's gesture so magnificently overturns. The 'axe's edge' is the weapon of puritanism, which has no authority but only a forced usurping power; it too is put on 'trial', but by a spirit the keener for being refined of indignation. These comments (I do not put them forward as indisputable) arise from reading the poem; and they relate in some way to its persuasive movement. To notice these reverberations of thought and imagery is to share in the enactment by which the poem advances towards its goal. Literary criticism would miss this meaning, if it were not concerned with the truth or falsehood of Marvell's final assertion.

Yeats hides behind a rhetorical question: 'How but in custom and in ceremony/Are innocence and beauty born?' But the thought is no less political than that which concludes the 'Horatian Ode'. Old values are being affirmed, as is their connection with forms of life—custom and ceremony—that must forbid the political activism of the day, or clothe it in unrecognizable habits. The movement towards the conclusion is again 'persuasive'. You could not regard these lines as an intrusion of mere prejudice, without experiencing a disintegration of the poem's mood. The reader who reacted with a peremptory 'Rubbish!' would be so distanced from the poem as to be indifferent to its quality. *If* the thought is rubbish, then so is the experience that has been enacted in the lines which lead up to it.

The last sentence contains a philosophy which I would like to set up for examination. The difficulty presented by such 'political' poems is this: they express definite, although not always pellucid, beliefs. They seem, too, to be informed by a persuasive intent. To use terms which are again not as clear as we might wish, the reader is being invited to assent to these beliefs, and something is being done to seek that assent, perhaps even to compel it. How then can he enjoy the poem and withhold his agreement? And what is this peculiar form of persuasion to which he is being exposed; how does it differ (if at all) from rational argument?

These questions seem less puzzling when asked of dramatic monologues. The dramatic monologue expresses an outlook only, as it were, in inverted commas, as does an actor on the stage. Here we have, not truth, but truthfulness. The dramatic monologue represents a character expressing his opinions; but it does not express an opinion. The inverted commas may be obvious—as in 'A Toccata of Galuppi.' Or they may be hidden, as in Baudelaire, Laforgue and the early Eliot, where the monologue has become an inner voice, a kind of tempter who, in order to scorn your obedience, says, 'see the world like this'. In either case the poem will be characterized by a certain distance between style and subject, the distance which we know as irony. The poet advances a thought, a feeling, an experience, only to abandon it at the moment when it might have seemed his own. You may love the product, but your love is the love for an orphaned child, encouraged by the thought that you are not responsible for the existence of this thing, which bears a real but unspoken debt of gratitude towards you for the sympathy which you may indulge at so little cost. This is the least painful and the most poignant form of human affection: *hypocrite lecteur, mon semblable, mon frère!*

But not all poems are dramatic monologues: surely neither the 'Horatian Ode' nor the 'Prayer for my Daughter' can be read as such, any more than Pope's moral epistles or the satires of Juvenal. And even in drama, we come across lines the political urgency of which creates a persuasive force that we cannot dismiss as the property, however disinherited, of someone with whom we sympathize but whose attitudes we need not adopt. Sometimes we are invited to identify, and not to sympathize. Consider the famous speech of Ulysses from *Troilus and Cressida*:

> Take but degree away, untune that string,
> And, hark, what discord follows! each thing meets
> In mere oppugnancy . . .

Shakespeare goes on to 'defend' this assertion, so repugnant to the ears of egalitarian man, with reflections that are in part philosophical, but which derive their persuasiveness, as does Marvell's Ode, from the manner in which they are carried by the verse. Shakespeare refers to authority and power, power and will, will and appetite, dramatizing, but not arguing, the thought that the distinction between these is socially necessary and yet artificial. Take degree away, and the artifact collapses; authority is reduced to appetite and appetite divides society into 'oppugnancy'. As Hegel might put it, civil society gives way to the universal 'I want'. It would be impossible to regard Shakespeare's thought as mere characterization. There would be no need, in such case, for philosophical subtlety, for that wrestling with truth which characterizes Shakespeare's greatest political speeches. The reader feels again the invitation to belief; the style may be that of Ulysses, but Ulysses becomes the embodiment of truth in a world torn by faction. Even in drama, then, we find the techniques of poetic 'persuasion'. Here the result is surprising, since, if we accept it, we must throw away all the political platitudes of our time. (It is interesting to compare the effectiveness of *Troilus* with the cold-hearted tableaux of Brecht, who makes so little effort to conceal his opinions, and yet who manages to detach them from the language of persuasion. The Brechtian vision is bleak, unfriendly, incapable of resounding in the mind beyond the tableaux that provide its sole illustration.)

Inverted commas, then, do not destroy persuasion, or veil every thought in irony. The persuasiveness of poetic thought, howsoever it may impose upon our prejudices, is intrinsic to it. It is the poem itself which persuades without coercing, which asks our agreement and disdains the reason why. Appreciation and agreement go together.

What then of falsehood? Let us consider another example. I am disposed—not, I think, from political prejudice, although prejudice leads one to ask more of those poets whose vision defies one's own—to find falsehood in A.L.T. Morton's 'Twilight Song'. It is, I think, the same kind of falsehood that Leavis finds in Lionel Johnson's effusion over the 'saddest of all kings', when comparing Johnson with Marvell. Morton, like Marvell, attempts to advance from bloody realities to a political moral: 'we will praise and will not bow down to twilight/And all men will rejoice and none will worship'. As a Marxist Morton feels safer with predictions than with observations: this might lead the reader to an attitude of scepticism that is not elicited by expressions of resolve. (Compare: 'I will not cease from Mental Fight/Nor shall my sword sleep in my hand . . .'.) If I find the advance towards this prediction unpersuasive it is not because the matter remains unproven. Whatever the quality of the writing it could hardly hope to *prove* something as ambitious as that, any more than Marvell could hope to prove the thought which, if true, makes Morton's prediction nonsense. The fault that strikes me is the *schematic* quality of Morton's imagery:

> Liebknecht lay bloody in his ditch. The head
> Of Rosa Luxemburg also . . .
>
> . . . . . .
> Grass springs up like swords
> From Liebknecht's ditch.

Morton's description of Liebknecht is no description: how could he have lain unbloody in that ditch? (Compare the real thought behind Marvell's: 'While round the armèd bands/Did clap their bloody hands', where 'bloody' anticipates blood that is not yet shed, by referring to blood that these hands once did shed but which no longer stains them. Something of motive, of spirit, is observed here.) Morton's effect is derived from the rhythmic assemblage of two proper names, and the invitation to the reader is something like this: remember Liebknecht and Rosa Luxemburg. The reader is persuaded to no attitude that he does not already have towards those two.

Consider too the image of the grass, (which rarely springs up like swords). It can be seen as anticipating the lifting of swords only by someone who already sees through the green fuse the force of a pre-existing anger. The image is a platitude, like the clenched fist of the heroic worker on the postage stamp. It derives persuasive power not from any intrinsic quality but from a prior readiness to accept it.

I consider Morton's poem because, like Marvell's, it purports to deal with actual events, and so the charge of falsehood can be made more particular. Morton's moral is irresolute, disguising desire in prediction, and the passage towards it is spasmodic and unobserved. It neither generates nor qualifies the emotion which it calls for; the poem consists of a series of signals for a feeling that is presupposed. Now that is one characteristic of a more general fault which has come to be known as 'sentimentality' (although the choice of this historically pregnant word should not mislead us). The sentimental emotion looks for an excuse, not an object. It cannot humble itself before the particular and take instruction from what it finds, but must bluster with abstractions which it protects from recalcitrant facts. The stanza that I considered from Marvell was tense with meaning, qualifying every invited emotion with resonances of afterthought. The sentimental separation between emotion and object is denied in every word.

In order to compare these two political poems I have had to shift from thought to feeling. The falsehood of the Morton poem resides in its sentimentality: feeling precedes and therefore disdains its object. To put it another way, the feeling is self-regarding; it loves itself first, and the world only afterwards, and only in so far as the world complies with a fixed emotional need. If there are forms of socialism which are not sentimental (let's not beg the question), then they can become persuasive in poetry only when the political thought is made integral to a feeling. The 'persuasive' quality of Marvell's 'Ode' comes about through the development of feeling. This development is entirely *objective*, consisting in comparisons and allusions that are built into the language of the verse, and which force us to observe events more closely than we could have observed them without their aid. Such statements of doctrine as there are follow according to a logic of feeling and not of argument. But that logic is nevertheless concerned with truth, since it takes its standard not from itself but from reality. In Marvell's poem a political vision is being compared with events, and the feelings integral to the vision are being tested.

> This was that memorable hour
> Which first assured the forced power:

Again 'memorable'. In repeating the idea the verse reminds us that memory is two-edged; there will be a time when the power which sought this memorability will also regret it. It gains the 'assurance' that it needs, and which, in default of legitimacy, is all that it can have. But assurance of what? A question lingers in the imagery of the verse: the edge of the axe is being tried.

We can return now to our question. The persuasion of poetry is not towards an abstract truth, considered in its generality. It is towards the truth of belief as it finds itself in feeling. Poetry involves observation, accuracy, a respect towards what is concrete: not the subsuming generality, but the perception of the actual. A political doctrine can be *tried* by poetry as by philosophical thought; but in the former case the test is in experience. The poem is exploring the extent to which a belief can be lived in the feelings of the man who possesses it. To what extent, the poem asks, do these beliefs encourage us to belong to and observe our world, to what extent do they separate us from it? Even the most abstract idea can be weighed in this balance and found wanting. And its deficiency will be a deficiency in truth.

But now it may be replied, any belief can pass such a test: it suffices that it gather to itself real and serious feeling: it suffices that it be *lived*. A test that passes everything, passes nothing. If poetry grants truth to all belief, then it grants truth to none. This brings us back to the problem. Richards described *The Waste Land* as achieving a complete severance between poetry and belief. Eliot seemed to have made poetry out of the *absence* of belief: and then, in *Four Quartets,* he poured into that absence a system of belief so subtle that few can tell whether it really belongs there, whether it adheres to the words or whether it slides away from them. The problem of Eliot has survived, among Marxists, among Leavisites, among New Critics and Old. Can this belief (or its absence) be lived without detriment to the individual soul? Some find solace in the vision of *Four Quartets,* others (like Leavis) find a deeply disguised rejection of experience, an experiment in living which failed. So clearly there *is* a genuine poetic test of truth. If Eliot could not persuade us of a particular belief then this must be because no one could.

I shall take a less familiar example. Here roughly translated, is the octet of the tenth poem in Book II of Rilke's *Sonnets to Orpheus:*

> All that we have acquired is threatened by the machine,
> So long as it dares, in spirit or obedience, to be.
> Where there was lovely hesitation of a happy hand
> It forces building from stones cut awkwardly.
>
> Nowhere does it refrain, that we might just *once* escape it
> And it, in the quiet factory, listen to anointing oil.
> It is life: it means us so to understand
> And with one resolve, must order, make and spoil.

Here is statement, and it is political. I imagine a certain kind of Marxist response. The machine is to be mastered, not implored. It is means and not end; nevertheless it is an indispensable means and the instrument of our salvation. Without the machine, our longed-for shortening of the working day will not happen; the hunting, fishing, and poetry-writing will remain confined to a leisured class. To invite the machine to stand idle and listen to its self-anointing—what is this but the quiescence of the leisured intellectual, who wishes to make subjective every objective reality which threatens his privilege? To live this vision is to surrender to beliefs which can be lived only in emotional detachment. The active self has given itself to self-surrender. We are invited to believe what destroys all active feeling. Here now is the sestet:

> But being is still enchanted for us; in a hundred
> Places it remains a source. A play of pure
> Powers, which touches no one, who does not kneel and
> wonder.

> Words still go softly out towards the unsayable.
> And music, always new, from palpitating stone
> Builds in useless space its godly home.

The lines have a persuasive intent. It might be the 'architecture d'aujourd'hui' that is being described; if so, we recognize our experience of that better thing which it has replaced: the 'palpitating stones' (*bebendsten Steinen*) that no machine could have cut for us. We have a description of architecture that touches the very heart of the distinction between the awkward starkness that no one has learned to tolerate, and the ancient music instilled by noble hesitations and godlike purposelessness. But there is a movement from the rejection of what is alien to us, to an acceptance of what remains. The emotion has been rescued from the fury of mere rejection, disciplined according to the precept of Zarathustra: 'Where you cannot love, pass by.'

The experience of architecture is a universal symbol for the spirit's attempt to find a correspondence between itself and the world. The movement of the sestet (whether or not successful) is towards self-affirmation. The poet states a thought the truth of which spells his dejection. But in the statement he searches for the innate qualification, the aspect that permits belief. The seriousness of the belief is not merely a matter of its truth, nor of the strength and complexity of the feelings that surrounds it. Seriousness involves a vision which makes room for the *subject*. Strength of feeling is not enough to guarantee his sense of self. Something more is needed. The point of a poetical test is that it brings this 'something more' into play. A political doctrine that does not survive the poetical test is one that must be rejected by anyone alert to poetry. For he will see that it is a doctrine that is at war with himself. And that is why poetry, but neither philosophy, nor science, can accomplish the final test of politics. In poetry words are used to convey absolute individuality of vision. It is this individuality which is captured in the Anglo-Saxon sense of 'mean'. Tried by the keen eye of Rilke, the machine may seem as deficient in meaning as the Marxist doctrine that seeks to defend it.

30   Humane Education

From *The American Scholar*, September 1980.

THE National Endowment for the Humanities, having been granted its charter by Congress, was also provided from the same source with a definition of its scope. 'The term "humanities" includes, but is not limited to, the study of the following: language, both modern and classical; linguistics; history; jurisprudence; philosophy; archaeology; comparative religion; ethics . . .' and also 'those aspects of the social sciences which have humanistic content and employ humanistic methods.' Certain features of this list raise intellectual questions, two of which will occupy me here. Is there any positive conception of a 'humanity'? And are there 'humanistic methods'? The purpose in asking these questions is to understand the nature of humane education.

Our present classification of university subjects reflects a complicated history. Until Bacon's *Advancement of Learning*, little attempt was made to distinguish genuine science from subjects of study which either did not or could not exhibit experimental method. 'Natural history' and 'natural philosophy' existed as fragmentary and encyclopaedic collections. While important and undifferentiated parts of the Greek corpus, they were tolerated with less patience in the Roman tradition of oratory, with its single-minded aim of producing (in Quintilian's words) *vir bonus, dicendi peritus*—the good man, skilled in speech. The disciplines of medicine and architecture, added to the Roman liberal arts by Varro, were almost immediately removed again by Martianus Capella, leaving the seven subjects which provided the basis of education from late antiquity to the Renaissance.

How did the idea of a humane education emerge from this tradition? Cicero used the term *humanitas* to express the general idea of cultural refinement—an idea later expressed as *civilitas* by John of Salisbury (cf. modern uses of the term 'civilized'). Petrarch intended to revive this idea as an educational aim when, in comparing his own intellectual standpoint with the traditions of scholasticism, he referred to the *studia humaniora*, the 'more human studies'. By the time of Leonardo Bruni (1436), the general designation of the classics, and the disciplines associated with them, as *studia humanitatis* was beginning to be conventional.

Our contemporary conception of the humanities has evolved out of this early Renaissance compendium by a process of steady elimination, followed by one of unsteady addition. If we ask what has been eliminated, the answer seems fairly clear—science. Now, it is true that the ancients (following Aristotelian thought) divided subjects into the theoretical and the practical, and believed this classification to correspond to a deep distinction among mental faculties. But the distinction was characterized obscurely, and important questions were left undecided. To which category, for example, does music belong? Together with geometry and astronomy, it was taught as part of the quadrivium, a practice that conflicted sharply with the descriptions of the educational nature of music given in the political works of Plato and Aristotle. And it would now be very unusual to think that music has an educational affinity with geometry. Likewise rhetoric—which is, superficially at least, a practical accomplishment—was studied in a quasi-theoretical way, so as to include classical languages, literature, and other subjects of bookish learning.

The scientific revolution brought with it the view that certain subjects have a special claim to objectivity. The subjects that we now know as sciences are characterized, first, by the attempt to understand the world as an entity independent of our ways of perceiving it, and, second, by their potentiality for 'progress'. The two features go together. If the world exists independent of our perception, then the task of understanding it will be cumulative. Learning will 'advance', sometimes retracing its steps but moving, in the long run, from ignorance to truth. Science involves prediction, experiment, theory, the division of the world into 'natural kinds'. It involves that complex but familiar thing called scientific method, the aim of which is the knowledge of how things are. As for the humanities, they are what remain when science is removed. Perhaps they are nearer to our apprehension of ourselves than any science; for they do not seem to be founded, as science is founded, on a sharp distinction between how things are and how things seem. But it is not clear what we can say about them, or why we should feel that they have anything in common, other than the fact that they are not yet scientific. The National Endowment's reference to the 'humanistic' parts of the social sciences reflects a sense that the scientific claims of those subjects have not yet been substantiated; they are therefore temporarily resident in the house of the humanities. But perhaps nothing remains in this house, or ought to remain there, for long.

Men are part of nature and are subjects of scientific inquiry. So there ought to be sciences, perhaps unborn, which will usurp the subject matter of the studies called humane. How, then, can we believe that there is anything objective in humane education? Are there limits to scientific inquiry, parts of nature which are recalcitrant to its methods? Or is there some other way of knowing the world than the way of science? I do not think it is coherent to suggest that there are limits to scientific inquiry. To say that there are parts of nature which lie beyond the purview of science is, in effect, to say that there are parts of nature which do not obey nature's laws. Any defence of the humanities which relies on this self-contradiction is dangerous, in that it discredits the cause which it pretends to uphold. It is unfortunate that so many modern American academics, in their desire to uphold traditional educational values, have had recourse to that contradiction, arguing as though the humanities were autonomous and valuable simply because they could not be understood by those opposed to them.

How should we defend them? We must show that there can be a study of natural objects which cannot be reducible to scientific inquiry. And we must show that this study is valuable; it must be a form of education. If it exists, then it will provide us with our positive conception of the humanities, our criterion for including, and also for excluding, potential members from the National Endowment's list. Nineteenth-century philosophical anthropology tried hard to identify this unscientific mode of knowledge. Under the influence of Kant and Vico, thinkers of the period were disposed to represent human things as having two contrasting aspects: nature and freedom. The more sensible among them did not refer to the two worlds of 'the empirical' and 'the noumenal'—the scientifically knowable and the arcane. Nor did they speak of facts which are inaccessible to science. They spoke rather of the world of science and the world of culture, which are in one sense the same world but which cannot be known in the same way. The world of culture, the 'human world', comes to us imbued with our way of knowing it. It is a reflection of ourselves, but a reflection made objective. To understand it we must cultivate the peculiar faculty—the faculty of *Verstehen*—which we use to understand ourselves.

Such doctrines, which find expression in Dilthey, in Weber, and in many others, are undeniably obscure. But that they might contain a truth is shown by a very simple example. A portrait consists of pigments spread upon a canvas, and from the scientific point of view that is *all* it contains. But of course it is also a law of nature that beings like us will react to portraits in certain complex ways. This law of nature has never been formulated, but in any case we can dispense with it. For we understand portraits without its aid. We see these coloured patches as a face and, seeing them so, gain access to the human reality of the picture. The face is not an additional feature of the portrait, above and beyond the coloured patches that make it up. But we do not see the face if we look only at the coloured patches. The human reality of these patches is not their scientific reality, because it comes to us mingled with our manner of perception. It is *we* who put the face in the picture; but it is there to stay, and we are obliged, if we can, to understand it.

I think that the suggestion that there is a 'human world' which is observable only to the person who has, and who cultivates, human understanding takes sustenance from such examples. It is obvious that the face in the picture is both objective—it belongs in the world—and yet not truly separable from our human capacity to recognize it. (It is only there for us; it is not there for a dog or a scientist.) The face is a tiny episode in what the Hegelians would call 'objective spirit'. And, as we know, there is an art in seeing pictures. The capacity to see this fragment of the human world can be cultivated, developed, educated.

The example has a certain rhetorical appeal, but it cannot stand alone as establishing the nature of humane education. We must show that there are modes of reflection proper to the understanding of the human world. These modes of reflection must not be mere skills. They must involve definite conceptual capacities: abilities to make comparisons, and to impose order on experience. I shall take architecture as an example. It would not be unreasonable to suggest that there is a conflict between those who regard architecture as a science, those who regard it as a skill, and those who regard it as something different from both. Now if to regard architecture as a skill is to regard it as a means to an end (however complicated the end and however sophisticated the means to it), then the first two parties will agree about what is to be taught in a school of architecture. The 'science' of architecture will be nothing more than the theory of a skill, concerned with representing, in theoretical terms, the means to given ends. The acquisition of the skill is the acquisition of the ability to employ those means, and so depends on their discovery.

The third party will not concede that architecture can be so easily defined. He will say that it involves something else—the exploration of style, the knowledge of the aesthetic properties of details, of materials, of manners, of light and shade. Is this knowledge practical or theoretical? You could put the difficulty in another way: architectural knowledge is not of means, but of ends. It is therefore not a skill, and is irreducible to the scientific methods that are subservient to skill. It retains something of the practical, for it involves knowing what to do, and something of the theoretical, since it requires classification and comparison. But the classifications and comparisons point not to scientific truth but to human interest; they are concerned with the understanding of architecture as a feature of the human, and not of the natural, world.

A very simple example of a nonscientific classification is that of ornamental marbles. These include porphyry (a silicate), onyx (an oxide), marble (a carbonate), and exclude limestone (chemically identical to marble and differing only in crystalline structure). The classification clearly does not name what philosophers would call a 'natural kind'; it is not the preface to a scientific explanation. The laws governing the behaviour and appearance of these stones would not use this concept but others, which the classification cuts across and to which it is irreducible. Nevertheless those laws would explain the properties of the stones which lead us to classify them as ornamental marbles. So in one sense the natural science of crystallography will generate all the truths of the matter. But it will not help us to understand the classification that we employ. Someone could remain ignorant of the nature of ornamental marbles, whatever the state of his scientific knowledge. The classification is genuine (there is something that a stone has to be in order to be an ornamental marble); yet it is a prelude not to scientific inquiry but to a complex aesthetic use. The appearance of an ornamental marble is understood only by those who are sensitive toward that use; they must become familiar with the place of ornamental marbles in our ways of perceiving and responding to buildings. One comes to understand the classification by learning to see the appearance of a material in a human context. That context endows the appearance with a meaning.

With this kind of classification we move about on the surface of things. We classify objects according to their felt significance, not according to the postulates of a predictive science. (In matters of human significance it is always the surface, and what can be brought to the surface, that counts.) It may be, therefore, that we cannot take for granted the ideals of convergence of opinion and of progress, which stem from the scientific view of the world. The end of our inquiry may not be a single body of recognized truths that state how things are, independent of our capacities to observe and discover them. In this more human world, our natural capacities to observe and discover, to feel and respond, enter into the description of how things are, and convergence, if it is to be secured at all, must be secured in some other way. Convergence persists as an ideal, but perhaps it is never to be realized: what is given is not the fact of it, but its common pursuit. Nevertheless, we are beginning to see that there may be distinctive educational processes through which this common pursuit can be advanced and retarded. How are these processes to be defined?

Whether or not architecture is to be considered as a 'humanity' (would that it were!), there are additions to our list of humanities that can be instantly recognized as illegitimate. Consider, for example, those second-order subjects or metadisciplines which are at present becoming fashionable. The guiding principle of these disciplines is that of relevance—education being conceived not as an end but as a means to some independent social goal. Examples in the humanities include 'Women's Studies' and 'Black Studies'—roughly 'For any underprivileged x, x Studies'. Many people oppose the suggestion that these constitute genuine subjects but cannot say why—which is indicative of the confusion common to all those who know that humane education is worthwhile and yet cannot find the reason. Can we explain their hostility?

Let us take a hypothetical example. 'Mathematics Studies' is a degree option for those who dislike the barren rigours of old-fashioned mathematics and who wish to see mathematics in its 'wider context' as a discipline potentially relevant to the problems facing 'industrial man'. This degree offers courses in the sociology of mathematics (which studies the effect of 'disprivileged background' on mathematical eminence, and of mathematical competence on social standing); the psychology of mathematics (which is very dry, except for the section devoted to the unconscious); the philosophy of mathematics (which, being unable to presuppose any competence in logic, stays with the jargon of 'dialectical' thought); and the history of mathematics; with options in 'mathematical art', 'Pythagorean cosmology', 'number symbolism' and 'the universal history of the number 2'. Nobody will suppose that such subjects produce understanding, either of mathematics or of anything else. It is impossible to gauge what qualities of mind would be adapted to them or what value or discipline would result from their pursuit. The subject of Mathematics Studies is pure fantasy, and even sociologists might consider that inflicting it on students would not be fair, or not before 'further research'. What is wrong is fairly evident: Mathematics Studies involves no critical reflection on a given field of inquiry and no methods which constrain that field. The true critical appraisal of mathematics is reserved for those with a mathematical understanding; those who emerge with a degree in this field cannot assess or dispute a mathematical proof, nor do they acquire any other intellectual accomplishment that would show itself in reasoned critical reflection, applicable beyond the range of examples which have nourished it.

It seems to me that analogous defects attend the other newly proposed additions to the humanities. Women's Studies is not defined by any process of critical reflection which constrains from within the matters to be studied, but by external interests whose focus is not education but politics. It is impossible to isolate the work of women poets from a tradition created by men; it is impossible to understand the social reality of womanhood without studying manhood; it is impossible to hold the jar of civilization to the light and expect the feminine and the masculine to separate themselves like oil and water, so that their properties can be independently observed. All we have, and all we shall ever have, is a collection of intellectual fragments: applications of this or that humane discipline by students who have neither the time nor the interest to master any of them, and the spawning of 'problems' that are as unreal as the subject which gives them academic respectability. But is the case of Women's Studies exactly like that of Mathematics Studies? I think they have this in common—that in both there is no intellectual relation between the things which are studied, and therefore no real field of study. By 'intellectual relation' I mean a relation by which knowledge of one thing can be brought to bear on questions about another. When this relation exists, then the field of study will be constrained by it, as mathematics is constrained by the discipline of mathematical proof.

We have the feeling that it is not just tradition which has created our idea of the 'humane' subject. The tradition has endured because it enshrines what is genuine. The sign of a genuine discipline is the existence of an intellectual constraint which unites its parts. It would be begging any questions to speak of method. But consider music or architecture. Is it not true to say that, as one comes to understand any one of the questions considered in these disciplines, so one finds it easier to understand the others? And is it not true that the mode of understanding in each case constrains the subject, forcing the student to recognize that some music or architecture is serious and some not, that some problems in musical analysis or architectural theory are problems and others mere confusion or bluff?

But the fact that certain subjects lead us to *believe* that they are genuine does not silence the sceptic. Many scientists, for example, find it difficult to recognize the limits of their subjects, and use their methods in areas where we feel (again without being able to say why) that they do not apply. People say that there is a science called economics and that it has some bearing on the government of nations. This may be an impertinence or it may be a serious truth; it is difficult to know which. Is this because there *is* a science, but its subject matter is unclear? Or because there is neither science nor subject? Or because government, as part of the human world, is to be understood, not scientifically, but with the aid of the education we call humane? I am inclined toward the third of those views, and hence see an enormous political significance in defining the nature and scope of the humanities. But the problem is difficult, perhaps insoluble. Our intuitions abandon us just here, where we need them most. The least that we can say is that the idea of a subject as constrained by an intellectual discipline has to be further examined, and something must be said about the peculiarity of a constraint that is not scientific. Should we speak of method here? Or should we try to give some other content to the notion of a common pursuit?

I think that three things can be said in answer to those questions. The first can be illustrated by returning to the example of ornamental marble, which showed that there can be a genuine classification, the application of which involves considerable understanding but which does not pass the barrier from *seeming* to *being*. It is a classification of appearances, but not the mere appearance of a classification. On the contrary, it focuses on human attitudes of the greatest significance and power. In understanding it we also understand those attitudes, in their objective, 'realized' form. So it seems that genuine knowledge can be enshrined in such classifications—a knowledge, to put it simply, of human nature. The whole art of architecture is like that. Properly understood, architecture involves a knowledge of the properties of materials, forms, and structures in terms of their resonance in the human spirit. Architecture is a study of the lived surface of things. Because this study constantly seeks to find what things belong together (as the parts of an architectural Order belong together), it is also a discipline. But it can be understood as such only if we see that the unifying principle must reside in an affinity that is perceived. Ornamental marbles share a common spirit; the origin of that spirit is in us, and the delight we take in them is in the human projection that they help us to achieve. The constraint implicit in humane education is always of that kind: it involves the discovery of spiritual relationships. These relationships are real, but not scientific. In understanding them we are understanding ourselves.

As we turn from architecture to literature, this last thought will seem both true and difficult. We know that criticism proceeds by comparison and analysis, and that it seeks for the spiritual significance of literature. We know, too, that it looks ridiculous as soon as it is divorced from the study of human nature and the values through which human nature finds enactment. But we find it very difficult to ascribe to literary criticism any such thing as a method, nor can we state in clear terms a single aim which it pursues. This points us to a second feature of the constraint that is intrinsic to the true humanity. The constraint has a kind of autonomy; it is resistant to scientific method and irreducible to it. When we try to import scientific method into a humane subject, we find that we are no longer talking about the same thing. This is illustrated by the many recent attempts to import the technicalities and theories of linguistics into the study of literature. The attempt, associated with names like 'semiology', 'semiotics', and 'hermeneutics', has led to nothing but intellectual confusion. What proudly announces itself as a method always turns out, on examination, to be an elaborate irrelevance. The sciences from which semiotics borrows its vocabulary are not concerned with the critical interpretation of literature, but with something quite different. They describe language as a natural object, obedient to laws which could be formulated and understood even by the man who could not speak the language and who had no knowledge of the human spirit which found expression through it. The technical terms of linguistics, in being twisted into critical usage, must therefore become metaphors, and the science suffers a systematic translation from theory to jargon. It then becomes necessary to remove the jargon in order to discover that the procedures of literary criticism, of musical analysis, or whatever, have remained entirely unchanged by its introduction. To prove this point is not easy, but I think that it can be shown (see my attempt in 'The Impossibility of Semiotics' on page 31).

This inherent resistance to scientific method is one of the most important features of humane education, showing it to be irreplaceable by science. If that is so, then there really is a positive conception of the humanities. Some subjects are humanities because they cannot make the passage from the *studia humanitatis* to the realm of scientific inquiry.

Why should that be so? What explains the impervious quality of a subject like literary criticism? Someone might say that these questions have no answer, that literary criticism, music, and so on are peculiar subjects and all their procedures are intrinsic. But to construe the autonomy of humane education so strictly is to risk losing sight of its value. An important feature of education is that it induces mental competence. It equips the student with habits of thought which are not merely exhausted by the subject that he studies but which enable him to extend his understanding in new and sometimes unforeseen directions. Writing early in the twelfth century, Hugh of Saint Victor, in his *Didascalion*, argued that this was true of the seven liberal arts. 'These seven [the ancients] considered so to excel all the rest in usefulness that anyone who had been thoroughly schooled in them might afterwards come to a knowledge of other subjects by his own inquiry and effort, rather than by listening to a teacher.' Clearly this feature is always in our minds when we try to decide whether a given subject constitutes 'an education'. It was the professed aim of Rhetoric to fit a man for public life. More recently, people have thought that Classics, or English, or even Philosophy might (in the right hands) constitute such an education, endowing a man with the capacity to perceive and understand not simply the matters which he had been taught but other matters which he had not. This is our picture of the civilized mind. But we cannot have such a picture if we insist on the absolute autonomy of the humanistic disciplines. So we must seek elsewhere for an explanation of their resistance to scientific method.

This leads me to my final point, which is that the distinction between humane and scientific understanding has a more general basis. Everything worthwhile in education stems from the attempt to answer the question 'Why?' A literary critic tells you why a certain word, line, or paragraph is as it is. The architect tells you why a window frame has the shape you see; the musician tells you why a given chord is inverted; and so on. All the learning that accumulates in the study of language, literature, and the arts is useless unless it brings the answer to such questions. But the scientist too asks 'Why?' He seeks the explanation of events, and looks for the laws of nature that provide it. But the question 'Why?' means something different in either case. The scientific 'Why?' seeks a cause and the laws from which causes emanate. The humane 'Why?' seeks a reason. This reason usually names no laws and forswears prediction; it is concerned to make the phenomenon intelligible. It enables the observer to see an order and reason in events; this order lies on the surface, like the meaning in a sentence or the spirit in a face.

All our examples of humane education involve subjects in which the 'Why?' of reason can be pursued with gathering momentum. Understanding one poem, you are more ready for the next; gradually a subject unfolds before you and becomes intelligible as an expression of the human spirit. If we want a general account of this 'Why?' of reason, and how it differs from the 'Why?' of cause, then we should look away from the world of objective spirit to humanity itself—to subjective spirit. It is there, in our instinctive understanding of ourselves and others, that the 'Why?' of reason has its fundamental use. We can see at once that it is not the 'Why?' of cause. A man's behaviour becomes intelligible when I see the world through his eyes. I see how one particular object can be desirable for him, another repulsive. I see the order in his experience: this does not mean explaining it or subsuming it under universal law, but understanding the complexities of perception that answer for him the question 'Why?'. I see why he would do what he did, feel what he did, and so on. The lived surface of his world is transmitted to me and, in knowing the reason why, I feel within myself the promptings of a motive that is his. This human understanding, so different from prediction, manipulation, or explanation, is the origin of our moral sense. The British moralists called it sympathy. Others have spoken of intuition, of empathy, of sensibility, of *Verstehen*. Vico, as Sir Isaiah Berlin has shown, attempted to give a complete theory of its nature. Yet one thing is sure. Whatever we call it, and however we analyse it, it exists. Moreover, it is indispensable to us, and irreplaceable by any natural science of man. Therefore we must defend as best we can the education which refines and embellishes it. This means that we must cease to fabricate those false humanities which turn attention away from the world of experience toward confused political goals, while depriving students of the education through which those goals can be understood.

31   The Politics of Culture

From *Conservative Essays*, edited by Maurice Cowling (Cassell, 1978).

IN THUCYDIDES' *History of the Peloponnesian War*, Book I, Archidamus, King of Sparta, exhorts his countrymen with the words: 'We are wise because we are not so highly educated as to look down upon our laws and customs . . .' Archidamus was not alone in thinking that education can destroy that respect for established custom which is the chief repository of common wisdom. The present day liberal would no doubt agree with him, hoping, like John Stuart Mill, to overthrow the 'despotism of custom' in the name of progress and enlightenment, and feeling a deep hostility to any form of 'wisdom' that cannot be made the exclusive property of an individualistic middle class—a class which finds its identity through doctrine and work rather than through inherited social position. Nevertheless, the thought remains that there might be some mode of education which can co-exist with the forms of popular feeling, that there might be what may be called a 'high culture' which is actually continuous with the 'common culture' from which it springs. It is that thought—common to the entire Hegelian tradition down to Adorno and Eliot—which will be explored in this essay.

On one view of these matters, high culture consists in nothing but specialized amusements and entertainments, amusements requiring rather higher educational attainments than say mud-wrestling or bear-baiting. High culture is nothing more nor less than the entertainment of the educated, and its quality bears no more essential relation to the health or well-being of a society than does the state of the nation's football team. Indeed, since the triumph of internationalism in these matters—a triumph already exhibited in the pan-Hellenic games, but given its full glory in our time by Hitler at the Berlin Olympics—people are likely to feel that the importance of a strong football team outweighs all the slender advantages to be gained from a theatre or an opera house. And of course, our football teams have no Pindar to celebrate them, and wear no crown more precious than the tin wreaths of Merseyside poets.

It is surprising to find how many of those who have reacted against the decadence of modern society have also shared that view of the place of high culture in social organization. They have defended high culture as the entertainment of the leisured class, because they have wished above all to defend the existence of that class and its necessity to a healthy social order. That is a serious and important outlook. But one is not forced to accept as a corollary to it what one might call the St Petersburg view—the view which sees high culture as the offshoot of an aristocratic order, and valuable only because of the value of that order. (We might call this the St Petersburg view partly after the spirit of that city, and partly in deference to its two most brilliant defenders, Stravinsky and Nabokov.) The other side of this view finds expression in a certain kind of Leninism, in particular in the cultural revolution of Chairman Mao, who clearly thought of the continuance of high culture as an obstacle to the destruction of the ruling class. In the face of such a conflict, between the crushing snobbery of St Petersburg and the self-righteous mediocrity of Leningrad, one cannot but be attracted by contemporary Western liberalism, which allows one to muddle along for a few more years, with neither iconoclastic fervour nor mute despair.

But perhaps we do not have to accept the premise—do not have to accept, that is, that there is any one kind of social order that is associated with the existence of high culture, or any one kind of social order that is served by its continuance. It is scarcely necessary to remind ourselves of the fact that, for us, high culture includes not only the aristocratic art of Racine and Molière, but also the bourgeois art of Dickens and Mann, the popular moralism of Bunyan and the folk poetry of the ancient Aegean. It is possible that T. S. Eliot was right to think that no genuine high culture can exist in a classless society. It would certainly be difficult to present an empirical refutation of his view, since the world has not seen, and never will see, a society that is truly 'classless'. But the issue is an obscure one, and for the purposes of our discussion we must regard all questions in this area as open ones.

Let us assume, therefore, that the St Petersburg view of culture is as unproven as it is discouraging. What do we put in its place? One view that is popular among historians—popular because it gives the illusion of method to a specious appetite for unmeaning facts—is that society is 'organic', so that high and common culture are separate manifestations of some common force or principle, the 'life-force' of the social order. On such a view all cultural manifestations are internally related to the health of a society, and changes in high culture necessarily reflect changes in the common culture that underlies it. The greatest exponent of that view was Hegel, whose indefatigable appetite for meaningful connections led him to see every aspect of society as necessarily connected with every other aspect, the whole being a manifestation of the world spirit at a particular moment in its compulsive evolution towards its highest manifestation in the person of Hegel. The idealist metaphysics which gave meaning to that view has been universally abandoned. But the view itself continues to exert its fascination, though perhaps less now than in 1926, when Spengler was able to write of the 'deep' connections between the differential calculus and the dynastic principle of politics in the age of Louis XIV, between the space-perspective of Western oil painting and the invention of the railway, between contrapuntal music and credit economics.

As is well known, Marx accepted the view that culture in all its forms is a sign of some deeper social process. But he gave to the idea of a sign a definite causal meaning. And the social essence, he thought, was to be found in labour, in the class struggle, and in the economic basis of the relationship between them. By the help of such conceptions he tried to give to the Hegelian theory the objectivity and explanatory power of a natural science. If he had succeeded in that, and succeeded moreover in showing the truth of his science, it might be thought that there would be nothing more to say—the connection between high culture and common culture would have been established, and it would be clear that the two cultures are simply separate effects of a common cause, the law of their relationship being seen as a causal one, and the pattern of their influence one on the other being describable only in terms of an all-embracing theory which removes autonomy from both.

Even if such a theory were true (and, as will be suggested later, its scientific pretensions are largely spurious), it would not have exhausted the matter. Consider a theory of psycholinguistics so exhaustive as to issue in laws which determine the utterance of every sentence. It tells us, for example, just when a man will say 'The house is white', and just when he will say 'Something is white'. In one sense, such a theory would provide a complete account of the relation between those sentences, since it would give the causal laws which determine their utterance. But in another sense it would be far from complete. For there is a connection between these sentences which is not causal, and yet which is of the first importance, a connection of meaning. It is that connection which is grasped in understanding the sentences, and a man may have a complete understanding of them while being ignorant of the causal laws which govern their utterance. He may also have a full knowledge of those causal laws and yet have no linguistic understanding. It could be that there is such a way of understanding the connection between high and common culture, a way which sees the connection more in terms of a concept of significance or meaning than in terms of some monolithic causal law. Such a connection would be *essentially* on the surface, and independent of the determinism of any 'economic' base. A man who understood the operation of the base might yet fail to see the meaning of what is explained. From the political point of view he would therefore be every bit as ignorant as if he knew no economics at all.

As a matter of fact, there is real evidence that the author of *Capital* was disposed to think in causal terms. The thought of his followers, however, has been largely analogical; it has consisted in the perception of connections in the absence of covering laws. Thus the 'fetishism of commodities' seems naturally to belong to mass production, and mass production to the presence of a controlling interest, and all three to that spirit of alienation which bedevils modern humanity. But the naturalness of those connections is established without recourse to any truly causal mode of reasoning. It proceeds, not by the discovery of genuine 'natural kinds'—entities which are the subject of theoretical laws—but rather by the invention of useful classifications—classifications which transform an inert body of facts into a live body of practical reasons.

The concepts introduced by Marxism have their *raison d'être* not in explanation but in practice. They are part of an attempt to understand the world, not as a material structure obedient to causal laws, but as a theatre of rational activity. And in this respect the Marxist notion of 'praxis' has much in common with the Christian notion of 'faith', both being designed to abolish the distinction between scientific and practical understanding in the hope that *practical* reasons could be given for *believing* something, rather as Pascal based his faith on a wager.

The argument for the abolition, however, is obscure, and must, unless we are to accept the entire Marxist theology, be treated with reserve. To classify objects according to their relation to our will is not *ipso facto* to divide them into scientifically respectable kinds, and so provides no explanation of the properties which we exploit in them. The explanation, when it is given, might therefore employ concepts which cut across the classifications necessary to practical understanding.

The desire to see all cultural activity as possessing a 'meaning' and as understandable in terms of that meaning, without recourse to a full explanatory science, is a familiar one. It is present in Burckhardt's theory of the state as a work of art; it dominates Freudian and Jungian analysis, and it is the stock in trade of art history and criticism. Its most recent manifestation—in the 'structuralism' of Lévi-Strauss and his followers—points to a cultural holism at least as grandiose as Hegel's. But the structuralist conception remains sketchy and confused. It tries to impose significance through the wholesale transportation of concepts from another intellectual sphere, and remain at one remove both from scientific explanation and from practical understanding. Nonetheless, as in Burckhardt, there is an interesting thought that we must try to express more coherently.

II

There is a tradition in political philosophy at least as old as Plato's *Republic*, which takes the analogy between the life of the individual and the life of the state very seriously. Whether it actually identifies its 'leviathan' with Hobbes's 'commonwealth', with the state, or with some entity such as Oakeshott's 'civil association', which is both morally vaster and politically smaller than the state, it sees the State or the society as a kind of super individual, and the organization and fulfilment of that larger individual are construed on the model of the organization and fulfilment of the smaller.

The analogy ought to bear directly on the present discussion. If it does, then the well known philosophical distinction between understanding a human being as an organism and understanding him as a person may also apply. There ought to be a particularly 'personal' way of *understanding* society. Indeed, the application of that distinction may provide us with a clue to the connection we are seeking, between high and common culture. To rehearse the distinction briefly: if someone does something, and we do not understand his action, we may seek to understand it in two separate ways. First we may seek for the causes of his behaviour, say, in his childhood, or in his neuro-physiological workings. Secondly, we may seek for the reason *why* he does what he does. Moreover, we may attempt to *change* our neighbour's behaviour in one of two ways, either by manipulation (that is, by employing whatever means might have the desired result), or by giving him reasons. In the second case we attempt to change his behaviour through his own agreement that it must be changed—we affect his behaviour by changing his aims.

From our present point of view, the interesting feature of rationality, so described, is its connection with self-consciousness, and the connection of both with the forms of communication, in particular with language. Another man's rationality enables us to affect his conception of his aims and purposes, by presenting him with reasons for doing, and reasons for feeling, that which he otherwise might not do or feel. A rational being, unlike a dog, does not have to be trained (or 'conditioned'); he may be educated instead. He may, that is, be given a new and better understanding of his situation, and through understanding he might achieve practical knowledge. Because of this we come to describe the behaviour of a rational being in terms that have only dubious or metaphorical application to animals, terms which locate their subject as an appropriate object of inter-personal feeling. We describe the actions of others as just, wise or outrageous; we are prepared to praise or blame them, to resent, reward or take revenge on them, in respect of what they do. In other words, dependent upon our special beliefs about rational conduct (beliefs about how that conduct arises, and how it might be changed), there are also special feelings and attitudes, the object of which is to be described in personal terms. There is something confused in resenting or taking revenge upon a horse or a dog. Animals are not, as we say, free agents. Which is tantamount to saying that their behaviour neither arises from, nor changes through, the operation of practical reason.

It is undeniable that, while we hesitate to extend the language of personal activity to the behaviour of animals, we feel no hesitation in extending it to the behaviour of states. It is certainly the case that we are given to describing the activities of states as just or unjust, as wise, courageous or disgraceful. We praise or blame nations for what they do: in recent years a nation has even been tried in a (strangely constituted) court of law. It seems then that we describe and react to the activity of states as we describe and react to the activity of people: we implicitly attribute to the state a character of rational agent, in addition to its character as political organism. Nor should we be surprised by this. To the extent that we recognize that an institution may be 'ailing' or 'flourishing', and that decisions are made uniquely for its well-being, then we will inevitably attribute to it a personal character. It is on this basis that the criminal law has gradually been extended to the activities of companies. And international companies, like nations, are now familiar objects of blame, resentment and the desire for revenge.

To make the analogy good, we must be prepared to speak of the state as in some way self-conscious—sufficiently self-conscious that it can itself make decisions, rather than merely having its decisions made for it. And indeed, a society or state does seem to have its self-conscious, decision-making part, just as it has its instinctive activity, which is the norm of day-to-day existence—the common culture (which, while being part of the consciousness of the individual, forms the *instinct* of society). The Hobbesian analogy suggests that the society, like the individual, has both an organic and a rational nature. While most of what it does it does unthinkingly, it also makes decisions, and those decisions may be foolish as they may be wise.

In understanding a man's actions in terms of the reasons for them, we are in effect understanding what an agent does in terms of a thought that he formulates. Sometimes the thought is not one that is formulated by the agent himself but by someone else, by a psychoanalyst, say, or a poet. But for it to be considered the real *reason* for what a man does he must in some sense be prepared to accept it as his. Suppose something similar were true of a society as a whole. In understanding society as a kind of super-rational agent we are in effect trying to understand social events in terms of a thought that is either 'uttered' or in some way 'accepted' by the society as the reason for what it does. It must be possible, if there is to *be* this kind of understanding, to identify the true 'thought processes' of the society, the thought processes which really provide the understanding that we are seeking.

If the analogy is to be significant we must say what it is for an articulate thought to provide the reason for a piece of behaviour, the reason in terms of which to understand it. The obvious suggestion is that the agent himself may *tell* us why he is doing what he does: what he says will contain his reason. But the suggestion is too simple: a man may be self-deceived, unconsciously determined, insincere, and in all those cases it might be that the real reason for his behaviour has to be discovered—even if he must be brought to 'accept' the reason if we are to be entitled to speak of it as his. More importantly, a man may not be sufficiently articulate to express in words the desires, aims and feelings which motivate his action. He may try, but he may find that the words he utters are unsatisfactory to him. He may feel that, if someone else were to offer him the words, then he would be able to say whether or not they captured his aim or emotion; but he may be unable to invent the words himself. Here we find one reason why a common culture tends always to realize itself in articulate proverbs, maxims, images and (where possible) texts, and in some received tradition of self-conscious reflection upon its own identity and history. There is a sense in which many of our aims, feelings and desires *fit* themselves to the forms of expression which our culture offers us, and depend upon that culture for the provision of their verbal form. Even the simple Homeric religion, which amounted to little more than a sense of belonging to a place and a community, had enough theology to translate that pious instinct into articulate thoughts and aims. Similarly, if we are to think of social activities as understandable in terms of articulate reasons for their occurrence, we will have to allow for the possibility that the real reason for some occurrence is not immediately available, that it is not expressed on the surface of activity, as it were, but has to be dis-covered. To discover the reason one will have to look to the articulate expressions which a society contains.

Among these articulate expressions there will be those which reveal transitory attitudes, and those which, on the contrary, express attitudes integral to the continuity of society, so that their destruction or trans-formation would strike at the roots of the social order. Among the transi-tory expressions one might further wish to distinguish those which express mere whims or velleities, and those which express a serious although impermanent social aim. (Examples are not hard to find. For the transitory and whimsical, one might consider the Victorian parlour song, or Bob Dylan; for the transitory but serious, D. H. Lawrence; for the enduring and essential, *The Divine Comedy*.) It is necessary to make these distinctions, not because of some preconceived idea of culture, but because they are essential to our analogy. In the case of the individual we do not regard each of his desires, nor each of his expressions of desire, as equally serious. And even among his transitory impulses we distinguish those which are properly desires, with a considered sense and aim, and those which are mere velleities, which can be opposed, ignored or over-come without detriment to the autonomy of their subject.

It is not absurd, therefore, to rule out of consideration a great many of a man's professed desires and reasons. Nor is it absurd in the case of society. An expression may be disregarded if it contains no serious attempt to understand or articulate the experience which compels it; for it will have no special authority as a guide to the desires and reasons of the community, however 'popular' it may be. It is for some such reason that the so-called 'popular' culture ('culture' which seeks to accommodate itself to the impulses, whatever they might be, of those designed to consume it) has so often been excluded from high culture. But that particular problem need not yet concern us. What belongs to high culture can be determined only when we know what high culture is and we will know that only when we have developed a theory which tells us what high culture is supposed to do. Once again, it will be best to start from a consideration of the individual.

An individual rational agent, because he makes decisions and has practical knowledge, is able to have not only desires but also ends. This is one of the fundamental distinctions between animals and men. It is only men who pursue things through a conception of their value. The acquisition of ends is an essential part of the education of practical reason, and it is an unavoidable consequence of rationality that the individual should not only desire things but also acquire this conception of their value.

However, a man may find himself wholly uncertain about his ends, about what he really is *doing* in making a certain decision. He might be prompted by an impulse which he rationalizes, without really being able to present, either to another or to himself, a picture of his aim which renders it desirable. But what is it to be certain of one's ends? There is a temptation to think of ends as matters that can be discussed round a table, as one might discuss means; one simply argues, as best one can, about the desirability of pursuing this or that. And it might seem that some such debate could be pursued at the political level, that the state, for example, uncertain of its aims, might appoint some committee of experts to decide on them. Indeed, one only has to remember the Eisenhower Commission on National Goals in order to realize how natural is the desire of government to appoint some 'committee of experts' to deal with any problem that it may encounter. Hence the dominance of modern politics by economic and political 'advisers', and the adherence to that 'managerial' conception of the state—that conception of the state as a body of experts directing the forces of society towards some defined, external aim— which Oakeshott has so effectively described in *On Human Conduct*.

While a committee of experts may be suited to discussing a problem of means, it is not at all clear that it is capable of contributing anything to our knowledge of ends. Ends are objects not of theoretical knowledge, but of practical certainty. Few people have any clear idea how we might reason about them, or settle any issue which involves them. In one important sense they elude explicit justification—not because they cannot be justified, but rather because their justification depends upon shared perceptions, a shared body of knowledge, and a common experience of the world. Ends are involved in how we *see* the world, how we understand it as an arena of action, how, indeed, we even formulate the practical problems which confront us. If we lack a sense of ends then what we lack is not so much a set of specifiable aims, in the way an engine might lack any rails to guide it, but rather a ready and certain response to practical situations, an ability to see practical problems not in the narrow framework of utility but in the wider framework of human satisfaction. In the last analysis, indeed, such matters can be revealed only *in concreto*; an abstract idea of value will never be a substitute for the immediate perception of what is right. Not to have that immediate perception—to live in a world that is not organized, as it were, according to a conception of human ends—is to risk losing oneself in a proliferation of means without meaning.

This is a point which is as important as it is obscure. The pursuit of a certain mechanical analogy has led to the belief (widely held but seldom stated) that an activity without an aim is merely aimless. So that if we are to consider political activity to be a form of rational activity, we have to ally it to certain aims—to an 'ideology' in Oakeshott's sense. Otherwise it is, as an activity, merely irrational. The politician must therefore be able to indicate the form of society at which he is aiming, why he is aiming at it, and what means he proposes for its realization.

Such a view is, for all its implicit popularity, deeply confused. It is clear that most human relations, and most activities that are worthwhile, are also 'aimless' in the above sense. There is no purpose for which they exist, nor could the agents and participants even begin to provide one. Nor ought they to try, since they could succeed only by either falsifying or brutalizing their experience. Suppose I were to approach another in the spirit of a given aim—there is something I have in mind in, and hope to achieve through, my relations with him. And suppose that the sole interest of my relation with the other is to be found in that aim. Now there is a sense in which I can still treat the other (to borrow Kant's terminology) not as a means only, but also as an end: for I may try to accomplish my aim by seeking his concurrence in it. I reason with him, I try to persuade him to do what I want him to do. But *if* that is my approach, then it is always possible that I shall not persuade him, or that he, in his turn, will dissuade me. A certain reciprocity arises, and the absolute authority of my aim—as the sole determining principle of what it is reasonable for me in these circumstances to do—must be abandoned. And there is nothing irrational in that. If my aim is abandoned in these circumstances it is because it has proved impossible or unjustifiable. It follows that, if I am to allow to another that degree of autonomy which his rational nature demands of me, I simply cannot approach him with a clearly delimited set of aims for *him*, and expect the fulfilment of those aims to be the inevitable, natural or even reasonable outcome of our intercourse. I might discover wholly new ends, or even lapse into that state of 'aimlessness' which is the norm of healthy human relationships. To refuse the possibility of that lapse is to treat the other not as an end, but as a means only, as wholly subordinate to the dictates of my will. That position is both repugnant and ultimately irrational.

So too, it might be suggested in the sphere of politics. A politician may very well have aims and ambitions for the society which he seeks to govern. But to seek to impose them come what may—to impose them, that is, without recognizing the society's right to give its reasons in return—that attempt can be carried through only at the cost of rationality and not to its advantage, however 'good in themselves' the ends might seem. It is the mark of rational intercourse that ends are not all predetermined, that some ends—and perhaps the most important ends—remain to be discovered, rather than imposed. It is by no means foolish, nor is it a sign of subservience to Mill's 'despotism of custom', to recognize that ends may be discovered through participating in the traditional arrangement in which they are alive. To participate in such an arrangement is to be possessed of certain perceptions, through which the value of conduct can be recognized. That value will not be the outcome of some all-embracing principle, applied abstractly, but on the contrary, it will proceed from an understanding of the here and now of politics. One might say that ends make sense in conduct, but for the most part resist translation into recipes. A politician cannot reasonably propose them until he has understood the social arrangement which he seeks to control, and having understood it, he may find that his ends cannot, in fact, be 'proposed' in the form of a programme. To propose a recipe in advance of understanding is a sentimental gesture: it involves regarding a society as an *excuse* for political emotion, rather than as a proper object of it. To avoid sentimentality is to attempt to understand the social object, and to measure one's feelings and aims accordingly; it is to recognize therefore that the society too has a voice, and that a rational man must be open to its persuasion.

Now if this human understanding of a social arrangement is to be possible, then it must be possible too to locate the true voice of society. The voice must reveal not transitory velleities or unpondered impulses but serious and accepted values. It must be a voice not only of reason but of the rational *identity* of the society. And identity here means identity through time. For it has been clear since the arguments of Kant and Hegel that only a being which is extended in time and conscious of its own extension in time can have a *reason* for what it does. Only such a being, therefore, can be a proper object of the feelings and reactions which we reserve for persons. It seems to follow that a society's voice must be informed by some sense of history, and of the values which have been alive in that history and which serve, as it were, to project it forward from past to future. Without that 'historical sense' the voice will reveal nothing comparable to decision or agency.

Among the claims that have been made for high culture—at least for certain paradigms of high culture, such as poetry and the theatre—are the claims that it embodies a shared moral experience, and that it conveys a sense of historical continuity, a sense that two periods are periods in the history of *one* state or nation, despite the changing conditions, the changing constitution, even the changed language and geographical location that might have intervened. By a 'sense of historical continuity' it is not intended to refer to any accumulation of factual knowledge, of dates, battles, policies and kings, but rather to an intuitive understanding of how *this* arrangement, with which one is, so to speak, inextricably mingled, has developed in time, and of what it contains by way of potentiality, not just for the future, but for the past. It is just such a sense of history that is presented by the Old Testament, and by Shakespeare in his historical plays. If these traditional claims for high culture could be upheld, then it would be possible to look upon high culture as an articulation of the true ends of social conduct. It would be possible to weigh the velleities of fashion against these true ends, as high culture reveals them to us. And that might lead us to say that a policy, which seems to satisfy the desires of many men, might actually be destructive of the social arrangement through which they obtain their satisfaction, destructive, that is, of its aims and identity. To insist on the absolute validity of the individual wish is to treat society—in Kant's phrase—as a means only and not as an end, as a means to the satisfaction of individual desire. Such an attitude is essentially revolutionary; it involves a stance of social murder. It is clearly that kind of consideration which is in the minds of those who argue—against the fashionable liberal defence of pornography—that no understanding of what is at issue will ever be achieved through an opinion poll or a count of hands, and that somebody who has lost all idea, for example, of what Shakespeare meant in referring to the 'expence of spirit in a waste of shame', is in this area not just wrong but politically incompetent.

III

If one could fill in all the gaps in that argument one would have succeeded not only in making sense of, but also in justifying the view of high culture that is to be found in the German idealists, and which finds expression in our own tradition of literary and historical reflection. But of course, the gaps are many, and wide. For example, the analogy can work only if one is prepared to say what it is for a society to 'accept' a high culture as its own authentic voice. And that is going to be very difficult. For it is hard enough to say what it is for the individual to accept some pronouncement as *his* reason for doing what he did. That is one of the outstanding problems in the philosophy of mind. In the social case the problem becomes formidable. It is not at all clear, for example, that the high culture which we so often identify as our own can be truly thought of as the voice of the society in which we find ourselves.

The difficulty here is twofold: First, the culture has lost that air of necessity with which it was once endowed, so that it is possible to doubt what was once seen as obvious—for example whether the study of Latin language and literature is essential to the transmission of English culture. Secondly, it is difficult even to recognize the unified society—the common culture—of which this high culture is the articulate expression. The rot of 'pluralism' has perhaps gone too far. Inevitably, therefore, the 'acceptance' of the voice by the society to which it is attributed will prove difficult to establish. Certainly it is hardly likely that we shall establish the point until some further description of the nature of a high culture is forthcoming. Does a high culture include only literary products, or does it embrace all forms of art? Does it include not only imaginative literature but also philosophy, history, theology, and other forms of unscientific speculation?

It will serve to generalize the argument slightly if an analogy is taken not from literature but from building. Culture, Arnold remarked, is at variance with 'our inaptitude for seeing more than one side of a thing, with our intense energetic absorption in the particular pursuit we happen to be following'. He connected that species of intensity with an increasing allegiance to mechanized, and, as he put it, 'external' forms of life, and some idea of the truth of this remark may be obtained from a study of contemporary architecture, in particular from that school of architecture known variously as constructivism and functionalism, which sees the study of building essentially in terms of the discovery of means to ends. On this view the work of the architect is to fulfil a commission, which may ask, say, for a certain number of rooms, a certain ease of communication, a certain amount of light, and so on, all confined to a given area of land. There is a soluble problem. Architects have developed ways of producing satisfactory solutions to such problems, using all the available techniques of modern engineering. There is no doubt that, in their intense application to the ends which are stipulated for them, they have usually succeeded very well in answering to those ends; much better, indeed than any architect constrained by the aesthetic values of the classical tradition. But the surprising thing is that people do not want to live and work in the resulting buildings. Nor do they want to look at them. And indeed the whole idea of new construction is fast becoming repugnant; people fight it whenever they can, in a sort of panic of apprehension that, if not always justified, is always understandable.

If we ask ourselves what has gone wrong we find immediately that our thought leads us back into the mysteries of culture—to the assumption that is made by some modern architects that aesthetic values are just one among many possible aims; as if by feeding them into a computer with the other relevant data, one could be certain that the resulting plan would satisfy aesthetic aims as well. That is precisely the philistine view of aesthetic value, which sees it both as a specifiable goal, in the way that a number of rooms may be a specifiable goal, and also a *limited* goal, which can .be weighed against other goals in one's search for an 'optimal' solution. But the fact is that what we naively dismiss as a mere 'matter of taste' is something which affects the whole quality of life. It is through working with one's eye on aesthetic value that one begins to perceive, in what one is doing, not just the limited ends which have been specified in the blue-print, but all the other satisfactions and desires to which one's work will minister. One sees the rightness and wrongness of what one is doing, not just in the light of an external purpose, but intrinsically. To lose that perception is to be bereft of a true human purpose; it would hardly be surprising if the end result were repugnant, not just to the self-consciously 'cultured', but also to the common man. And of course an aesthetic value, being part of culture, must be acquired through the forms of education that are proper to the transmission of culture. It will never be born out of 'engineering studies' narrowly conceived, out of the study of means in isolation from any cultivation of a sense of ends.

Might one not suggest, therefore, that what is a fault in the architects of a building is also a fault in the architects of a state, that the subtle but real dissatisfaction which proceeds from the one fault will proceed also from the other, and therefore that the replacement of social architecture by social engineering is no more desirable than is an allegiance to the functionalist programme in building? If so, then must one not agree with Arnold in thinking that government by philistines is an evil, not just to the man who can perceive these things, but also, and more especially, to the man who can't?

Index